IRISH DRUIDS

AND

OLD IRISH RELIGIONS

IRISH DRUIDS

AND

OLD IRISH RELIGIONS

JAMES BONWICK

DORSET PRESS

This edition published by Dorset Press.
a division of
Marboro Books Corporation.
1986 Dorset Press.

ISBN 0-88029-070-6

Printed in the United States of America

M9 8 7 6 5 4 3

PREFACE.

IRELAND, whether viewed from an antiquarian or an ethnological point of view, is one of the most interesting countries in the world. It is not the less an object of attention from the fact, that in its early history there are traces of nearly every kind of pagan belief.

It is curious that its literary treasures should have been so long neglected. Of late years, thanks to literary and scientific societies, including the new association fostered by Sir C. Gavan Duffy, Irish MSS. have engaged much thoughtful investigation.

The author of this work, conscious of the importance of inquiry into ancient faiths, has collected such information upon Irish religions as a lengthened course of general reading has thrown in his way, since it may benefit those who have less leisure or opportunity for research. He is content to state various views, presented in quotations from writers, rather than to put forth any special conjectures of his own. Examinations of old myths and folklore will often throw light upon current notions of nationalities.

This sketch of the ancient Irish mind might help to confirm the conviction that Religion, in the sense of a reverence for something beyond the individual, has been ever associated with human nature. Anything, however apparently absurd to some of us, that tends to restrain vice, and exalt virtue, is not to be despised in the development of our race. The heathen Irish had a worshipful spirit. As to their morals, they certainly honoured woman more than did the favoured Jews or accomplished Greeks.

The Druids, forming one subject of this publication, are still an enigma to us. They were, doubtless, neither so grandly wise, nor so low in reputation, as represented by tradition. Their ethical lessons must have assuredly prepared the way for Christian missions.

However open to criticism in literary merit, the book claims some kindly consideration, as coming from one who, in his seventy-seventh year, retains a confiding hope in the march of human intellect, and the growth of human brotherhood.

JAMES BONWICK.

Norwood.
   January 1, 1894.

CONTENTS.

PAGE

PREFACE V

PART I.

IRISH DRUIDS.

WHO WERE THE DRUIDS? I
WELSH OR BRITISH DRUIDISM 2
IRISH DRUIDISM 10
ST. PATRICK AND THE DRUIDS 27
OPINIONS ON IRISH DRUIDS 31
IRISH BARDS 37
ISLE OF MAN DRUIDISM 44
FRENCH DRUIDISM 45
GERMAN DRUIDISM 49
DRUIDICAL MAGIC 50
NEO-DRUIDISM 62
DRUIDICAL BELIEF 64
DRUIDICAL MYSTICISM 71

PART II.

EARLY RELIGIONS OF THE IRISH.

INTRODUCTION 76
IRISH SUPERSTITIONS 79
IRISH MAGIC AND TUATHA DE DANAANS 101
IRISH GODS 116
IDOL-WORSHIP 157

Contents.

	PAGE
SERPENT FAITH	168
SUN-WORSHIP	189
FIRE-WORSHIP	198
STONE-WORSHIP	211
ANIMAL-WORSHIP	224
THE SHAMROCK, AND OTHER SACRED PLANTS	232
WELL-WORSHIP	238
HOLY BELLS	244
IRISH CROSSES	247
THE SACRED TARA HILL	257
ROUND TOWER CREED	263
OSSIAN THE BARD	274
THE CULDEES OF DRUIDICAL DAYS	279
THE FUTURE LIFE, OR LAND OF THE WEST	286
ANCIENT IRISH LITERATURE	303
THE LIA FAIL, OR THE STONE OF DESTINY	313
INDEX	321
AUTHORITIES CITED	325

IRISH DRUIDS.

WHO were the Druids?
This question has agitated the minds of the learned for a long period ; and various, as well as contradictory, have been the replies. Tradition preserves their memory as of a pious and superior race, prominently associated with the British Isles and France, and, in a lesser degree, with Belgium, Holland, Germany, and the lands of Scandinavia.

Much romance has been long attached to them. We hear their chants in the Stone Circles. We listen to the heaven-inspired utterances of the Archdruid, as he stands on the capstone of a cromlech, in the eye of the sun, surrounded by the white-robed throng, with the bowed worshippers afar. We see the golden sickle reverently cutting off the sacred mistletoe. We follow, in imagination, the solemn procession, headed by the cross-bearer. We look under the old oak at the aged Druid, instructing disciples in mystic lore, in verses never to be committed to writing. We gaze upon the assembly of kings and chieftains, before whom the wise men debate upon some points of legislation.

Then, again, we recognize the priests as patriots, resisting the invaders of their homes, and loudly chanting the Battle Hymn. We are at the convocation of Brehons, in their deliberations on law, and, awestruck, wait upon the observers of sun and stars, or of the signs of the times in the investigation of terrestrial phenomena. We go with them to the judgment upon offenders of an unwritten code, and witness the dread ordeal, or the fiery human sacrifice.

But our inquiry is, What has Irish tradition or literature to say to these interesting details concerning Druids?

Were the Irish Druids like those of whom we read belonging to other lands? Did they spring up from among the Irish people, or were they strangers from another and distant shore? Could they have formed a distinct community, like the tribe of Levi, intermarrying among themselves only? Amidst much ignorance, and even barbarism, can the Druids have been distinguished by the learning and refinement attributed to them?

With our conceptions of the ancient religions of Ireland, should we credit the Druids with the introduction of Sun worship, Serpent reverence, and the adoration of Idols? Were they, on the contrary, new comers, arriving subsequent to the establishment of these various forms of paganism, and merely known a little before the rise of Christianity in Erin?

WELSH OR BRITISH DRUIDISM.

Druidism has been of late years so persistently appropriated by the Welsh, that English, Scotch, and Irish have seemed to have no part in the property. Even Stonehenge has been claimed by the Welsh, on the very doubtful story of the Britons, Cæsar's Teutonic *Belgæ*, being driven by Romans to Wales. The true Welsh—the Silures, or Iberians—were in the land before the Romans appeared. Gaels from Ireland, Cymry from Scotland and England, Belgæ from Germany, Bretons, Britons, Saxons, Normans,

English, Irish, and Flemings go to make up the rest. We know nothing of Welsh prehistoric races.

Even allowing cromlechs, circles, and pillar-stones to be called Druidical, there are fewer of these stone remains in Wales than in Scotland, Ireland, England, or France. As to other antiquities, Ireland is richer than Wales in all but Roman ruins.

It is hard upon Ireland that her Druids should have been so long neglected, and the honours of mystic wisdom become the sole possession of Wales. It is true, however, that the Irish have been less eager about their ancestral glory in that aspect, and have not put forward, as the Welsh have done, a Neo-Druidism to revive the reputation of the ancient Order. But Ireland had its *Druids*, and traditionary lore justifies that country in the acknowledgment of those magi or philosophers.

The Welsh have a great advantage over the Irish in the reputed possession of a literature termed Druidical. They assume to know who the Druids were, and what they taught, by certain writings conveying the secret information. The Irish do not even pretend to any such knowledge of their Druids. The Welsh, therefore, look down with pity upon their insular neighbours, and plume themselves on being the sole successors of a people who were under true Druidical teaching, and whose transmitted records reveal those mysteries.

The revival of the ancient faith, in the organization called *Druids of Pontypridd,*—having members in other parts of Wales, but claiming a far larger number of adherents in America,—has given more prominence to Druidical lore. The fact of the late simple-minded but learned Archdruid, Myfyr Morganwg, a poet and a scholar, after thirty years' preaching of Christianity, publicly proclaiming the creed of his heathen forefathers, has naturally startled many thoughtful minds. The writer can affirm, from personal knowledge of Myfyr, that he was no pretender, but an absolute believer in the tenets he taught ; it is not therefore surprising that students of anthropology should inquire into this revival.

Such teaching is quite different from the *Neo-Druidism* which arose a few years ago, and whose imaginative interpretation of writings in Welsh, under the names of Taliesin, &c., were endorsed by several distinguished ministers of the Christian religion. Neo-Druidism was brought forward at Eisteddfods, and works were written to show that Welsh Druidism was simply the truth as recorded in the biblical account of the Hebrew Patriarchs.

The Pontypridd Archdruid held quite another doctrine. He embraced within his fold not only Abraham, Isaac, and Jacob, but the promulgators of Hindooism, Buddhism, and all the ancient systems of so-called idolatry. He recognized his principles in them all, as they simply represented the forces of Nature, under the guise of personalities.

The mantle of the octogenarian leader has fallen upon Mr. Owen Morgan, better known as *Morien*, long an able and voluminous writer for the Press. His version of Welsh Druidism can be studied in the recently published *Light of Britannia*. He assumes for his Druids the priority of learning. From the mountains of Britain proceeded the light which produced the wisdom of Egypt, Babylon, Persia, India, Phœnicia, Judea, and Greece.

They who deem this too large a draft upon faith for acceptance, will assuredly discover in that unique work a mass of curious facts bearing upon ancient science, and be constrained to admit that the *Light of Britannia* is not the product of unreasoning Welsh enthusiasm, but is among the most candidly expressed books ever printed.

It was Dr. Lanigan who asserted, " The Christian mission-

aries early opened schools in opposition to Druids." It was
the opinion of Arthur Clive that much Druidism "blended
with the Christian learning of the seventh and subsequent
centuries." The same might be affirmed of Welsh Druidism.
Alluding to an astronomical MS. of the fourteenth century,
Clive says, "I believe that it, or rather the knowledge
which it contains, is a Druidic survival, a spark transmitted through the dark ages." Gomme tells us, "that
Druidism continued to exist long after it was officially
dead can be proved."

Dr. Moran, Bishop of Ossory, in his *Irish Saints*, asso-
ciates the Welsh Saint David with an Irish Druid. St.
David was the son of an Irish Christian lady. He came
to Menevia, on the Welsh promontory, made a fire on the
shore, and its smoke filled the land. The Bishop then
goes on to say:—

"The owner of the district was an Irishman, named
Baya, a pagan and a Druid. He was one of those successful rovers who years before had carved out territories for
themselves on the Welsh coast, and continued to hold
them by the sword. He was filled with horror when he
saw the smoke that arose from St. David's fire, and cried
out to those that were with him, 'The enemy that has lit
that \fire shall possess this territory as far as the smoke has
spread.' They resolved to slay the intruders, but their
attempt was frustrated by a miracle. Seeing this, Baya
made a grant of the desired site, and of the surrounding
country, to St. David, whose monastery quickly arose."

Welsh patriotic zeal would receive a shock from Professor
O'Curry's statement. "It appears then that it was from
Erinn that the Isle of Mona (Anglesey) received its earliest
colony; and that that colony was of a Druidical people."
This view has been supported by other testimony. The
Welsh Cerrig Edris (Cader Idris) has been identified

with the Irish Carrick. Carrick Brauda of Dundalk, like
Carig Bradyn of Mona, was renowned for astronomical
observations.

Owen Morgan, in the *Light of Britannia*, has brought
forward authorities to support his theory that the Welsh, at
any rate, could claim for ancestors the Druids of classical
writers. But Leflocq declares the language of the so-called
Welsh Druids of the early Christian centuries is modern ;
and that even Sharon Turner—"for the mythological poems
dare not assign them to the sixth century, nor attribute
them to Taliesin." He considers the mystery of the
Bards of Britain consists of a number of Christian sentences,
interpreted according to the arbitrary system of modern
mysticism ; and concludes, "Such are the narrow bases of
the vast pre-conceived system of our days as to the true
religion of the Gauls."

But Rhys in *Celtic Britain* asserts that "the Goidelic
Celts appear to have accepted Druidism, but there is no
evidence that it ever was the religion of any Brythonic
people." Again, "The north-west of Wales, and a great
portion of the south of it, had always been in the possession
of a Goidelic people, whose nearest kinsmen were the
Goidels of Ireland."—"The Brythonic Celts, who were
polytheists of the Aryan type ; the non-Celtic natives
were under the sway of Druidism ; and the Goidelic Celts,
devotees of a religion which combined polytheism with
Druidism." He says the word *Cymry* "merely meant
fellow-countrymen" ; though, as he adds, "The Cymry
people developed a literature of their own, differing from
that of the other Brythonic communities." He makes
Carlisle the centre of their influence before coming down
into Wales.

The assumptions of Welsh advocates may not be very
satisfactory to scholars, and all we know of Irish Druids

furnishes little evidence for romantic conclusions ; but why should tradition hold so tenaciously to the theory ? Making all allowance for extravagance of views, and their variety, it is not easy to explain these early and particular accounts.

Although Welsh Druidism is represented by Welsh writers as being so different from the Gaulish, as pictured by French authors, or the Irish of Irish scholars, a few words may be allowed from the publication of the enthusiastic Morien of Wales.

" It is evident," says he, " that the Druid believed in the eternity of matter in an atomic condition, and also in the eternity of water ; and that the passive, that is, the feminine principle of the Divine nature, pervaded both from eternity."— " He imagined a period before creation began, when darkness and silence pervaded illimitable space."—" The Sun is the son of the Creator, who is referred to by the Druids as the higher sun of the circle of Infinitudes above the Zodiacal Sun."—" Wherever the solar rites relating to the ancient worship had been performed, those places were still regarded by the masses as sacred."

The *Annwn* of Morien is Hades or Erebus, and that "of northern ideas is cold." Of the Archdruid he says, " The Divine Word incarnate, such was our Druidic High Priest ;" especially when standing on the Logan stone. The Holy Greal was the cauldron of Ceridwen, or Venus. The Druids' ecclesiastical year commenced at midnight, March 20—21.

God was regarded through the symbol of three letters /|\ or rods, representing the light, or descent of rays, the true Logos. Hu, the divine Sun, was the *Menw* incarnate. The grave is the matrix of *Ced*, who bears the same relation to Venus as the Creator does to Apollo the Sun. The twelve battles of Arthur, or the Sun, relate to the signs of the Zodiac. Morien observes two sects in Druidism—the

party of the Linga, and that of the Logos.   His Druidism is
simply solar worship,—or, in another sense, pure Phallicism.
According to him, " The Christian religion is scientifically
arranged on the most ancient framework of British
Druidism."

A perusal of Morien's *Light of Britannia* will give the
reader an explicit account of the mystery of Welsh
Druidism, but fail to prove its identity with Irish Druidism;
although the connection of Ireland with Wales was most
intimate before the Danish invasion, traditional Irish saints
having converted to Christianity their wilder neighbours of
North and South Wales, as they did of those in Cornwall
and other places.

The Druid, according to Morien, and his distinguished
master, the Archdruid Myfyr Morganwg, was a more
picturesque individual than the person figured by Irish
writers, and he is strictly associated with so-called Druidical
circles, cromlechs, &c.   Stonehenge and Abury, not less
than Mona and Pontypridd, are claimed as the scenes of
their performances.   All that tradition has represented
them, or poets have imagined them, the Druids were in the
estimation of modern Welsh authorities.

> " Theirs were the hands free from violence,
> Theirs were the mouths free from calumny,
> Theirs the learning without pride,
> And theirs the love without venery."

They were more than what Madame Blavatsky said—" only
the heirs of the Cyclopean lore left to them by generations
of mighty hunters and magicians."   They were, as Diodorus
declared, " Philosophers and divines whom they (Gauls) call
Saronidæ, and are held in great veneration."   Myfyr left it
on record, " That the Druids of Britain were Brahmins is
beyond the least shadow of a doubt."

Much has been written about Druids' dress, their

ornaments, and the mysteries of their craft,—as the glass boat, the cup, the cross, &c. Archdruid Myfyr, at Pontypridd (not Dr. Price), explained to the present writer, his processional cross, with movable arms; his wonderful egg, bequeathed from past ages; his *Penthynen*, writing rods, or staff book; his rosary,—used by ancient priests, not less than by modern Mahometans and Christians; his glass beads; his *torque* for the neck; his breastplate of judgment; his crescent adornments; his staff of office, &c.

The staff or *Lituus* was of magical import. Wands of tamarisk were in the hands of Magian priests. The top of such augur rods were slightly hooked. One, found in Etruria, had budded in the hand. The *barsom*, or bundle of twigs, is held by Parsee priests. Strabo noted twigs in hand at prayer. The *Thyrsus* had several knots. Prometheus hid the fire from heaven in his rod.

Glass was known in Egypt some three or four thousand years before Christ. Amber beads—Hesiod's tears of the sisters of Phœbus—were in use by Phœnicians, brought probably from the Baltic. Torques have been found in many lands. As Bacon remarked, " Religion delights in such shadows and disguises."

Nash, in his remarks upon the writings of Taliesin, writes :—" The only place in Britain in which there is any distinct evidence, from the Roman authorities, of the existence of Druids, should be the Isle of Anglesey, the *seat of the Irish population* before the migration (from Scotland) of the Cambrian tribes, the ancestors of the modern Welsh." He thus fixes the Irish Druids in Wales.

While history and philology are tracing the great migration of Cambrians into North Wales from *Scotland*, where their language prevailed before the Gaelic, why is North Britain so little affected with the mysticism associated with Welsh Druidism ? A natural reply would be, that this

peculiar manifestation came *into* Wales subsequent to the
Cambrian migration from the Western Highlands through
Cumberland to the southern side of the Mersey, and did not
originate with the Cambrian Druids. It must not be forgotten that two distinct races inhabit Wales ; the one,
Celtic, of the north ; the other, Iberian, dark and broad-
shouldered, of the south. Some Iberians, as of Spain and
North Africa, ·retain the more ancient language ; others
adopted another tongue. Many of the so-called Arabs, in
the Soudan, are of Iberian parentage.

No one can read Morien's most interesting and suggestive
Light of Britannia, without being struck with the remarkable parallel drawn between the most ancient creeds of
Asia and the assumed Druidism of Wales. The supposition
of that industrious author is, that the British Druids were
the originators of the theologies or mythologies of the Old
World.

Ireland, in his calculation, is quite left out in the cold.
Yet it is in Ireland, *not in Wales*, that Oriental religions had
their strongest influence. That country, and not Wales,
would appear to have been visited by Mediterranean
traders, though tradition, not well substantiated, makes
Cornwall one of their calling-places.

IRISH DRUIDISM.

Turning to Irish Druidism, we may discern a meaning,
when reading between the lines in Irish MSS., but the
mystery is either not understood by the narrators, or is
purposely beclouded so as to be unintelligible to the
vulgar, and remove the writers (more or less ecclesiastics)
from the censure of superiors in the Church. Elsewhere, in
the chapter upon " Gods," History, as seen in lives of Irish
heroes and founders of tribes, is made the medium for the

communication, in some way, of esoteric intelligence. If the Druids of Erin were in any degree associated with that assumed mythology, they come much nearer the wisdom of British Druids than is generally supposed, and were not the common jugglers and fortune-tellers of Irish authorities.

As the popular Professor O'Curry may be safely taken as one leading exponent of Irish opinion upon Irish Druids, a quotation from his able Lectures will indicate his view :—

"Our traditions," says he, "of the Scottish and Irish Druids are evidently derived from a time when Christianity had long been established. These insular Druids are represented as being little better than conjurers, and their dignity is as much diminished as the power of the King is exaggerated. He is hedged with a royal majesty which never existed in fact. He is a Pharaoh or Belshazzar with a troop of wizards at command ; his Druids are sorcerers and rain-doctors, who pretend to call down the storms and the snow, and frighten the people with the fluttering wisp, and other childish charms. They divined by the observation of sneezing and omens, by their dreams after holding a bull-feast, or chewing raw horseflesh in front of their idols, by the croaking of their ravens and chirping of tame wrens, or by the ceremony of licking the hot edge of bronze taken out of the rowan-tree faggot. They are like the Red Indian medicine men, or the Ange-koks of the Eskimo, dressed up in bull's-hide coats and bird-caps with waving wings. The chief or Arch-Druid of Tara is shown to us as a leaping juggler with ear-clasps of gold, and a speckled cloak ; he tosses swords and balls into the air, and like the buzzing of bees on a beautiful day is the motion of each passing the other."

This, perhaps, the ordinary and most prosaic account of the Irish Druid, is to be gathered from the ecclesiastical annals of St. Patrick. The monkish writers had assuredly no high opinion of the Druid of tradition ; and, doubtless, no respect for the memory of Taliesin or other members of the Craft.

Nevertheless, we should bear in mind that these same authorities took for granted all the stories floating about concerning transformations of men and women into beasts and birds, and all relations about gods of old.

O'Beirne Crowe has some doubt about Druid stories and primitive missionaries. He finds in the Hymn of St. Patrick the word *Druid* but once mentioned ; and that it is absent alike in Brocan's *Life of St. Brigit*, and in Colman's Hymn. "Though Irish Druidism," says he, " never attained to anything like organization, still its forms and practices, so far as they attained to order, were in the main the same as those of Gaul."

Those Christian writers admitted that the Druids had a literature. The author of the *Lecan* declared that St. Patrick, at one time, burnt one hundred and eighty books of the Druids. "Such an example," he said, "set the converted Christians to work in all parts, until, in the end, all the remains of the Druidic superstition were utterly destroyed." Other writers mention the same fact as to this burning of heathen MSS. Certainly no such documents had, even in copies, any existence in historic times, though no one can deny the possibility of such a literature. The Welsh, however, claim the possession of Druidic works. But the earliest of these date from Christian times, bearing in their composition biblical references, and, by experts, are supposed to be of any period between the seventh and twelfth centuries. Villemarque dates the earliest Breton Bards from the sixth century; other French writers have them later.

At the same time, it must be allowed that early Irish MSS., which all date since Christianity came to the island, contain references of a mystical character, which might be styled Druidical. Most of the Irish literature, professedly treating of historical events, has been regarded as having covert allusions to ancient superstitions, the individuals mentioned being of a mythical character.

A considerable number of such references are associated with Druids, whatever these were thought then to be. Miracles were abundant, as they have been in all periods of Irish history. The Deity, the angels, the spirits of the air or elsewhere, are ever at hand to work a marvel, though often for little apparent occasion. As the performances of Saints are precisely similar to those attributed to Druids, one is naturally puzzled to know where one party quits the field and the other comes on.

A large number of these references belong to the Fenian days, when the Tuatha Druids practised their reported unholy rites. Thus, Teige was the father of the wife of the celebrated Fenian leader, Fionn MacCumhaill, or Fionn B'Baoisgne, slain at Ath-Brea, on the Boyne. But Matha MacUmoir was a Druid who confronted St. Patrick. St. Brigid was the daughter of the Druid Dubhthach. The Druid Caicher foretold that the race he loved would one day migrate to the West.

In Ninine's Prayer it is written—

"We put trust in Saint Patrick, chief apostle of Ireland ;
He fought against hard-hearted Druids."

As told by T. O'Flanagan, 1808, King Thaddy, father of Ossian, was a Druid. Ierne was called the Isle of learned Druids. Plutarch relates that Claudius, exploring, "found on an island near Britain an order of Magi, reputed holy by the people." Tradition says that Parthalon, from Greece, brought three Druids with him. These were Fios, Eolus, and Fochmarc ; that is, observes O'Curry, "if we seek the etymological meaning of the words, *Intelligence*, *Knowledge*, and *Inquiry*."

The Nemidians reached Ireland from Scythia, but were accompanied by Druids; who, however, were confounded by the Fomorian Druids. At first the Nemidians were victorious, but the Fomorian leader brought forward his most powerful spells, and forced the others into exile. Beothach, Nemid's grandson, retired with his clan to northern Europe, or Scandinavia; where "they made themselves perfect in all the arts of divination, Druidism, and philosophy, and returned, after some generations, to Erinn under the name of the Tuatha de Danaan." The last were most formidable Druids, though overcome in their turn by the Druids of invading Milesians from Spain.

There were Druids' Hills at Uisneath, Westmeath, and Clogher of Tyrone. The *Draoithe* were wise men from the East. Dubhtach Mac Ui' Lugair, Archdruid of King Mac Niall, became a Christian convert. The Battle of Moyrath, asserted by monkish writers to have taken place in 637, decided the fate of the Druids. And yet, the *Four Masters* relate that as early as 927 B.C., there existed Mur Ollavan, the *City of the Learned*, or Druidic seminary.

Bacrach, a Leinster Druid, told Conchobar, King of Ulster, something which is thus narrated:—"There was a great convulsion. 'What is this?' said Conchobar to his Druid. 'What great evil is it that is perpetrated this day?' 'It is true indeed,' said the Druid, 'Christ, the Son of God, is crucified this day by the Jews. It was in the same night He was born that you were born; that is, in the 8th of the Calends of January, though the year was not the same.' It was then that Conchobar believed; and he was one of the two men that believed in God in Erinn before the coming of the faith."

Among the names of Druids we have, in *Cormac's Glossary*, Serb, daughter of Scath, a Druid of the Connaught men ; Munnu, son of Taulchan the Druid ; and Druien, a Druid prophesying bird. D. O. Murrim belonged to Creag-a-Vanny hill ; Aibhne, or Oibhne, to Londonderry. We read of Trosdan, Tages, Cadadius, Dader, Dill, Mogruth, Dubcomar, Firchisus, Ida, Ono, Fathan, Lomderg the bloody hand, and Bacrach, or Lagicinus Barchedius, Arch-druid to King Niall.

Druidesses were not necessarily wives of Druids, but females possessed of Druidical powers, being often young and fair.

Some names of Druidesses have been preserved ; as Geal Chossach, or Cossa, *white-legged*, of Inisoven, Donegal, where her grave is still pointed out to visitors. There was Milucradh, Hag of the Waters, reported to be still living, who turned King Fionn into an old man by water from Lake Sliabh Gullin. Eithne and Ban Draoi were famous sorcerers. Tradition talks of Women's Isles of Ireland, as of Scotland, where Druidesses, at certain festivals, lived apart from their husbands, as did afterwards Culdee wives at church orders. On St. Michael, on Sena Isle of Brittany, and elsewhere, such religious ladies were known. Scotch witches in their reputed powers of transformation were successors of Druidesses.

Several ancient nunneries are conjectured to have been Druidesses' retreats, or as being established at such hallowed sites. At Kildare, the retreat of St. Brigid and her nuns, having charge of the sacred fire, there used to be before her time a community of Irish Druidesses, virgins, who were called, from their office, *Ingheaw Andagha, Daughters of Fire*. The well-known Tuam, with its nine score nuns, may be an instance, since the word *Cailtach* means either *nun* or *Druidess*. On this, Hackett remarks, " The

probability is that they were pagan Druidesses." Dr.
O'Connor notes the Cluan-Feart, or sacred Retreat for
Druidical nuns. It was decidedly dangerous for any one
to meddle with those ladies, since they could raise storms,
cause diseases, or strike with death. But how came Pliny
to say that wives of Druids attended certain religious rites
naked, but with blackened bodies? Enchantresses, possessed of evil spirits, like as in ancient Babylon, or as in
China now, were very unpleasant company, and a source
of unhappiness in a family.

The Rev. J. F. Shearman declared that Lochra and Luch-
admoel were the heads of the Druids' College, prophesying
the coming of the Talcend (St. Patrick), that the first was
lifted up and dashed against a stone by the Saint, the other
was burnt in the ordeal of fire at Tara, that the Druid
Mautes was he who upset the Saint's chalice, and that Ida
and Ona were two converted Druids.

The Synod of Drumceat, in 590, laid restrictions on
Druids, but the Druids were officially abolished after the
decisive Battle of Moyrath, 637. The bilingual inscription
of Killeen, Cormac—IV VERE DRVVIDES, or "Four
True Druids," was said to refer to Dubhtach Macnlugil
as one of the four, he having been baptized by Patrick.

Dr. Richey may be right, when he says in his *History of
the Irish People*:—"Attempts have been made to describe
the civilization of the Irish in pre-Christian periods, by the
use of the numerous heroic tales and romances which still
survive to us ; but the Celtic epic is not more historically
credible or useful than the Hellenic,—the *Tain Bo* than
the *Iliad*." It is probable that the readers of the fore-
going tales, or those hereafter to be produced, may be
of the same opinion. Not even the prophecy of St.
Patrick's advent can be exempted, though the Fiacc Hymn
runs :—

" For thus had their prophets foretold then the coming
Of a new time of peace would endure after Tara
Lay desert and silent, the Druids of Laery
Had told of his coming, had told of the Kingdom."

Ireland had a supply of the so-called Druidical appendages and adornments. There have been found golden
torques, gorgets, armillæ and rods, of various sorts and
sizes. Some were twisted. There were thin laminæ of
gold with rounded plates at the ends. Others had penan-
nular and bulbous terminations. Twisted wire served for
lumbers or girdle-torques. A twisted one of gold, picked
up at Ballycastle, weighed 22 oz. Gorgets are seen only
in Ireland and Cornwall. The Dying Gladiator, in Rome,
has a twisted torque about his neck.

The gold mines of Wicklow doubtless furnished the
precious metal, as noted in *Senchus Mor.* Pliny refers
to the golden torques of Druids. One, from Tara, was
5 ft. 7 in. long, weighing 27 ozs. A *Todh*, found twelve
feet in a Limerick bog, was of thin chased gold, with con-
cave hemispherical ornaments. The *Iodhan Moran*, or
breastplate, would contract on the neck if the judges gave
a false judgment. The crescent ornament was the Irish
Cead-rai-re, or sacred ship, answering to Taliesin's *Cwrwg
Gwydrin*, or glass boat. An armilla of 15 ozs. was recovered in Galway. The glass beads, cylindrical in shape,
found at Dunworley Bay, Cork, had, said Lord Londes-
borough, quite a Coptic character. The Druid glass is
Gleini na Droedh in Welsh, *Glaine nan Druidhe* in Irish.

The Dublin Museum—Irish Academy collection—contains over three hundred gold specimens. Many precious
articles had been melted down for their gold. The treasure-
trove regulations have only existed since 1861. Lunettes
are common. The Druids' tiaras were semi-oval, in thin
plates, highly embossed. The golden breast-pins, *Dealg Oir*,
are rare. Some armillæ are solid, others hollow. Fibulæ

bear cups. Torques are often spiral. *Bullæ* are amulets of lead covered with thin gold. Circular gold plates are very thin and rude. Pastoral staffs, like pagan ones, have serpents twisted round them, as seen on the Cashel pastoral staff.

Prof. O'Curry says—"Some of our old glossarists explain the name *Druid* by *doctus*, learned ; and *Fili*, a poet, as a lover of learning." But Cormac MacCullinan, in his glossary, derives the word *Fili* from *Fi*, venom, and *Li*, brightness ; meaning, that the poet's satire was venomous, and his praise bright or beautiful. The Druid, in his simple character, does not appear to have been ambulatory, but stationary. He is not entitled to any privileges or immunities such as the poets and Brehons or judges enjoyed. He considers the Druids' wand was of yew, and that they made use of ogham writing. He names Tuath Druids ; as, Brian, Tuchar Tucharba, Bodhbh, Macha and Mor Rigan ; Cesarn Gnathach and Ingnathach, among Firbolgs ; Uar, Eithear and Amergin, as Milesians.

For an illustration of Irish Druidism, reference may be made to the translation, by Hancock and O'Mahoney, of the *Senchus Mor*. Some of the ideas developed in that Christian work were supposed traditional notions of earlier and Druidical times.

Thus, we learn that there were eight Winds : the colours of which were white and purple, pale grey and green, yellow and red, black and grey, speckled and dark, the dark brown and the pale. From the east blows the purple wind ; from the south, the white ; from the north, the black ; from the west, the pale ; the red and the yellow are between the white wind and the purple, &c. The thickness of the earth is measured by the space from the earth to the firmament. The seven divisions from the firmament to the earth are Saturn, Jupiter, Mercury, Mars, Sol, Luna, Venus. From the moon to the sun is 244 miles ;

but, from the firmament to the earth, 3024 miles. As the shell is about the egg, so is the firmament around the earth. The firmament is a mighty sheet of crystal. The twelve constellations represent the year, as the sun runs through one each month.

We are also informed that "Brigh Ambui was a female author of wisdom and prudence among the men of Erin— after her came Connla Cainbhrethach, chief doctor of Connaught. He excelled the men of Erin in wisdom, for he was filled with the grace of the Holy Ghost; he used to contend with the Druids, who said that it was they that made heaven and the earth and the sea—and the sun and moon." This *Senchus Mor* further stated that "when the judges deviated from the truth of Nature, there appeared blotches upon their cheeks."

It is not surprising that Dr. Richey, in his *Short History of the Irish People*, should write :—" As to what Druidism was, either in speculation or practice, we have very little information.—As far as we can conjecture, their religion must have consisted of tribal divinities and local rites. As to the Druids themselves, we have no distinct information." He is not astonished that "authors (from the reaction) are now found to deny the existence of Druids altogether." He admits that, at the reputed time of St. Patrick, the Druids "seem to be nothing more than the local priests or magicians attached to the several tribal chiefs,—perhaps not better than the medicine-men of the North-American Indians."

As that period was prior to the earliest assumed for the Welsh Taliesin, one is at a loss to account for the great difference between the two peoples, then so closely associated in intercourse.

The opinion of the able O'Beirne Crowe is thus expressed :—"After the introduction of our (Irish) irregular system of Druidism, which must have been about the second century of the Christian era, the *filis* (Bards) had to fall into something like the position of the British bards. —But let us examine our older compositions—pieces which have about them intrinsic marks of authenticity— and we shall be astonished to see what a delicate figure the Druid makes in them." On the supposition that Druidism had not time for development before the arrival of the Saint, he accounts for the easy conversion of Ireland to Christianity.

It is singular that Taliesin should mention the sun as being sent in a coracle from Cardigan Bay to Arkle, or Arklow, in Ireland. This leads Morien to note the "solar drama performed in the neighbourhood of Borth, Wales, and Arklow, Ireland."

Arthur Clive thought it not improbable that Ireland, and not Britain, as Cæsar supposed, was the source of Gaulish Druidism. "Anglesey," says he, "would be the most natural site for the British Druidical College. This suspicion once raised, the parallel case of St. Colum Kille occupying Iona with his Irish monks and priests, when he went upon his missionary expedition to the Picts, occurs to the mind." Assuredly, Iona was a sacred place of the Druids, and hence the likeness of the Culdees to the older tenants of the Isle.

Clive believed the civilization of Ireland was not due to the Celt, but to the darker race before them. In Druidism he saw little of a Celtic character, "and that all of what was noble and good contained in the institution was in some way derived from Southern and Euskarian sources." May not the same be said of Wales? There, the true Welsh—those of the south and south-east—are certainly not the light Celt, but the dark Iberian, like to the darker Bretons and northern Spaniards.

Martin, who wrote his *Western Islands* in 1703, tells us

that in his day every great family of the Western Islands
kept a Druid priest, whose duty it was to foretell future
events, and decide all causes, civil and ecclesiastical. Dr.
Wise says, " In the *Book of Deer* we meet with Matadan,
' The Brehon,' as a witness in a particular case. The laws
found in the legal code of the Irish people were administered by these Brehons. They were hereditary judges of
the tribes, and had certain lands which were attached to
the office. The successors of this important class are the
Sheriffs of counties."

The learned John Toland, born in Londonderry, 1670,
who was a genuine patriot in his day, believed in his
country's Druids. In the Hebrides, also, he found harpers
by profession, and evidence of ancient Greek visitants. In
Dublin he observed the confidence in augury by ravens.
He contended that when the Ancients spoke of Britain as
Druidical, they included Ireland ; for Ptolemy knew Erin
as *Little Britain*. He recognized Druids' houses still
standing, and the heathen practices remaining in his
country.

" In Ireland," said he of the Druids, " they had the
privilege of wearing six colours in their Breacans or robes,
which are the striped Braceæ of the Gauls, still worn by
the Highlanders, whereas the king and queen might have
in theirs but seven, lords and ladies five," &c. He had
no doubts of their sun-worship, and of Abaris, the Druid
friend of Pythagoras, being from his own quarters. While
he thought the Greeks borrowed from the northern Druids,
he admitted that both may have learned from the older
Egyptians.

Rhys, as a wise and prudent man, is not willing to
abandon the Druids because of the absurd and most
positive announcements of enthusiastic advocates ; since
he says, " I for one am quite prepared to believe in a

Druidic residue, after you have stripped all that is mediæval and Biblical from the poems of Taliesin. The same with Merlin." And others will echo that sentiment in relation to Irish Druidism, notwithstanding the wild assumptions of some writers, and the cynical unbelief of others. After all eliminations, there is still a substantial residue.

One may learn a lesson from the story told of Tom Moore. When first shown old Irish MSS., he was much moved, and exclaimed, "These could not have been written by fools. I never knew anything about them before, and I had no right to have undertaken the History of Ireland."

An old Irish poem runs :—

> "Seven years your right, under a flagstone in a quagmire,
>   Without food, without taste, but the thirst you ever torturing,
>   The law of the judges your lesson, and prayer your language ;
>   And if you like to return
>   You will be, for a time, a Druid, perhaps."

Druid Houses, like those of St. Kilda, Borera Isle, &c., have become in more modern days *Oratories* of Christian hermits. They are arched, conical, stone structures, with a hole at the top for smoke escape. Toland calls them "little arch'd, round, stone buildings, capable only of holding one person." They were known as *Tighthe nan Druidhneach*. There is generally in many no cement. The so-called Oratory of St. Kevin, 23 ft. by 10 and 16 high, has its door to the west. The writer was supported by the Guide at Glendalough, in the opinion of the great antiquity of St. Kevin's *Kitchen*. The house at Dundalk is still a place of pilgrimage.

The one at Gallerus, Kerry, has a semi-circular window. Of these oratories, so called, Wise observes, "They were not Christian, but were erected in connection with this early, let us call it, Celtic religion. If they had been

Christian, they would have had an altar and other Christian emblems, of which, however, they show no trace. If they had been Christian, they would have stood east and west, and have had openings in those directions.—The walls always converged as they rose in height."

Irish Druids lived before the advent of Socialism. They appear to have had the adjudication of the law, but, as ecclesiastics, they delivered the offenders to the secular arm for punishment. Their holy hands were not to be defiled with blood. The law, known as the *Brehon* Law, then administered, was not socialistic. Irish law was by no means democratic, and was, for that reason, ever preferred to English law by the Norman and English chieftains going to Ireland. The old contests between the Irish and the Crown lay between those gentlemen-rulers and their nominal sovereign. So, in ancient times, the Druids supported that Law which favoured the rich at the expense of the poor. They were not Socialists.

They were, however, what we should call *Spiritualists*, though that term may now embrace people of varied types. They could do no less wonderful things than those claimed to have been done by Mahatmas or modern Mediums. They could see ghosts, if not raise them. They could listen to them, and talk with them ; though unable to take photos of spirits, or utilize them for commercial intelligence.

It would be interesting to know if these seers of Ireland regarded the ghosts with an imaginative or a scientific eye. Could they have investigated the phenomena, with a view to gain a solution of the mysteries around them ? It is as easy to call a Druid a deceiver, as a politician a traitor, a scientist a charlatan, a saint a hypocrite.

As the early days of Irish Christianity were by no means either cultured or philosophical, and almost all our knowledge of Druids comes from men who accepted what would now only excite our derision or pity, particularly indulging the miraculous, we are not likely to know to what class of modern Spiritualists we can assign the Druids of Erin.

Our sources of knowledge concerning the Druids are from tradition and records. The first is dim, unreliable, and capable of varied interpretation. Of the last, Froude rightly remarks—" Confused and marvellous stories come down to us from the early periods of what is called History, but we look for the explanation of them in the mind or imagination of ignorant persons.—The early records of all nations are full of portents and marvels ; but we no longer believe those portents to have taken place in actual fact.—Legends grew as nursery tales grow now."

There is yet another source of information—the preservation of ancient symbols, by the Church and by Freemasons. The scholar is well assured that both these parties, thus retaining the insignia of the past, are utterly ignorant of the original meaning, or attach a significance of their own invention.

Judging from Irish literature—most of which may date from the twelfth century, though assuming to be the eighth, or even fifth—the Druids were, like the Tuatha, nothing better than spiritualistic conjurers, dealers with bad spirits, and always opposing the Gospel. We need be careful of such reports, originating, as they did, in the most superstitious era of Europe, and reflecting the ideas of the period. It was easy to credit Druids and Tuaths with miraculous powers, when the Lives of Irish Saints abounded with narratives of the most childish wonders, and the most needless and senseless display of the miraculous. The destruction of Druids through the invocation of Heaven by the Saints, though nominally in judgment for a league with evil spirits, was not on a much higher plane than the powers for mischief exercised by the magicians.

Such tales fittingly represented a period, when demoniacal possession accounted for diseases or vagaries of human action, and when faith in our Heavenly Father was weighed down by the cruel oppression of witchcraft.

Still, in the many credulous and inventive stories of the Middle Ages, may there not be read, between the lines, something which throws light upon the Druids? Traditional lore was in that way perpetuated. Popular notions were expressed in the haze of words. Lingering superstitions were preserved under the shield of another faith.

Then, again, admitting the common practice of rival controversialists destroying each other's manuscripts, would not some be copied, with such glosses as would show the absurdities of the former creeds, or as warnings to converts against the revival of error?

Moreover,—as the philosophers, in early Christian days of the East, managed to import into the plain and simple teaching of Jesus a mass of their own symbolism, and the esoteric learning of heathenism,—was it unlikely that a body of Druids, having secrets of their own, should, upon their real or assumed reception of Christianity, import some of their own opinions and practices, adapted to the promulgation of the newer faith? No one can doubt that the Druids, to retain their influence in the tribe, would be among the first and most influential of converts; and history confirms that fact. As the more intelligent, and reverenced from habit, with skill in divination and heraldic lore, they would command the respect of chiefs, while their training as orators or reciters would be easily utilized by the stranger priests in the service of the Church.

But if, as is likely, the transition from Druidism to Christianity was gradual, possibly through the medium of

Culdeeism, the intrusion of pagan ideas in the early religious literature can be more readily comprehended. As so much of old paganism was mixed up in the Patristic works of Oriental Christendom, it cannot surprise one that a similar exhibition of the ancient heathenism should be observed in the West. O'Brien, in *Round Towers*, writes—" The Church Festivals themselves in our Christian Calendar are but the direct transfers from the Tuath de Danaan Ritual. Their very names in Irish are identically the same as those by which they were distinguished by that earlier race." Gomme said, " Druidism must be identified as a non-Aryan cult."

Elsewhere reference is made to the Culdees. They were certainly more pronounced in Ireland, and the part of Scotland contiguous to Ireland, than in either England or Wales.

Ireland differs from its neighbours in the number of allusions to Druids in national stories. Tradition is much stronger in Ireland than in Wales, and often relates to Druids. On the other hand, it differs from that of its neighbours in the absence of allusions to King Arthur, the hero of England, Scotland, Wales, and Brittany. Rome, too, was strongly represented in Britain, north and south, but not in Ireland.

It is not a little remarkable that Irish Druids should seem ignorant alike of Round Towers and Stone Circles, while so much should have been written and believed concerning Druidism as associated with circles and cromlechs in Britain and Brittany. Modern Druidism, whether of Christian or heathen colour, claims connection with Stonehenge, Abury, and the stones of Brittany. Why should not the same claim be made for Irish Druids, earlier and better known than those of Wales ?

As megalithic remains, in the shape of graves and circles,

are found all over Europe, Asia, and northern Africa, why were Druids without association with these, from Japan to Gibraltar, and confined to the monuments of Britain ? Why, also, in Ossian, are the *Stones of Power* referred to the Norsemen only ?

In the Irish Epic, *The Carrying off of the Bull of Cuâlnge*, the Druid Cathbad is given a certain honourable precedence before the sovereign. That the Druids exercised the healing art is certain. Jubainville refers to a MS. in the Library of St. Gall, dating from the end of the fourteenth century, which has on the back of it some incantations written by Irish seers of the eighth or ninth century. In one of them are these words—" I admire the remedy which Dian-Cecht left."

Though a mysterious halo hangs about the Irish Druids, though they may have been long after the Serpent-worshippers, and even later than the Round Tower builders, tradition confidently asserts their existence in the Island, but, doubtless, credits them with powers beyond those ever exercised. The love for a romantic Past is not, however, confined to Ireland, and a lively imagination will often close the ear to reason in a cultured and philosophical age.

ST. PATRICK AND THE DRUIDS.

Let us see what the biographers of St. Patrick have to relate about the Druids.

A work published at St. Omer, in 1625, by John Heigham, has this story :—" One day as the Saint sayd masse in the sayd church, a sacrilegious magitian, the child of perdition, stood without, and with a rodd put in at the window, cast down the chalice, and shed the holy sacrament, but God without delay severely punished so wicked a sacrilege, for the earth opening his mouth after a most strange manner, devoured the magitian, who descended alive downe to hell."

Again :—" A certain magitian that was in high favor with the King, and whome the King honoured as a god, opposed himself against S. Patricke, even in the same kind that Simon Magus resisted the apostle S. Peter ; the miserable wretch being elevated in the ayre by the ministery of Devils, the King and the people looked after him as if he were to scale the heavens, but the glorious Saint, with the force of his fervent prayers, cast him downe unto the ground, where dashing his head against a hard flint, he rêdred up his wicked soule as a pray to the infernnall Fiendes."

The *Tripartite* Life of St. Patrick relates :—" Laeghaire MacNeill possessed Druids and enchanters, who used to foretell through their Druidism and through their paganism what was in the future for them." Coming to a certain town, the Saint, according to history, " found Druids at that place who denied the Virginity of Mary. Patrick blessed the ground, and it swallowed up the Druids."

The book of 1625 is the authority for another story :— " Two magitians with their magicall charmes overcast all the region with a horrible darkness for the space of three dayes, hoping by that meanes to debar his (Patrick's) enterance into the country." Again :—" Nine magitians côspired the Saint's death, and to have the more free accesse to him, they counterfeited thēselves tó be monks, putting on religious weeds ; the Saint, by divine information, knew thē to be wolves wraped in sheeps cloathing ; making, therefore, the signe of the crosse against the childrē of Satan, behould fire descended from Heaven and consumed them all nine." He is also reported to have caused the death of 12,000 idolaters at Tara.

St. Patrick contended with the Druids before King

Laeghaire at Tara. One, Lochra, hardened the King's heart against the preaching ; so " the Saint prayed that he might be lifted out and die, even as St. Peter had obtained the death of Simon Magus. In an instant Lochra was raised up in the air, and died, falling on a stone." This Lochra had, it is said, previously foretold the Saint's visit :—

> " A Tailcenn (baldhead) will come over the raging sea,
> With his perforated garments, his crook-headed staff,
> With his table (altar) at the east end of his house,
> And all the people will answer—'Amen ! Amen ! ' "

The authoress of *Ireland, the Ur of the Chaldees*, ventured to write :—" When the Apostle of Ireland went there, the people believed him, for he taught no new doctrine." She thought Druidism not very unlike Christianity. Dr. O'Donovan, upon the *Four Masters*, observes :—" Nothing is clearer than that Patrick engrafted Christianity on the pagan superstitions with so much skill that he won the people over to the Christian religion before they understood the exact difference between the two systems of beliefs ; and much of this half pagan, half Christian religion will be found, not only in the Irish stories of the Middle Ages, but in the superstitions of the peasantry of the present day." Todd sees that worldly wisdom in " dedicating to a Saint the pillar-stone, or sacred fountain."

It is not necessary to discuss the question as to the individual Saint himself, around which so much controversy has raged. They who read theology between the lines of old Irish history may be induced to doubt whether such a person ever existed, or if he were but a Druid himself, such being the obscurity of old literature.

St. Bridget's early career was associated with the Druids. A miracle she wrought in the production of butter caused her Druidical master to become a Christian.

Colgan contended that St. Patrick, by "continually warring with Druids, exposed his body to a thousand kinds of deaths." In *The Guardsman's Cry of St. Patric*, which declares "Patric made this hymn," we are informed that it was "against incantations of false prophets, against black laws of hereticians, against surroundings of idolism, against spells of women, and of smiths, and of Druids."

The *Annals of the Kingdom of Ireland by the Four Masters* mentions a number of stories relative to Irish Druids, then believed to have once ruled Erin. St. Patrick was a youthful slave to Milcho, a Druidical priest. Gradwell's *Succat*, therefore, says, "He must often have practised heathenish rites in the presence of his household, and thus excited the horror of his Christian slave."

Scoto-Irish Druids.

St. Columba, the Culdee, was much the same as St. Patrick in his mission work, and his contests with Druids. He changed water into wine, stilled a storm, purified wells, brought down rain, changed winds, drove the devil out of a milk-pail, and raised the dead to life. All that tradition acknowledged as miraculous in the Druids was attributed equally to Columba as to Patrick.

Adamnan of Iona tells some strange stories of his master. One tale concerns Brochan the Druid. "On a certain day, Brochan, while conversing with the Saint, said to him, 'Tell me, Columba, when do you propose to set sail?' To which the Saint replied, 'I intend to begin my voyage after three days, if God permits me, and preserves my life.' Brochan then said, 'You will not be able, for I will make the winds unfavourable to your voyage, and I will create a great darkness over the sea.'" The wind rose, and the darkness came. But the Saint put off, and "the vessel ran against the wind with extraordinary speed, to the wonder of the large crowd."

The Saint wanted the Druid to release an Irish female captive, which he declined to do. But, says Adamnan, "an angel sent from heaven, striking him severely, has broken in pieces the glass cup which he held in his hand, and from which he was in the act of drinking, and he himself is left half dead." Then he consented to free the Irish girl, and Columba cured him of the wound.

OPINIONS ON IRISH DRUIDS.

Leflocq wrote his *Études de Mythologie Celtique* in 1869, observing, "Some represented the Druids as the successors of the Hebrew patriarchs, the masters of Greek philosophy, the forerunners of Christian teaching. They have credited them with the honours of a religious system founded upon primitive monotheism, and crowned by a spiritualism more elevated than that of Plato and St. Augustine." One might perceive little of this in Irish tales, like the preceding. Leflocq is justified in adding, "One will be at first confounded by the extreme disproportion which exists between the rare documents left by the past, and the large developments presented by modern historians."

Pliny speaks thus of the Druids, "A man would think the Persians learned all their magic from them;" and Pomponius Mela affirmed, "They profess to have great knowledge of the motions of the heavens and the stars." Others write in the same strain. Who, then, were the Druids of Greeks and Romans? Why did Cæsar recognize such as living in Gaul? Why did Jamblichus make Pythagoras a disciple of Gaulish priests? Why did St. Clement say the Druids had a religion of philosophy ; and St. Cyril, that they held but one God ? Why should Origen, like the foe of early Christianity, Celsus, believe that the Druids of Gaul had the same doctrines as the Jews ?

Himerius speaks of Abaris, the sage, from Scythia, but well acquainted with Greek, with this description :—" Abaris came to Athens, holding a bow, having a quiver hanging from his shoulders, his body wrapt up in a plaid, and wearing trousers reaching from the soles of his feet to his waist." Cicero knew Divitiacus, who professed the know-ledge of Nature's secrets, though regarded as a Hyperborean.

Could these have been the Scythians from Tartary, the descendants of the wise men who gave their religion and the arrow-headed letters to Assyrian-Semitic conquerors, who had come down as Turanian roamers to the Plains of Babylon, and whose Chaldæan faith spread even to Egypt and Europe ?

It would seem more probable—with respectful consider-ation of the learned Morien, who makes Wales the teacher of the world—that wisdom should emanate from a people cultured long before Abrahamic days, though subsequently regarded as rude shepherd Scythians, than proceed from a western land preserving no monuments of learning.

Then, the dress, the staff, the egg, and other things associated with Druids, had their counterpart in the East, from, perhaps, five thousand years before our Christian era.

As to so-called Druidical monuments, no argument can be drawn thence, as to the primary seat of this mysticism, since they are to be seen nearly all over the world.

An instance of the absurd ideas prevalent among the ancients respecting Druids is given in Dion Chrysostom :— " For, without the Druids, the Kings may neither do nor consult anything ; so that in reality they are the Druids who reign, while the Kings, though they sit on *golden* thrones, dwell in spacious palaces, and feed on costly dishes, are only their ministers." Fancy this relating to either rude Irish or Welsh. Toland makes out that Lucan spoke to one ; but Lucan said it not. The *Edinburgh Review* of 1863 may well come to the conclusion that " the place they really fill in history is indefinite and obscure."

Madame Blavatsky has her way of looking at them. They were "the descendants of the last Atlanteans, and what is known of them is sufficient to allow the inference that they were Eastern priests akin to the Chaldæans and Indians." She takes, therefore, an opposite view to that held by Morien. She beheld their god in the Great Serpent, and their faith in a succession of worlds. Their likeness to the Persian creed is noticed thus :—" The Druids understood the morning of the Sun in Taurus ; therefore, while all the fires were extinguished on the first of November, their sacred and inextinguishable fires alone remained to illumine the horizon, like those of the Magi and the modern Zoroastrians."

Poppo, a Dutchman of the eighth century, wrote *De officiis Druidum ;* and Occo, styled the last of the Frisian Druids, was the author of a similar work. Worth, in 1620, and Frickius of 1744, were engaged on the same subject. It is curious to notice St. Columba addressing God as " My Druid," and elsewhere saying, " My Druid is Christ the Son of God." The Vates were an order known in Irish as *Faidh.* Some derive *Druid* from *Druthin,* the old German for God. The word *Druith* is applied to a Druidess.

While many treat the Druids as religious, O'Curry asserts, " There is no ground whatever for believing the Druids to have been the priests of any special positive worship." Then Vallencey declares that " Druidism was not the established religion of the Pagan Irish, but Buddhism." Yet Lake Killarney was formerly *Loch Lene,* the Lake of Learning.

The mystical, but accomplished, Massey tell us, "An Irish name for Druidism is *Maithis*, and that includes the Egyptian dual Thoth called Mati, which, applied to time, is the Terin or two Times at the base of all reckoning"— "likely that the Druidic name is a modified form of Tru-Hut."—" In Egypt *Terut* signifies the two times and before, so the Druidic science included the knowledge of the times beforehand, the coming times."

Toland, one of the earliest and most philosophical Irish writers on this subject, thus spoke of them in his *History of the Druids*—" who were so prevalent in Ireland, that to this hour their ordinary word for magician is *Druid* (Drai), the art magic is called *Druidity* (Druid-heacht), and the wand, which was one of the badges of the profession, the rod of Druidism (Slatnan Druidheacht)."

Windele, in Kilkenny records, expressed this view :— " Druidism was an artfully contrived system of elaborate fraud and imposture.   To them was entrusted the charge of religion, jurisprudence, and medicine.   They certainly well studied the book of Nature, were acquainted with the marvels of natural magic, the proportions of plants and herbs, and what of astronomy was then known ; they may even have been skilled in mesmerism and biology."   He thought that to the Druid " exclusively were known all the occult virtues of the whole *materia medica*, and to him belonged the carefully elaborated machinery of oracles, omens, auguries, aëromancy, fascinations, exorcisms, dream interpretations and visions, astrology, palmistry, &c."

As this may demand too much from our faith, we may remember, as Canon Bourke says, that " the youth of these countries have been taught to regard the Pagan Druids as educated savages, whereas they had the same opportunity of acquiring knowledge, and had really possessed as much as the Pagans of the Peloponnesus."   We should further bear in mind the assurance of the Irish historian, O'Curry, that "there are vast numbers of allusions to the Druids, and of specific instances of the exercise of their vocation—be it magical, religious, philosophical, or educational—to be found in our old MSS."

Has not much misapprehension been caused, by authors concluding that all varieties of religion in Ireland proceeded from a class of men who, while popularly called Druids, may not have been connected with them? We know very far more about these varieties of faith in Ireland, before Christianity, than we do about any description of religion in Wales; and yet the Druidism of one country is reported as so different from that in the other immediately contiguous. Such are the difficulties meeting the student of History.

The Irish Druidical religion, like that of Britain and Gaul, has given rise to much discussion, whether it began, as some say, when Suetonius drove Druids from Wales, or began in Ireland before known in either Britain or Gaul, direct from the East.

"The Druidical religion," says Kenealy in the *Book of God*, "prevailed not only in Britain, but likewise all over the East." Pictet writes, "There existed very anciently in Ireland a particular worship which, by the nature of its doctrines, by the character of its symbols, by the names even of its gods, lies near to that religion of the Cabirs of Samothrace, emanated probably from Phœnicia." Mrs. Sophie Bryant thinks that "to understand the Irish non-Christian tradition and worship, we should understand the corresponding tradition and worship, and their history, for all the peoples that issued from the same Aryan home." Ledwich is content with saying, that "the Druids possessed no internal or external doctrine, either veiled by symbols, or clouded in enigmas, or any religious tenets but the charlatanerie of barbarian priests and the grossest Gentile superstition."

While Professor O'Curry had " no ground whatever for believing the Druids to have been the priests of any special positive worship,"—and Vallencey could say, " From all I could collect from Irish documents, relative to the religion of the heathen Irish, it appears that the Druidical religion never made a part of it,"—popular opinion has always been in the other direction. Yet Vallencey would credit Druids with some religion, when he mentions the Druidical oracular stone,—in Irish *Logh-oun*, in Cornish *Logan*,—" into which the Druids pretend that the *Logh*, or divine affluence, descended when they consulted it."

Dr. Richey depreciates the Druid, when writing of the early Irish missionaries : " They did not encounter any Archdruid as the representative or head of a national religion,—they found no priesthood occupying a definite political position which the ministers of the new religion could appropriate." The Welsh Archdruid Myfyr took higher ground, when saying, " This Gorsedd has survived the bardic chairs of Greece and Rome—it has survived the institutions of Egypt, Chaldæa, and Palestine." He declared, " Druidism is a religious system of positive philosophy, teaching truth and reason, peace and justice." He believed of Druids what Burnouf thought of the Hindoo Rishis, that their metaphysics and religion " were founded on a thorough grasp of physical facts."

Morien, his favourite disciple, boldly avows that Druidism, like Freemasonry, was a philosophy, founded on natural law, and not religion in the ordinary sense of that term. So L. Maclean regarded Ossian's heroes " for the greater part cabalistic, and indicative of the solar worship. Phion (Fingal) bespeaks the Phœnician ; Cual, the Syrian or Dog-star worshipper, of which Conchulain with his *crios* or belt is but a variation." In Smith's *Dictionary of the Bible*, the religion of the Phœnicians is described in the way Morien has done that of the Druids;—"a personification of the forces of nature, which, in its more philosophical shadowing forth of the Supreme powers, may be said to have represented the male and female principles of production."

The Sabbath—a Babylonian word—was, it is said, kept on the 1st, 8th, 15th, 22nd, 29th of months, as with the Magi of the East. Philo says all nations of antiquity kept the seventh day holy. Porphyry mentions the same thing of the heathen. Professor Sayce finds it was a day of rest with ancient Assyrians, as Dr. Schmidt of temple pagan worship. Eusebius asserted that almost all philosophers acknowledged it. The Roman Pontiffs regulated the Sabbath, and Roman school-boys had then a holiday. The Persian word *Shabet* is clearly of Assyrian origin. The authoress of *Mazzaroth* says, " The Assyrians, Babylonians, Egyptians, Chinese, and the natives of India were acquainted with the seven days division of time, as were the Druids." The sun, moon, and five planets were the guardians of the days.

IRISH BARDS.

The BARDS proper occupied a high position in Ireland. The Ollamhs had colleges at Clogher, Armagh, Lismore, and Tamar. On this, Walker's *Historical Memoirs*, 1786, observes that " all the eminent schools, delectably situated, which were established by the Christian clergy in the fifth century, were erected on the ruins of those colleges." They studied for twelve years to gain the *barred* cap and title of Ollamh or teacher. They were *Ollamhain Re-dan*, or *Filidhe*, poets. They acted as heralds, knowing the genealogy of their chiefs. With white robe, harp in hand, they encouraged warriors in battle. Their power of satire was dreaded ; and their praise, desired.

There is a story of the Ard Ollamh, or Archdruid, sending to Italy after a book of skins, containing various chosen compositions, as the *Cuilmeun*, &c. As heralds they were called *Seanachies*. As Bards they sang in a hundred different kinds of verse. One Ollamh Fodhla was the Solon of Ireland ; Amergin, the singer, lived 500 B.C. ; Torna Egeas, was last of the pagan bards. Long after, they were patriots of the tribes—

> " With uncouth harps, in many-colour'd vest,
>   Their matted hair with boughs fantastic crown'd."

The *Statutes of Kilkenny* (Edward III.) made it penal to entertain any Irish Bard ; but Munster Bards continued to hold their annual Sessions to the early part of last century. Carolan, the old blind harper, called last of the Bards, died in 1738.

Bards sang in the Hall of Shells : shells being then the cups. There were hereditary bards, as the O'Shiels, the O'Canvans, &c., paid to sing the deeds of family heroes. A lament for Dallan ran—

> " A fine host and brave was he, master of and Governor,
>   Ulla ! Ullalu !
>   We, thrice fifty Bards, we confessed him chief in song and war—
>   Ulla ! Ullalu ! "

In the far-famed Trinity College Library is *The Dialogue of the Two Sages*, in the Irish Fenian dialect, giving the qualifications of a true Ollamh. Among the famous bards were, Lughar, "acute poet, Druid of Meidhbh" ; Olioll, King of Munster ; Oisin, son of Cormac, King of Tara, now nearly unintelligible to Irish readers ; Fergus finbel of the *Dinn Senchus ;* Oisin, the Fenian singer ; Larghaire, whose

poem to the sun was famous ; Lughaidh, whose poem of
the death of his wife Fail is of great antiquity ; Adhna,
once chief poet of Ireland ; Corothruadh, Fingin, &c.
Fergus Finbheoil, *fair lips*, was a Fenian Bard.

Ireland's Mirror, 1804, speaks of Henessey, a living seer,
as the Orpheus of his country. Amergin, brother of Heber,
was the earliest of Milesian poets. Sir Philip Sydney
praised the Irish Bards three centuries ago. One, in
Munster, stopped by his power the corn's growth ; and the
satire of another caused a shortness of life. Such rhymes
were not to be patronized by the Anglo-Normans, in the
Statute of 1367. One Bard directed his harp, a shell of
wine, and his ancestor's shield to be buried with him. In
rhapsody, some would see the images of coming events pass
before them, and so declare them in song. He was surely
useful who rhymed susceptible rats to death.

The Irish war odes were called *Rosg-catha*, the Eye of
Battle. Was it for such songs that Irish-Danes were cruel
to Bards ? O'Reilly had a chronological account of 400
Irish writers. As Froude truly remarks, "Each celebrated
minstrel sang his stories in his own way, adding to them,
shaping them, colouring them, as suited his peculiar genius."
It was Heeren who said of the early Greek bards, "The
gift of song came to them from the gods." Villemarque
held that Irish Bards were "really the historians of the
race."

Walker's *Irish Bards* affirms that the "Order of the
Bards continued for many succeeding ages invariably the
same." Even Buchanan found "many of their ancient
customs yet remain ; yea, there is almost nothing changed
of them in Ireland, but only ceremonies and rites of religion." Borlase wrote, "The last place we read of them in
the British dominions is Ireland." Blair added, "Long
after the Order of the Druids was extinct, and the national

religion changed, the Bards continued to flourish, exercising the same functions as of old in Ireland." But Walker claimed the *Fingalians* as originally Irish. Sir I. Ferguson, in his *Lays of the Western Gael*, says, " The exactions of the Bards were so intolerable that the early Irish more than once endeavoured to rid themselves of the Order." Their arrogance had procured their occasional banishment. Higgins, in *Celtic Druids*, had no exalted opinion of them, saying, " The Irish histories have been most of them filled with lies and nonsense by their bards." Assuredly a great proportion of their works were destroyed by the priests, as they had been in England, Germany, France, &c.

The harp, according to Bede, was common in the seventh century. St. Columba played upon the harp. Meagor says of the first James of Scotland, " On the harp he excelled the Irish or the Highland Scots, who are esteemed the best performers on that instrument." Ireland was the school of music for Welsh and Scotch. Irish harpers were the most celebrated up to the last century. Ledwich thought the harp came in from Saxons and Danes. The Britons, some say, had it from the Romans. The old German harp had eighteen strings; the old Irish, twenty-eight; the modern Irish, thirty-three. Henry VIII. gave Ireland the harp for an armorial bearing, being a great admirer of Irish music ; but James I. quartered it with the arms of France and England. St. Bernard gives Archbishop Malachy, 1134, the credit of introducing music into the Church service of Ireland.

The Irish *cruit* was the Welsh *crwdd* or *crwth.* Hugh Rose relates, that " a certain string was selected as the most suitable for each song." Diodorus Siculus recorded that "the bards of Gaul sang to instruments like lyres." The *crotals* were not Bardic, but bell cymbals of the Church. They were hollow spheres, holding loose bits of metal for rattling, and connected by a flexible shank. The *corn* was a metallic horn ; the drum, or *tiompan*, was a tabor ; the *piob-mela*, or bagpipes, were borrowed from the far East ; the bellows to the bag thereof were not seen till the sixteenth century. The Irish used *foghair*, or whole tones, and *foghair-beg*, or semi-tones. The *cor*, or harmony, was *chruisich*, treble, and *cronan*, base. The names of clefs were from the Latin. In most ancient languages the same word is used for Bard and Sage. Lönnrot found not a parish among the Karelians without several Bards. Quatrefages speaks of Bardic contests thus : " The two bards start strophe after strophe, each repeating at first that which the other had said. The song only stops with the learning of one of the two."

Walker ungallantly wrote, " We cannot find that the Irish had female Bards," while admitting that females cried the *Caoine* over the dead. Yet in *Cathluina* we read, " The daughter of Moran seized the harp, and her voice of music praised the strangers. Their souls melted at the song, like the wreath of snow before the eye of the sun."

The Court Bards were required, says Dr. O'Donovan, to have ready seven times fifty chief stories, and twice fifty sub-stories, to repeat before the Irish King and his chiefs. Conor Mac Neasa, King of Ulster, had three thousand Bards, gathered from persecuting neighbouring chiefs.

" Musician, herald, bard, thrice may'st thou be renowned,
And with three several wreaths immortally be crowned."

Brehons—Breitheamhain—were legislative Bards ; and, said Walker, in 1786, they " promulgated the laws in a kind of recitative, or monotonous chant, seated on an eminence in the open air." According to McCurtin, the Irish Bards of the sixth century wore long, flowing garments, fringed and ornamented with needlework. In a *Life of Columba*, 1827, it is written, " The Bards and Sennachees retained their office, and some degree of their former estimation among the nobility of Caledonia and Ireland, till the accession of the House of Hanover."

" Nothing can prove," says O'Beirne Crowe, " the late introduction of Druidism into our country more satisfactorily than the utter contempt in which the name *bard* is held in all our records.—After the introduction of our irregular system of Druidism, which must have been about the second century of the Christian era, the *Filis* (bard) had to fall into something like the position of the British Bards— hence we see them, down to a late period—practising incantations like the Magi of the continent, and in religious matters holding extensive sway."

Ossianic literature had a higher opinion of the Bards ; as, " Such were the words of the Bards in the days of the Song ; when the King heard the music of harps and the tales of other times. The chiefs gathered from all their hills, and heard the lovely sound. They praised the voice of Cona, the first among a thousand bards." Again, " Sit thou on the heath, O Bard ! and let us hear thy voice. It is pleasant as the gale of the spring, that sighs on the hunter's ear, when he wakens from dreams of joy, and has heard the music of the spirits of the hill.—The music of Cardil was like the memory of joys that are past, pleasant, and mournful to the soul. The ghosts of departed Bards heard it." " My life," exclaimed Fingal, " shall be one stream of light to Bards of other times." Cathmor cried, " Loose the Bards. Their voice shall be heard in other ages, when the Kings of Temora have failed."

Keating, amusingly credulous as an *Irish historian*, records with gravity the story of an ancient militia, numbering nine thousand in time of peace, who had both serjeants and colonels. Into the ranks of these *Fine Eirion* no one was admitted unless proved to be a poetical genius, well acquainted with the twelve books of poetry.

The *Dinn Seanchas* has poems by the Irish Bard of the second century, Finin Mac Luchna ; and it asserts that "the people deemed each other's voices sweeter than the warblings of the melodious harp." On Toland's authority we learn that, for a long time after the English Conquest, the judges, Bards, physicians, and harpers held land tenures in Ireland. The O'Duvegans were hereditary Bards of the O'Kellies ; the O'Shiels were hereditary doctors ; the O'Brodins, hereditary antiquaries ; the Maglanchys, hereditary judges. The Bards were Strabo's hymn-makers.

Mrs. Bryant felt that "The Isle of Song was soon to become the Isle of Saints ;" and considered "Ireland of the Bards knew its Druids simply as men skilled in all magical arts, having no marked relation either to a system of theology, or to a scheme of ceremonial practice."

The *Brehon Law* gives little information respecting Druids, though the Brehons were assumed to have been originally Druid judges. St. Patrick has the credit of compiling this record.

These Brehons had a high reputation for justice ; and yet it is confessed that when one was tempted to pass a false sentence, his chain of office would immediately tighten round his neck most uncomfortably as a warning. Of the Brehons, it is said by the editors—O'Mahony and Richey—"The learning of the Brehons became as useless to the public as the most fantastic discussions of the Schoolmen, and the whole system crystallized into a form which rendered social progress impossible." Though those old Irish laws were so oppressive to the common people, and so favourable to the hereditary chiefs, it was hard indeed to get the people to relinquish them for English laws.

In 1522, English law existed in only four of the Irish counties ; and Brehons and Ollamhs (teachers) were known to the end of the seventeeth century. The founding of the book of Brehon Law is thus explained :—" And when the men of Erin heard—all the power of Patrick since his arrival in Erin—they bowed themselves down in obedience to the will of God and Patrick. It was then that all the professors of the sciences (Druids) in Erin were assembled, and each of them exhibited his art before Patrick, in the presence of every chief in Erin.—What did not clash with the Word of God in the written law, and in the New Testament, and with the consciences of the believers, was confirmed in the laws of the Brehons by Patrick, and by the ecclesiastics and the chieftains of Erin."

ISLE OF MAN DRUIDISM.

The Isle of Man lies just between Ireland and Wales. Let us examine what can be shown about these matters therein.

Boetius, translated by Alfred the Great, had a particularly doubtful story to tell ; too similar, alas ! to the narratives of early Christian writers. " Cratilinth, the Scottish King, A.D. 277," said he, " was very earnest in the overthrow of Druidism in the Isle of Mon and elsewhere ; and upon the occasion of Dioclesian's persecution, when many Christians fled to him for refuge, he gave them the Isle of Mon for their residence." He relates that Mannanan Beg " was the establisher and cultivator of religion after the manner of the Egyptians.—He caused great stones to be placed in the form of a circle."

Train, in his *History of Man*, refers to Mannanan Beg, Mac-y-Leirr, of the first century, having kept the Island under mist by his nêcromancy. " If he dreaded an enemy, he would cause one man to seem a hundred, and that by Art Magic." King Finnan, 134 B.C., is said to have first established Druids there. The Archdruid was known as *Kion-druaight*, or *Ard-druaight*. Plowden thought the Druids emigrated thither after the slaughter at Mona ; others declare Mona to have been an Irish Druidical settlement. Sacheverell refers to Druidical cairns on the tops of hills, which were dedicated to the Sun, and speaks of hymns having what were called cairn tunes. Train says, " So highly were the Manx Druids distinguished for their knowledge of astronomy, astrology, and natural philosophy, that the Kings of Scotland sent their sons to be educated there." He thought that until 1417, "in imitation of the practice of the Druids, the laws of the Island were locked up in the breasts of the Deemsters." The old rude edifices of stone are still called *Tinan Druinich*, or Druids' houses. McAlpine says that *Druid* in Manx is *Magician*.

FRENCH DRUIDISM.

The *Deroo* of Brittany were more ancient, said Henri Martin, than those Druids known to Romans ; being "primitive Druids, a sacerdotal caste of old Celts." Yet Forlong, who believed the Gallic coast tribes long traded and intermarried with the Phœnicians, saw "abundant evidences for their worshipping Astarte and Herakles." They were Saronidæ, or judges. They were the builders, masons, or like Gobhan Saer, free smiths. Of Saer, O'Brien in his *Round Towers* says—" The first name ever given to this body (Freemasons) was *Saer*, which has three significations : firstly, *free ;* secondly, *mason ;* and thirdly, *son of*

God." Keane calls him "one of the Guabhres or Cabiri, such as you have ever seen him represented on the Tuath de Danaan Cross at Clonmacnoise."

A Breton poem, *Ar Rannou*, a dialogue between a Druid and his pupil, is still sung by villagers, as it may have been by their ancestors, the *Venite* of Cæsar's story. The seat of the Archdruid of Gaul was at Dreux.

French writers have interested themselves in the Druidic question. The common impression is that Druids were only to be found in Brittany; but other parts of France possessed those priests and bards. Certainly the north-west corner, the region of megalithic remains, continued later to be their haunt, being less disturbed there. It was in Brittany, also, that the before-mentioned Oriental mysticism found so safe a home, and was nurtured so assiduously. But Druids were equally known in the south, centre, and north-east of France.

Dijon Druids, or the *Vacies*, were described in 1621 by Guenebauld of Dijon in *Le Reveil de Chyndonax, Prince des Vacies Drvydes Celtiqves Düonois*. Upon the tomb of the Archdruid Chyndonax was found an inscription in Greek, thus rendered by the Dijon author—

> " En ce tombeau, dans le sacré boccage
> Du Dieu Mithras, est contenu le corps
> De Chyndonax grand Prestre ; mechant hors,
> Les Dieux Sanneurs le gardent de dommage."

Numbers of the learned went to view the inscription, and an urn found within the tomb. Mithras was a form of Apollo, or the Sun. There are other evidences of the southern Gaulish Druids using Greek characters, beyond Cæsar's assertions.

Guenebauld spoke of the prohibition of the Druidical religion by the Emperors Augustus, Tiberias, and Claudius ; adding that the Druids " furent chassez du mont Drvys or

Drvyde proche d'ostum, a cause de leur trop cruel sacrifice d'hommes." He declared that after the general Edict of Claudius " il ne s'en treuva plus, parmy les Gaulois." When banished from Gaul, they retired to Britain, though Druid-esses were mentioned as being at Dijon in the time of Aurelian.

Beaudeau, in 1777, published *Memoire à consulter pour les anciens Druides Gaulois*, intended as a vindication of them against the strictures of Bailly in his letters to Voltaire. He had a great belief in the astronomical skill of the Druids, from their use of the thirty years cycle, the revolution period of the planet Saturn.

At the Congress of Arras, in 1853, the question debated was—" Up to what period Roman polytheism had pene-trated into Belgic Gaul ;—and up to what period continued the struggle between Polytheism and Christianity ? " The French author remarks, " The Romans did but one thing— gave the names of their gods to the divinities of the people of Fleanderland. And these divinities—what were they ? Evidently those of the country from which the people had been forced to flee."

Dezobry and Bachelets, in their *Dictionnaire de Biogra-phie*, &c., affirm that " the Celtic word *derouyd* (from *de* or *di*, God, and *rhoud* or *rhouid*, speaking) signifies Interpreter of the gods, or one who speaks from the gods. According to others, the etymology should be, in the Gaelic language, *druidheacht*, divination, magic ; or, better, *dern*, oak, and *wydd*, mistletoe." Acknowledging the ancient renown of their knowledge, it is admitted to be imperfectly known to us, though Pythagoreans pretended to be the founders thereof. The French authors had the following account of the Druids' great charm—

" They carried suspended from their neck, as a mark of dignity, a serpent's egg—a sort of oval ball of crystal, that in the time of Pliny tradition pretended to be the product of the foam of a quantity of serpents, grouped and interlaced together. This egg has been the origin of a crowd of superstitions, which, up to a century ago, were in vogue in Cornwall, Wales, and the mountains of Scotland ; they continued to carry these balls of glass, called *serpent stones*, to which they attributed particular virtues."

Druidesses of Gaul had a sanctuary on the Isle of Sena, Finisterre. Druidism in France was condemned as late as 658, by the Council of Nantes ; and, later on, by the Capitularies of Charlemagne. Renan supposed that Druidism remained a form exclusively national. Justin's remark, that "the Greek colony of Marseilles civilized the Gauls," may help to explain how Gaulish Druids knew Greek, and how some French writers traced Druidism to the Phocians of Southern Gaul. Then, again, we have Ammianus Marcellinus saying, " The Druids were formed into fraternities as the authority of Pythagoras decreed." Cæsar, in his account of Gaulish Druids, had clearly in his mind his own country's faith. They were like his own augurs, and their Archdruid was his *pontifex maximus.*

D'Arbois de Jubainville, in his account of Irish Mythology, has, of course, references to the Druids. He lays emphasis on the difference between those of Gaul and those of our islands. The judicial authority was vested in the *Filé.* These need not, like the Druids proper, celebrate sacrifices. He traces the word *file*, a seer, from the same root as the Breton *givelout*, to see.

The French author records that Polyhistor, Timagenus, Valerius Maximus, and others wrote of the north-western men holding Pythagorean doctrines ; but he adds, that while a second birth was regarded by the Pythagoreans as a punishment of evil, it was esteemed by the others as a privilege of heroes.

GERMAN DRUIDISM.

Louis de Baecker, 1854, gave an account of Teutonic Druidism, similar to that of the Belgæ of Britain, in his *De la Religion du Nord de la France avant le Christianisme.* He, unlike men of the Welsh Druidic school, joins Dr. Ledwich, and some Irish authorities, in tracing Druidism to the German and Scandinavian races; saying, " The religion of our pagan ancestors was that of Odin or Woden." But he evidently refers to north-eastern France rather than north-western, as he derives the religion from the Edda. In the book *Volu-Spa,* or the Priestess, the first song of the poetic Edda, he discovers what Ossian and other British and Irish bards describe as Spirits of the air, of earth, of waters, of plains, and woods. " Cæsar was deceived," says he, " when he said that the Germans had neither priests nor religious ceremonies ; for Tacitus mentions them in his *Germania* in the most formal manner." By the way, if Cæsar was so mistaken about the Germans, whom he knew so well, is his evidence about Gaulish Druids worth much ?

Baecker's northern Gauls had priests of various kinds. The sacrificers were called *Blodmanner,* or *Pluostari ;* the sustainers of order were *Ewart* and *Gotes-ewart ;* the pro- tectors of sacred woods, *Harugari, Parawari,* or *Wihes- mart ;* the prophets, *Spamadhr, Wizago, Vitega, Veitsga, Weissager, Wetekey.* The Priestesses were the *Vaulur.* The horse, bull, boar, and sheep were sacrificed. " It was in the middle of the wood," he writes, " that the Belgæ offered their sacrifices." The Belgic Britons, doubtless, had a similar Druidism.

Cæsar asserts that the Germans had no Druids, while he credits the German Belgæ of South Britain with having them.

DRUIDICAL MAGIC.

As to magical arts, exercised by Druids and Druidesses, the ancient Irish MSS. are full of stories about them. Joyce has said, " The Gaelic word for *Druidical* is almost always applied where we should use the word *magical*—to spells, incantations, metamorphoses, &c." Not even China at the present day is more given to charms and spells than was Ireland of old. Constant application of Druidic arts upon the individual must have given a sadness and terror to life, continuing long after the Druid had been supplanted.

It was a comfort to know that magician could be pitted against magician, and that though one might turn a person into a swan or horse, another could turn him back again.

Yet, the *chewing of one's thumb* was sometimes as effectual a disenchanter as the elevation or marking of the cross in subsequent centuries. Thus, when Fionn was once invited to take a seat beside a fair lady on her way to a palace, he, having some suspicion, put his thumb between his teeth, and she immediately changed into an ugly old hag with evil in her heart. That was a simple mode of detection, but may have been efficacious only in the case of such a hero as Fionn. Certainly, many a bad spirit would be expelled, in a rising quarrel, if one party were wise enough to put his thumb between his teeth.

Charm-mongers, who could take off a spell, must have been popular characters, and as useful as wart-removers. It is a pity, however, that the sacred salmon which used to frequent the Boyne is missing now, when examinations are so necessary, as he or she who bit a piece forgot nothing ever after. Balar, the Fomorian King, was a good-natured fellow, for, finding that a glance from his right eye caused death to a subject, he kept that eye constantly closed.

One way of calling spirits from the deep, to do one's will, was to go to sleep with the palms of both hands upon the cheek. The magic cauldron was not in such requirement as with the Welsh. But it was a Druidic trick to take an idol to bed, lay the hands to the face, and discover the secret of a riddle in dreams. Another trick reminds one of the skill of modern spiritualistic mediums, who could discover the history of a man by a piece of his coat; for, Cormac read the whole life of a dog from the skull.

Healing powers were magical. Our forefathers fancied that a part of enjoyment in heaven was fighting by day and feasting at night, the head cut off in daylight conflict resuming its position when the evening table was spread. The rival forces of Fomorians and Danaans had Druids, whose special work was to heal the wounded at night, so as to be ready for the next morning's battle.

In the *Story of Deirdri* it is written, "As Conor saw this, he went to Cathbad the Druid, and said to him, 'Go, Cathbad, unto the sons of Usnach, and play Druidism upon them.'" This was done. "He had recourse to his intelligence and art to restrain the children of Usnach, so that he laid them under enchantment, that is, by putting around them a viscid sea of whelming waves."

Nothing was more common than the raising of Druidic fogs. It would be easier to do that in Ireland or Scotland than in Australia. The *Story of Cu* speaks of a King Brudin who "made a black fog of Druidism" by his *draoidheacht*, or magic. Druidic winds were blasting, as they came from the East. The *Children of Lir* were made to wander on the Irish Sea till the land became Christian.

A wonderful story in an old MS. respecting Diarmuid is connected with the threatened divorce of the lovely Mughain, as no prince had appeared to her husband the King. "On this," says the chronicler, "the Queen went

to Finnen, a Magus (Druid) of Baal or Belus, and to
Easbad, named Aedha, son of Beg, and told them she was
barren. The Reataire (chief Druids) then consecrated some
water, of which she drank, and conceived ; and the produce
of her womb was a white lamb. 'Woe is me!' said Mughain,' to bring forth a four-footed beast.' 'Not so,' replied
Finnen, 'for your womb is thereby sanctified, and the
lamb must be sacrificed as your first-born.' The priests
blessed the water for her, she drank, and conceived. Say
the priests, 'You shall now bring forth a son, and he shall
be King over Ireland.' Then Finnen and Easbad Aedha
blessed the Queen and the seed of her loins, and giving
her more consecrated water, she drank of it, and called
his name *Aedh Slaines,* because he was saved from the
sacrifice."

Well might Vallencey exclaim, " The whole of this story
is strong of Chaldæan Paganism, and could not have been
invented by any Christian monks whatever."

Cuchulainn of Ulster was much given to magic. He
caught birds by it. He left his wife to be with a lady in
fairy-land. Caught by spells, he was brought back home.
He drank the draught of forgetfulness that he might not
remember fairy-land, and she drank to forget her jealousy.
All this is in *Leabhar na-h-Uidhré.*

When the Danaans raised a storm to drive off the invading hosts of Milesians, this was the spell used by Milesius, as told in the *Book of Invasions:*—" I pray that they
reach the land of Erinn, these who are riding upon the
great, productive, vast sea—that there may be a King for
us in Tara,—that noble Erinn be a home for the ships and
boats of the son of Milesius."

By the 14th Canon of the Synod at Armagh, as asserted
for the year 448, a penance was exacted for any sooth-
saying, or the foretelling of future events by an inspection

of animals' entrails, as was the practice with the Druids. It is curious to see how this magic was, by the early writers, associated with Simon Magus ; so much so, that, as Rhys observes, " The Goidelic Druids appear at times under the name of the School of Simon Druid."

Fionn was once coursing with his dog Bran, when the hare suddenly turned into a lady weeping for the loss of her ring in the lake. Like a gallant, the hero dived down and got it ; but all he had for his trouble was to be turned by her into a white-haired old man. On another occasion he was changed into a grey fawn. But Fionn endured the metamorphoses of twenty years as a hog, one hundred a stag, one hundred an eagle, and thirty a fish, besides living one hundred as a man. The heroine Caer had to be alternate years a swan and a woman.

The *Kilkenny Transactions* refer to one Liban, transformed for three hundred years as a fish, or, rather a mermaid, with her lap-dog in the shape of an otter after her. Bevan, however, caught her in a net, had her baptized, and then she died. In the *Fate of the Children of Lir*, we read of Aoife, second wife of Lir, jealous of her husband's children by his first mate, turning them into four swans till her spell could be broken. This happened under the Tuath rule, and lasted nine hundred years. They are reported to have said, " Thou shalt fall in revenge for it, for thy power for our destruction is not greater than the Druidic power of our friends to avenge it upon thee." However, having musical qualities, they enjoyed themselves in chanting every night. At last they heard the bell of St. Patrick. This broke the spell. They sang to the High King of heaven, revealed their name, and cried out, " Come to baptize us, O cleric, for our death is near."

An odd story of the Druid Mananan is preserved in the *Ossian Transactions.* It concerned a magical branch, bearing nine apples of gold. They who shook the tree were lulled to sleep by music, forgetting want or sorrow.

Through that, Cormac, grandson of Conn of the hundred fights, lost his wife Eithne, son Cairbre, and daughter Ailbhe. At the end of a year's search, and passing through a dark, magical mist, he came to a hut, where a youth gave him a pork supper. The entertainer proved to be Mananan. The story runs, " After this Mananan came to him in his proper shape, and said thus : ' I it was who bore these three away from thee ; I it was who gave thee that branch, and it was in order to bring thee to this house. It was I that worked magic upon you, so that you might be with me to-night in friendship.' " It may be doubted if this satisfied King Cormac.

A chessboard often served the purpose of divination. The laying on of hands has been from remote antiquity an effectual mode for the transmission of a charm. But a *Magic Wand* or *Rod*, in proper hands, has been the approved method of transformation, or any other miraculous interposition. Here is one *Wand* story relative to the romance of Grainne and Diarmuid :—" Then came the Reachtaire again, having a Magic Wand of sorcery, and struck his son with 'that wand, so that he made of him a cropped pig, having neither ear nor tail, and he said, ' I conjure thee that thou have the same length of life as Diarmuid O'Duibhne, and that it be by thee that he shall fall at last.' "

This was the boar that killed, not the Syrian Adonis, but a similar sun-deity, Diarmuid. When Fionn, the disappointed husband, in pursuit of the runaway, found the abductor dying, he was entreated by the beautiful solar hero to save him. " How can I do it ? " asked the half-repentant Fionn. " Easily," said the wounded one ; " for when thou didst get the noble, precious gift of divining at the Boinn, it was given thee that to whomsoever thou shouldst give a drink from the palms of thy hands, he should after that be young and sound from every sickness." Unhappily, Fionn was so long debating with himself as to this gift to his enemy, that, when he walked towards him with the water, life had departed from the boar-stricken Irish Adonis.

Dr. W. R. Sullivan has a translation of the *Fair of Carman*, concerning three magicians and their mother from Athens :—

" By charms, and spells, and incantations, the mother blighted every place, and it was through magical devastation and dishonesty that the men dealt out destruction. They came to Erin to bring evil upon the Tuatha de Danann, by blighting the fertility of this isle. The Tuatha were angry at this ; and they sent against them Ai, the son of Allamh, on the part of their poets, and Credenbel on the part of their satirists, and Lug Laeban, *i. e.* the son of Cacher, on the part of their Druids, and Becuille on the part of the witches, to pronounce incantations against them. And these never parted from them until they forced the three men over the sea, and they left a pledge behind them, *i. e.* Carman, their mother, that they would never return to Erin."

A counter-charm is given in the *Senchus Mor.* When the Druids sought to poison St. Patrick, the latter wrote over the liquor :—

" Tubu fis fri ibu, fis ibu anfis,
Fris bru uatha, ibu lithu, Christi Jesus."

He left it on record that whoever pronounced these words over poison or liquor should receive no injury from it. It might be useful with Irish whisky ; only the translator adds that the words of the charm, like most of the charms of the Middle Ages, appear to have had no meaning.

Spiritualism, in all its forms, appears to have been practised by the Irish and Scotch Druids. Dr. Armstrong's
Gaelic Dictionary has an account of the Divination of the
Toghairm, once a noted superstition among the Gaels, and
evidently derived from Druid-serving ancestors. The so-
called prophet " was wrapped in the warm, smoking roue of
a newly slain ox or cow, and laid at full length in the
wildest recess of some lonely waterfall. The question was
then put to him, and the oracle was left in solitude to
consider it." The steaming body cultivated the frenzy for
a reply, although " it was firmly believed to have been
communicated by invisible beings."

Similar traditions are related by Kennedy, in *Fictions of
the Irish Celts*. One of the tales is of Sculloge, who spent
his father's gold. While out hunting he saw an old man
betting his left hand against his right. At once he played
with him for sixpence, but won of the ancient Druid a
hundred guineas. The next game won, the old fellow was
made to rebuild the Irishman's mill. Another victory
brought him as wife a princess from the far country. But
Sabina, when married, besought him to have no more to do
with old Lassa Buaicht of the glen.

Things went on well a good while, till the man wanted
more gold, and he ventured upon a game. Losing, he was
directed to bring the old Druid the *Sword of Light*. Sabina
helped her husband to a Druidic horse, that carried him to
her father's castle. There he learned it was held by another
brother, also a Druid, in an enchanted place. With a black
steed he leaped the wall, but was driven out by the magic
sword. At last, through Fiach the Druid, the sword was
given to Lassa Buaicht. The cry came, " Take your Sword
of Light, and off with his head." Then the un-spelled wife
reappeared, and the couple were happy ever after.

Conn of the Hundred Battles is often mentioned in

connection with Druids. One of the Irish MSS. thus introduces the Magical Stone of Tara:—" One evening Conn repaired at sunrise to the battlements of the Ri Raith or Royal fortress at Tara, accompanied by his three Druids, Mael, Bloc, and Bluicné, and his three poets, Ethain, Corb, and Cesare ; for he was accustomed every day to repair to this place with the same company, for the purpose of watching the firmament, that no hostile aërial beings should descend upon Erin unknown to him. While standing in the usual place this morning, Conn happened to tread on a stone, and immediately the stone shrieked under his feet so as to be heard all over Tara, and throughout all Bregia or East Meath. Conn then asked his Druids why the stone had shrieked, what its name was, and what it said. The Druids took fifty-three days to consider, and returned the following answer :—' *Fal* is the name of the stone ; it came from Inis Fal, or the Island of Fal. It has shrieked under your royal feet, and the number of the shrieks, which the stone has given forth, is the number of Kings that will succeed you.' "

At the Battle of Magh Tuireadh with the Fomorians, it is said that the chief men of the Tuatha de Danann " called their smiths, their brass-workers, their sorcerers, their Druids, their poets, &c." The Druids were engaged putting the wounded in a bath of herbs, and then returning them whole to the battle ranks.

Nash, who showed much scepticism respecting Druids in Britain, wrote :—" In the Irish tales, on the contrary, the magician under the name of Draoi and Drudh, magician or Druid, *Draioideacht*, *Druidheat*, magic plays a considerable part." The Cabiri play a great part according to some authors ; one speaks of the " magic of Samhan, that is to say, Cabur." A charm against evil spirits, found at Poitiers, is half Gallic, half Latin. Professor Lottner saw that " the Gallic words were identical with expressions still used in Irish."

We are told of a rebel chief who was helped by a Druid against the King of Munster, to plague the Irish in the south-west by magically drying up all the water. The King succeeded in finding another Druid who brought forth an abundant supply. He did but cast his javelin, and a powerful spring burst forth at the spot where the weapon fell. Dill, the Druidical grandfather of another King of Munster, had a magical black horse, which won at every race.

Elsewhere is a chapter on the Tuatha de Danaans, concerning whom are so many stories of Druids. Attention is drawn by Rhys to " the tendency of higher races to ascribe magical powers to lower ones ; or, rather, to the conquered."

A Druid's counsel was sometimes of service. A certain dwarf magician of Erregal, Co. Derry, had done a deal of mischief before he could be caught, killed, and buried. It was not long before he rose from the dead, and resumed his cruelties. Once more slain, he managed to appear again at his work. A Druid advised Finn Mac Cumhail to bury the fellow the next time head downward, which effectually stopped his magic and his resurrection powers.

Fintain was another hero of antiquity. When the Deluge occurred, he managed by Druidic arts to escape. Subsequently, through the ages, he manifested himself in various forms. This was, to O'Flaherty, an evidence that Irish Druids believed in the doctrine of metempsychosis. Fintain's grave is still to be recognized, though he has made no appearance on earth since the days of King Dermot.

It is not safe to run counter to the Druids. When King Cormac turned against the Craft, Maelgenn incited the

Siabhradh, an evil spirit, to take revenge. By turning himself into a salmon, he succeeded in choking the sovereign with one of his bones. It was Fraechan, Druid of King Diarmaid, who made the wonderful *Airbhi Druadh,* or Druidical charm, that caused the death of three thousand warriors.

A King was once plagued by a lot of birds wherever he went. He inquired of his Druid Becnia as to the place they came from. The answer was, " From the East." Then came the order—" Bring me a tree from every wood in Ireland." This was to get the right material to serve as a charm. Tree after tree failed to be of use. Only that from the wood of Frosmuine produced what was required for a charm. Upon the *dichetal,* or incantation, being uttered, the birds visited the King no more.

In the *Book of Lecan* is the story of a man who underwent some remarkable transformations. He was for 300 years a deer, for 300 a wild boar, for 300 a bird, and for the like age a salmon. In the latter state he was caught, and partly eaten by the Queen. The effect of this repast was the birth of Tuan Mac Coireall, who told the story of the antediluvian colonization of Ireland. One Druid, Trosdane, had a bath of the milk of thirty white-faced cows, which rendered his body invulnerable to poisoned arrows in battle.

A Druid once said to Dathi, " I have consulted the clouds of the man of Erin, and found that thou wilt soon return to Tara, and wilt invite all the provincial Kings and chiefs of Erin to the great feast of Tara, and there thou shalt decide with them upon making an expedition into Alba, Britain, and France, following the conquering footsteps of thy great-uncle Niall." He succeeded in Alba, but died in Gaul. A brother of his became a convert to St. Patrick.

Grainne, the heroine of an elopement with the beautiful hero Diarmuid, or Dermot, fell into her trouble through a Druid named Daire Duanach MacMorna. She was the daughter of King Cormac, whose grave is still shown at Tara, but she was betrothed to the aged, gigantic sovereign Fionn the Fenian. At the banquet in honour of the alliance, the Druid told the lady the names and qualities of the chiefs assembled, particularly mentioning the graceful Diarmuid. She was smitten by his charms, particularly a love-mark on his shoulder, and readily agreed to break her promised vows in order to share his company. When she fled with him, Fionn and his son pursued the couple, who were aided in their flight by another Druid named Diorraing, styled a skilful man of science.

A fine poem—*The Fate of the Son of Usnach*—relates the trials of Deirdri the Fair. Dr. Keating has this version : " Caffa the Druid foreboded and prophesied for the daughter (Deirdri, just born), that numerous mischiefs and losses would happen the Province (Ulster) on her account. Upon hearing this, the nobles proposed to put her to death forthwith. ' Let it not be done so,' cried Conor (King), ' but I will take her with me, and send her to be reared, that she may become my own wife.' " It was in her close retreat that she was seen and loved by Naisi, the son of Usnach, and this brought on a fearful war between Ulster and Alba.

The *Book of Leinster* has the story of one that loved the Queen, who returned the compliment, but was watched too well to meet with him. He, however, and his foster-brother, were turned, by a Druidic spell, into two beautiful birds, and so gained an entrance to the lady's bower, making their escape again by a bird transformation. The King had some suspicion, and asked his Druid to find out the secret. The next time the birds flew, the King had his watch; and, as soon as they resumed their human appearance, he set upon them and killed both.

The *Book of Leinster* records several cases of Druids taking opposite sides in battle. It was Greek meeting Greek. The northern Druids plagued the southern men by drying up the wells; but Mog Ruth, of the South, drove a silver tube into the ground, and a spring burst forth. Ciothrue made a fire, and said a charm with his mountain-ash stick, when a black cloud sent down a shower of blood. Nothing daunted, the other Druid, Mog Ruth, transformed three noisy northern Druids into stones.

Spiritualism, as appears by the *Banquet of Dun na n-Gedh*, was used thus:—" This is the way it is to be done. The poet chews a piece of the flesh of a red pig, or of a dog or cat, and brings it afterwards on a flag behind the door, and chants an incantation upon it, and offers it to idol gods; and his idol gods are brought to him, but he finds them not on the morrow. And he pronounces incantations on his two palms; and his idol gods are also brought to him, in order that his sleep may not be interrupted. And he lays his two palms on his two cheeks, and thus falls asleep. And he is watched in order that no one may disturb or interrupt him, until everything about which he is engaged is revealed to him, which may be a minute, or two, or three, or as long as the ceremony requires—one palm over the other across his cheeks."

The author of *The Golden Bough*, J. G. Frazer, judiciously reminds us that "the superstitious beliefs and practices, which have been handed down by word of mouth, are generally of a far more archaic type than the religions depicted in the most ancient literature of the Aryan race." A careful reading of the chapter on the "Superstitions of the Irish" would be convincing on that point.

Among ancient superstitions of the Irish there was some relation to the *Sacred Cow*, reminding one of India, or even of the Egyptian worship of Apis. The *Ossianic Transactions* refer to this peculiarity.

There was the celebrated *Glas Gaibhne*, or Grey Cow of the Smith of the magical Tuaths. This serviceable animal supplied a large family and a host of servants. The Fomorians envied the possessor, and their leader stole her. The captive continued her beneficent gifts for many generations. Her ancient camps are still remembered by the peasantry. Another story is of King Diarmuid Mac Cearbhail, half a Druid and half a Christian, who killed his son for destroying a Sacred Cow. But Owen Connelan has a translation of the *Proceedings of the Great Bardic Institute*, which contains the narrative of a cow, which supplied at Tuaim-Daghualan the daily wants of nine score nuns ; these ladies must have been Druidesses, the word *Caillach* meaning equally *nuns* and *Druidesses*. As W. Hackett remarks, " The probability is that they were pagan Druidesses, and that the cows were living idols like Apis, or in some sense considered sacred animals."

One points out the usefulness of the Irish Druids in a day when enchantments prevailed. Etain, wife of Eochaid, was carried off by Mider through the roof, and two swans were seen in the air above Tara, joined together by a golden yoke. However, the husband managed to recover his stolen property by the aid of the mighty spell of his Druid.

NEO-DRUIDISM.

Edward Davies, author of *Mythology and Rites of British Druids*, was one of those who, with Jolo Morganwg, regarded the Arkite theory as having its foundation in Genesis. But,

as Professor Rhys says, " when one turns to Davies's authorities for his unhesitating statements of the kind, no doubt
one is a little dismayed at first, and not a little inclined
to doubt him altogether, and, in disposing of his Helio-
Arkite absurdity, dispose of the Druids with them."

The *Modern Druidism*, or *Bardism*, about which a few
years ago there was considerable excitement in Wales,
must not be confounded with the Druidism of Myfyr and
Morien, who sought the revival of what was declared by
others to be a mystical paganism. The Bardism of this
century, brought forward by Welsh clergymen, like *Ab Ithel*,
&c., was founded upon the so-called Welsh *Triads* of the
Middle Ages, which were interpreted in a *quasi* Christian
light, and presumed to have been the relics of the Scriptural
Patriarchal system.

The Rev. John Williams was, perhaps, the best exponent
of Bardism, though all its advocates recognized in it the
Church of England ideas of this century, and yet hardly
of the High Church order. The *Patriarchal Religion of
Britain*, by the Rev. Dr. James, made many converts to the
system. But the ceremonies associated with it have something of the Masonic character. This is the Summary of
the Bardo-Druidic creed :—

There was one God. There were five elements—earth,
water, fire, air, and heavens. The soul—refined, vital, and
imperishable—is a lapsed intelligence, regaining happiness
by transmigration. Creation improved as man improved,
and animals gradually became men. Man develops by
experience in different states of being. Celestial beings
aid man in development. Ultimately all will be happy,
and evil finally extinguished. All these views were
gathered from the said Triads, though regarded by many
pious Welshmen as teaching opposed to Christianity.

Morien's reading of the Triads is something very different ; for *The Light of Britannia* has no Bardo-Druidic creed.

DRUIDICAL BELIEF.

Immortality was adjudged to be a Druidic creed.

The *Inverness Gaelic Society's Journal* has this affirm-ation : " They looked for an immortality more substantial than the rewards of fame, in a heroic state in the far-off spirit land, to which the bards, it would appear, issued the passport.—There lay the realms of mystery." Beyond that, however, was "the roofless house of lasting doom," to which illustrious spirits eventually passed. As a Skye tale implies, there was a happier region in the *Beyond*, from which there was no return. The ghosts, that ap-peared, came, as they are said by Spiritualists of our day still to come, from a sort of pleasant Purgatory, where they enjoyed awhile a free and easy condition of existence.

Ammianus Marcellinus recorded : " The Druids, who united in a Society, occupied themselves with profound and sublime questions, raised themselves above human affairs, and sustained the immortality of the soul." On the other hand, Archbishop Whately, and many more, maintained that there was no proof of immortality independent of revelation.

This idea of life had, however, a peculiar connection with pre-existence and transmigration. Thus, George Eliot refers to their finding "new bodies, animating them in a quaint and ghastly way with antique souls." So Wordsworth—

" Our life's star
Hath had elsewhere its setting,
And cometh from far."

The soul descended into the womb of nature to be re-born

in another body. Cæsar ascertained that Druids "are anxious to have it believed that souls do not die, but after death pass from one to another." Troyon fancied men of the Stone Age accepted reincarnation; since they buried their dead crouching, to imitate the babe in the womb. Lord Brougham asserted that the ancients "all believed in the soul's pre-existence." Theosophists hold that Druids recognized the Karmic land. Mormons share the like faith. Morien refers to souls waiting in the Sea of Annwn, to be called up to inhabit new bodies. Taliesin sang, "My original country is the land of Cherubim."

What said the Irish upon immortality?

Their word *Nullog, newbeily*, implied regeneration. Their many tales of transmigration, or life under varied conditions, are well known. An old MS. has this of a ghost :—

> " Fionn never slept a calm sleep
> From that night to the day of his death."

This, says O'Kearney, "is a poetical licence, and evidently refers to the time when the spirit of Fionn, according to the Druidic doctrine of the transmigration of souls, should assume mortality in some other shape and character, and revisit the earth." The same author—noting the dialogue between St. Patrick and Oisin the Fenian, who had been three hundred years in the Land of Youth—observes, "It is doubtful if St. Patrick ever saw the real Oisin, but only some Druid or old Seanchaidhe who believed himself to be Oisin revived."

Donald Ross, taking the creed of the old Scots, said, "They held a modified form of Pythagorean metempsychosis; for the soul is represented as emigrating into the lower animals, and even into trees, stones, and other inanimate objects." Two versions are given of the lives of Tuan Mac Coireall; one, that he lived 100 years as a man, 300 as a deer, 300 as a boar, 300 as a bird, and 300 as a salmon; the other was, that he was 100 years a man, 20 a hog, 30 a stag, 100 an eagle, and 30 a fish. To this day butterflies are spoken of as souls of some deceased persons.

Dr. A. G. Richey, Q. C., when quoting from pre-Christian MSS., is careful to intimate that they were "not more historically credible or useful than the Hellenic—the *Tain Bo* than the *Iliad.*" He gives the wonderful adventures of Fintan, who passed through many lives on earth, and appeared to St. Patrick. He was for a year beneath the waters of the Deluge, but in a fast sleep. A couple of verses of the poem will suffice.

> "I was then in Ireland,—
> Pleasant was my condition
> When Partholon arrived
> From the Grecian country in the East.
> After that the Tuatha De arrived,
> Concealed in their dark clouds;
> I ate my food with them,
> Although at such a remote period."

Dr. H. Waddell, dealing with the Druids, points out— "Purification by fire for body and soul, and assimilation thereby to the purest essence of the universe, were the fundamental ideas of their creed—the infallible means of the highest and most acceptable apotheosis." Rhys remarks—"That they believed in a dominant faith and transmigration is pretty certain."

"Irish transmigration," remarks O'Beirne Crowe, "means the soul's passing from man into other animals—man and all subordinate animals included. This is Irish trans-migration, called by the Greeks, transformation of one body into another, while the Gaulish is transmigration of a soul into the body of another human being." He adds—"But is this transformation a Druidic doctrine? Most certainly not ; it is purely Pythagorean, and must have for many centuries preceded Druidism in this strange land of ours."

The revival of Reincarnation, by Madame Blavatsky, and the Theosophists under the eloquent Mrs. Besant, shows the persistency of the idea that so entranced the semi-civilized Irish long ago, and seemed so satisfactory a way to account for the existence of man after death.

Transmigration being found in Ireland, has led some to assert their conviction that Buddhist missionaries conveyed it thither. The *Soc. des Antiquaires de France* had an article, from the pen of Coquebert-Montbret, advancing this opinion, relying upon the known ardour and extensive proselytism of early Buddhist missionaries. He knows the Irish deity *Budd* or *Budwas,* and asks if that be not *Buddha.* In the Hebrides, spirits are called *Boduchs*, and the same word is applied to all heads of families, as the Master. The Druids were, says one, only an order of Eastern priests, located in Britain, adoring Buddwas.

The St. Germain Museum has, in its Gaulish department, an altar, on which is represented a god with the legs crossed after the manner of the Indian Buddha. That relic is the fourth of the kind found in France. Anderson Smith, in his *Lewisiana*, writes reluctantly—" we must accept the possibility of a Buddhist race passing north from Ireland." This means, that Ireland is to be regarded as the source of so many Buddhist significations which are discovered on the west of Scotland, and in the Hebrides.

It has been generally accepted that Druidism was Celtic in origin and practice, because Cæsar found it in Gaul and Britain. But he records three races in Gaul itself—the Celtic, the German, and the Aquitani. The Britons were, to him, Belgæ, or of German connection. He knew nothing of Ireland or Wales, in which two countries he would have seen the fellows of his Aquitani, a darker people than either Celt or German. Prof. Rhys, one of the highest living authorities, was justified in thinking that Druidism was "probably to be traced to the race or races which preceded the Celts in their possession of the British Isles." The Iberians, with dark eyes and hair, belonged to these Isles, as well as in north-west and south-west Gaul. In Brittany, as in Wales, to this day, the Iberian and Celt may be seen side by side.

A discussion has arisen in French scientific journals, as to the apparently different views of Druidism in writings attributed to Pythagoras and to Cæsar. Hermand pointed out their contradiction. Lamariouze remarked—"One says there were in all Celtic lands neither temples nor statues; the other, on the contrary, would declare he had found the worship of Roman divinities, and consequently temples, statues, images." Pythagoras was told by a Druid that he believed " in one Divinity alone, who is everywhere, since He is in all."

Lamariouze failed to see any decided difference in the two authorities, saving the modification occasioned by the Roman domination. He saw in one of the constituents and principles of the Gaulish religion the proscription of temples and idols, recalling the well-known fact of the destruction of the temple of Delphi by the same people. He points out that Cæsar spoke of a *likeness* to Roman idols, not the idols themselves, especially in the relation of so many of Mercury.

Of the Gaulish Druids, Lamariouze said—" Besides these purely spiritual beliefs, they permitted a material worship for the people. They permitted the adoration of God in that which the ancients named the Elements."

Some hold that the Druids were either strangers from afar, or an esoteric body of the learned, who permitted the vulgar to indulge their heathenish practices, while they themselves maintained loftier conceptions. The early Christian missionaries seemed to have adopted a like policy in allowing their converts considerable liberty, especially if safe-guarded by a change of names in their images. For instance, as Fosbroke's *British Monarchism* says, " British churches, from policy, were founded upon the site of Druidical temples."

The three *rays* of the Druids, three yods, *fleur-de-lis*, broad arrow, or otherwise named, may have represented light from heaven, or the male attributes, in the descending way, and female ones when in the reversed position. They may have been Buddhist, or even ancient Egyptian—and may have symbolized different sentiments at different times, or in different lands.

As Druids, like other close bodies, wrote nothing, we depend upon outside pagans, and Christian teachers, for what we know of their doctrines. Doubtless, as many Spanish Jews kept secretly their old faith after the enforced adoption of Christianity, so may some Irish monks have partly retained theirs, and even revealed it, under a guise, in their writings, since ecclesiastical authority shows that Druidism was not wholly extinct in the sixteenth century.

While some authorities imagined the Druids preceded the ordinary polytheistic religion, others taught that they introduced pantheism. Amédée Thierry, in *Histoire des Gaulois*, found it based on pantheism, material, metaphysical, mysterious, sacerdotal, offering the most striking likeness to the religions of the East. He discovered no historic light as to how the Cymry acquired this religion, nor why it resembled the pantheism of the East, unless through their early sojourn on the borders of Asia.

" The empire of Druidism," says he, " did not destroy the religion of exterior nature, which had preceded it. All learned and mysterious religions tolerate an undercurrent of gross fetishism to occupy and nourish the superstition of the multitude."

Again he writes—"But in the east and south of Gaul, where Druidism had not been imposed at the point of the sword, although it had become the prevailing form of worship, the ancient religion preserved more independence, even under the ministry of the Druids, who made themselves its priests. It continued to be cultivated, if I may use the word, following the march of civilization and public intelligence, rose gradually from fetishism to religious conceptions more and more purified." Was it in this way that Druids found their way to Britain and Ireland?

Cæsar, who saw nothing of the religion among these islands, was told that here was the high seat of Druidism. His observations on religion were not so keen as those on the art of war. Thierry regarded Druidism as an imported faith into Gaul, and partly by means of force. Strabo heard that Druids spoke Greek. Tacitus may say our rude ancestors worshipped Castor and Pollux ; but Agricola, who destroyed Druids in Mona, found no images in the woods.

Baecker remarked that "the Celtic history labours under such insuperable obscurity and incertitude, that we cannot premise anything above a small degree of verisimilitude." And *Ireland's Mirror* ventured to write—"On no subject has fancy roamed with more licentious indulgence than on that of the Druids and their Institutions. Though sunk in the grossest ignorance and barbarism, their admirers have found them, in the dark recesses of forests, secluded from mankind, and almost from day, cultivating the abstrusest sciences, and penetrating the sublimest mysteries of nature—and all this without the aid of letters or of experiments."

This is not the opinion of some modern devotees of

Druidism in these islands, who imagine, under Druidic control, the existence of a primal and exalted civilization.

O'Curry thought it probable " that the European Druidical system was but the offspring of the Eastern augury, somewhat less complete when transplanted to a new soil."

DRUIDICAL MYSTICISM.

However orthodox the Irish of the present day may be esteemed, there must have been a fair amount of mysticism in the past amongst so imaginative a race.   Perhaps this quality brought them into some disrepute with the Church, down to the time when the Pope gave their country to the Norman King of England, in order to bring the people into more consistent faith.   Even St. Bernard, in his *Life of Malachy*, referred to the Irish as " Pagans, while calling themselves Christians."

John Scotus Erigena, the learned Irishman of the ninth century, was certainly mystical in his views. He spoke of God as the essence of all things ; of the Divine *Dark* and Supreme *Nothing ;* of creation being only an eternal self-unfolding of the Divine Nature ; of all things resolved or self-drawn to God ; of time and space, of modes of conception of the present state, &c.

Gould's *History of Freemasonry* refers to the connection between the Druids and Freemasons.   The Papal Bull of 1751 against the latter might have been applied to the former :—

" The strict bond of secrecy—the oath to keep secret— at variance with civil and canon law—of ill repute amongst wise and good men."   Clement XII. was followed in his condemnation of Freemasons by Benedict XIV.

The Zohar of the Kabbala taught that the "narrative of the Doctrine was its cloak—the simple look only at the garment." Clement of Alexandria wrote, " The mysteries of the Faith are not to be divulged to all.—It is requisite to hide in a mystery the wisdom spoken." Even Augustine admitted that what " is now called the Christian religion really was known to the ancients." Druidism may, therefore, have had its secrets.

It is well to recollect, as Professor Rhys points out, that " what may seem to one generation of men a mere matter of mythology, is frequently found to have belonged to the serious theology of a previous one ; " and that " early man is not beneath contempt, especially when he proves to have had within him the makings of a great race, with its highest notions of duty and right."

No one can deny that Wales—somehow or other, at a certain period, assuredly long after the establishment of Christianity in these Islands, and suspected by many, from philological investigations, to have been about the twelfth century—received a flood of mystical learning, conveyed in Welsh *Triads* of great beauty, but great obscurity. This mystical learning, conveyed in a Christian guise, is asserted to be a re-statement, in refined symbolism, of those ancient creeds, and associated with ideas drawn from megalithic monuments, as cromlechs and circles.

The Irish literature of the same period in the Middle Ages, though less tinctured than the Welsh with the Mediæval mysticism, is not without a trace of it. England, judging from the sudden admixture of religious symbols, previously unknown in the Churches of that same era, was likewise affected. French literature shares the same suspicion, Brittany in particular, and especially in connection with the myths of Arthur, and the Quest of the Holy Grail. Morien is right in placing this French development of Pagan mysticism alongside that of his Welsh.

The Early Lives of St. Patrick, containing many foolish

stories of Druids, of raising the dead, and striking dead the opponents of the Saint, have no reference to this Oriental mysticism ; but the latter appears in later Lives of the Irish and Welsh Saints.

Whence came this occultism into the Church ?

The introduction of it may be largely attributed to the Templars. They were accused of magic, and lost everything thereby. As students, not less than fighting monks, they learned much of Oriental mysticism, and may have been a prominent means of introducing ancient heresies into Britain and France. Their destruction from the orthodox point of view was justified. No one can look at *that* symbol in the roof of London Temple Church, and on English Church banners elsewhere, without recognizing the heathenism so conspicuous in Welsh Druidism.

But why this Eastern philosophy should find a special retreat in the Triads of mediæval Wales is by no means clear. It is, however, a singular fact that the introduction of this mysticism appeared almost simultaneously in the *Sufuism* of Persian Mahometanism, as exhibited in the poems of Hafiz, Sadi, &c., and is still to be found in the sect of the Dancing Dervishes. Did it reach Wales through Spain and France ? There is little or no evidence of Gnosticism —so full of more ancient and pagan symbolism—penetrating to the British Isles ; though the later development of the Middle Ages abounded in Gnostic ideas.

As this peculiarity would appear to have entered Wales in the early Norman period, during the Crusades, why was it not evidenced in Ireland ? Did the Norman conquerors, who became more Irishy than the Irish, from their devotion to the Irish Brehon law, which gave chiefs so much power and property, decline to patronize therein the new learning ?

The Irish King of Ulster, Mongân, recollected his first life as *Find*, though two centuries before. Tuan was twice

born as a man. "The idea," says Jubainville, "that a soul
could in this world re-clothe successively several different
physical forms, was a natural consequence of a Celtic
doctrine well known in antiquity. This doctrine is that
the deceased who have left in the tomb their body deprived
of life, find in exchange a living body in the mysterious
country which they go to inhabit, under the bewitching
sceptre of the powerful King of the Dead."

That there has been an esoteric learning in the Past,
which has come down to us in the form of Christian and
Masonic Symbolism, is now by many accepted as a truth.
The Mason's Tools must have been used once, though now
merely badges of the worthy Craft. We may, therefore,
be excused citing a remarkable letter, reproduced in
Melville's costly work, *Veritas*, professedly dealing with
the esoteric laws of the Medes and Persians, which cannot
alter. The letter is signed by Mr. Henry Melville, and
by Mr. Frederick Tennyson, brother of the late Lord
Tennyson, and is addressed as follows :—

"To the Most Worshipful the Grand Master of Ireland,
His Grace the Duke of Leinster :

"The Petition of the Undersigned,

"Humbly Sheweth—

"That we, Master Masons, are in possession of the knowledge
of the 'Lost Secrets of Masonry.' We can prove that the Mysteries
were Masonic, inasmuch as by the usage of the Symbols now unwit-
tingly worn by Companions and Masters, Celestial Laws are framed
in accordance with the Sacred Writings, and by these Laws are
obtained the true interpretation of the Lost Mysteries.

"That in former ages the learned rulers retained the Masonic
mysteries for the use and benefit of the Craft, and these Mysteries
were not to be divulged under a lesser penalty than Death. Such
mystic secresy might have been advisable and requisite in ages past,
but such retention of knowledge your Petitioners verily believe to be
no longer necessary, as the advancement of truth is now the policy of
the civilized world, more especially so of the British nation.

"Your Petitioners, therefore, humbly pray, Most Worshipful Sir, that you will be pleased to order a Commission of learned and intelligent Brethren to be appointed to inquire and decide—

" 1st—Whether the knowledge we profess was in former times considered Masonic.

" 2nd—Whether the Lost Mysteries were, and consequently still are, celestial truths.

" 3rd—Whether truth should be published to mankind under the sanction of the Grand Lodge, provided always that these Lost truths interfere not with the Mysteries and Ritual of Modern Masonry.

" And, lastly, whether, under all considerations, the Grand Lodge of Ireland will assist, fraternally, the dissemination of the recovered truths, which will enlighten the most 'enlightened Chiefs' of this present generation.

(*Signed*)   HENRY MELVILLE,
FREDERICK TENNYSON."

We were acquainted with Mr. Melville in Tasmania some fifty years ago, when he had been long engaged in an investigation of ancient learning, and had even then come to the conclusion that heathen mythology was but a disguise, concealing scientific truths.

Occultism, in these modern days, as in Madame Blavatsky's *Theosophy*, or Morien's *Light of Britannia*, attempts to explain, even to the vulgar many, the secret mysteries supposed to have been cherished by the IRISH DRUIDS.

PART II.

EARLY RELIGIONS OF THE IRISH.

INTRODUCTION.

ONE of the most philosophical statements from Max Müller is to this effect: "Whatever we know of early religion, we always see that it presupposes vast periods of an earlier development." This is exhibited in the history of all peoples that have progressed in civilization, though we may have to travel far back on the track of history to notice transformations of thought or belief. When the late Dr. Birch told us that a pyramid, several hundreds of years older than the Great Pyramid, contained the name of *Osiris*, we knew that at least the Osirian part of Egyptian mythology was honoured some six or seven thousand years ago. What the earlier development of religion there was, or how the conception of a dying and risen Osiris arose, at so remote a period, may well excite our wonder.

Professor Jebb writes—"There was a time when they (*early man*) began to speak of the natural powers as persons, and yet had not forgotten that they were really natural powers, and that the persons' names were merely signs." Yet this goes on the assumption that religion—or rather dogmas thereof—sprang from reflections upon natural phenomena. In this way, the French author of *Sirius* satisfied himself, particularly on philological grounds, that the idea of God sprang from an association with thunder and the barking of a dog.

We are assured by Max Müller, that religion is a word that has changed from century to century, and that " the word rose to the surface thousands of years ago." Taking *religion* to imply an inward feeling of reverence toward the unseen, and a desire to act in obedience to the inward law of *right*, religion has existed as long as humanity itself. What is commonly assumed by the word *religion*, by writers in general, is dogma or belief.

The importance of this subject was well put forth by the great Sanscrit scholar in the phrase, " The real history of man is the history of religion." This conviction lends interest and weight to any investigations into the ancient religion of Ireland ; though Plowden held that " few histories are so charged with fables as the annals of Ireland."

It was Herder who finely said, " Our earth owes the seeds of all higher culture to a religious tradition, whether literary or oral." In proportion as the so-called supernatural gained an ascendancy, so was man really advancing from the materialism and brutishness of savagedom. Lecky notes " the disposition of man in certain stages of society towards the miraculous." But was Buckle quite correct in maintaining that " all nature conspired to increase the authority of the imaginative faculties, and weaken the authority of the reasoning ones " ?

It is not to be forgotten in our inquiry that, as faiths arose in the East, science has exerted its force in the West.

Fetishism can hardly be regarded as the origin of religion. As to those writers who see in the former the deification of natural objects, Max Müller remarks, " They might as well speak of primitive men mummifying their dead bodies before they had wax to embalm them with."

Myth has been styled the basis of religion not less than of history ; but how was it begotten ?

Butler, in *English, Irish, and Scottish Churches*, writes—

"To separate the fabulous from the probable, and the probable from the true, will require no ordinary share of penetration and persevering industry." We have certainly to remember, as one has said, that "mythic history, mythic theology, mythic science, are alike records, not of facts, but beliefs." Andrew Lang properly calls our attention to language, as embodying thought, being so liable to mis-conception and misinterpretation. Names, connected with myths, have been so variously read and explained by scholars, that outsiders may well be puzzled.

How rapidly a myth grows, and is greedily accepted, because of the wish it may be true, is exemplified in the pretty story, immortalized by music, of Jessie of Lucknow, who, in the siege, heard her deliverers, in the remote distance, playing "The Campbells are coming." There never was, however, a Jessie Brown there at that time; and, as one adds, Jessie has herself "been sent to join William Tell and the other dethroned gods and goddesses."

In the *Hibbert Lectures*, Professor Rhys observes, "The Greek myth, which distressed the thoughtful and pious minds, like that of Socrates, was a survival, like the other scandalous tales about the gods, from the time when the ancestors of the Greeks were savages." May it not rather have been derived by Homer, through the trading Phœnicians, from the older mythologies of India and Egypt, with altered names and scenes to suit the poet's day and clime?

It would scarcely do to say with Thierry, "In legend alone rests real history—for legend is living tradition, and three times out of four it is truer than what we call History." According to Froude, "Legends grew as nursery tales grow now.—There is reason to believe that religious theogonies and heroic tales of every nation that has left a record of itself, are but practical accounts of the first impressions produced upon mankind by the phenomena of day and night, morning and evening, winter and summer."

Such may be a partial explanation ; but it may be also assumed that they were placed on record by the scientific holders of esoteric wisdom, as problems or studies for elucidation by disciples.

The anthropological works of Sir John Lubbock and Dr. Tylor can be consulted with profit upon this subject of primitive religious thought.

Hayes O'Grady brings us back to Ireland, saying, " Who shall thoroughly discern the truth from the fiction with which it is everywhere entwined, and in many places altogether overlaid ?—There was at one time a vast amount of zeal, ingenuity, and research expended on the elucidation and confirming of these fables ; which, if properly applied, would have done Irish history and archæology good service, instead of making their very names synonymous among strangers with fancy and delusion."

After this we can proceed with the Irish legends and myths, the introduction to this inquiry being a direction to the current superstitions of the race.

IRISH SUPERSTITIONS.

THE peculiar superstitions of a people will often throw a light upon their ancient faiths. Baring-Gould has remarked, " Much of the religion of the lower orders, which we regard as essentially divine, is ancient heathenism, refined with Christian symbols." Whatever doubt may be felt as to this, all must admit the underlying paganism of some customs, credences, or sayings. Gomme tells us that "the local fetishism to be found in Aryan countries simply represents the undying faith of the older race."

Dr. Todd, in his work on *Irish Religion*, ventured on more tender ground, when he wrote concerning the "Guardsman's Cry" of St. Patrick—"The prayer which it contains against women, smiths, and Druids, together with the invocation of the powers of the sky, the sun, fire, lightning, &c., proves that, notwithstanding the undoubted piety and fervent Christian faith of the author, he had not yet fully shaken off the pagan prejudices." Giraldus Cambrensis declared that the Irish, at the conquest by Henry II., justified their condemnation by the Pope, "being more ignorant than all other nations of the first principles of the faith."

The legends of the English and French might be shown to contain a vast amount of questionable common sense and faith ; but our present inquiry is to trace the underlying opinions of the ancient Irish.

Leaving outside the so-called Druidical megalithic monuments, about the origin of which, in circles, pillars, &c., we know little or nothing beyond speculation, and which are scattered almost all over the globe, we notice in the Irish certain notions and practices connected with stones that reflect the manners of former times.

The stone of Cuamchoill, near Tipperary, produced blindness on those who gazed on it. Stones of Speculation, *Liath Meisieth*, used to draw fire, were much revered. One object in the Irish Museum, of brass cased in silver, six inches by four, has the precious crystal in the centre, set round with coloured stones. The footprints of the angel Victor were to be seen on a stone in Down County, as the celestial being alighted to deliver his message from on high to St. Patrick.

In the *Glimpses of Erin*, by S. and Alice Milligan, an interesting notice occurs of the *Brash* or *Bullan* stones, in Cork Co., though there is a specimen at the Seven

Churches of Glendalough. " The upper surface of this monument," say they, " is indented with four deep basin-shaped hollows. Two of them, the smallest, are quite close to each other at one edge ; the other two, of larger size, are at the opposite edge. The devotee placed his or her knees in the smaller hollows ; and, repeating a certain number of prayers, dropped an offering of some minute article into the larger. This operation, with certain rounds and washings at the Well, was deemed a specific for rheumatic pains and other ailments."

It is added, of the *Brash* superstition, " This is a pagan cultus, which all the power of Christianity, the personal influence of the cleric, and national education, have not been able to obliterate." A respectable farmer declared that he was not above saying a prayer at the " blessed stone " when he came that way. The water found in hollows of Bullan stones was held good for bad eyes.

Upright *Standing Stones*, or *Dallans*, the same authorities assure us, are reverenced as in idolatrous India. Mr. Milligan says, " The Inismurray women kneel before these stones, and pray that they may be delivered from the perils of childbirth." St. Bridget's stone at the Faughard, Louth, has a raised work round it, with St. Bridget's pillar near it upon steps, round which the devotees walk.

The *Clocha breca*, or speckled stones of Inismurray, Sligo, are thus described by Dr. O'Donovan—

" They are round stones, of various sizes, and arranged in such order that they cannot be easily reckoned ; and, if you believe the natives, they cannot be reckoned at all. These stones are turned, and, if I understand them rightly, their order changed by the inhabitants on certain occasions, when they visit the shrine to wish good or evil against their neighbours." An *aeir*, or *long-curse*, has been often thus hurled against a private enemy.

There is no account of the people, as recorded of some Celts, worshipping a bloody spear, or one placed in a vase upon the altar, as with the Scythians ; but Spenser, in Queen Elizabeth's time, observed the Irish drink blood in a certain ceremony, and swear by the right hand of their chiefs.

Solinus, in the early Christian centuries, must have heard strange tales of Erin, when he left this record—" It is a surly, savage race. The soldier in the moment of victory takes a draught of his enemy's blood, and smears his face with the gore. The mother puts her boy's first food, for luck, on the end of her husband's sword, and lightly pushes it into the infant's mouth, with a prayer to the gods of her tribe that her son may have a soldier's death."

The *Evil Eye* was an object of dread, and penalties concerning it are conspicuous in the old Brehon laws. The *Suil Bhaloirs,* or *Balor eye,* relates to one Balor, who was able by an eye to strike a foe dead. Love potions, on the contrary, are referred to in many ancient songs.

Persons were put under vows to do or not to do a thing. They were said to be under *Gesa.* This was often imposed with certain spells or charms.

Raising the wind—so valuable a power in sailing days— was the privilege of a few, and had its votaries down to the last century. Windbound fishermen of the Hebrides, too, used to walk, sunwise, round the chapel of Fladda, in Fladdahuan Isle, and pour water upon a round, bluish-looking stone. This effectually raised a wind. The gods then kept the wind in bags. Not so long ago, old women in the Shetlands would sell wind to sailors.

Dreams have played a great part in Ireland. In St. Patrick's *Confession* they are referred to. Professor O'Curry explains the meaning attached to them by the peasantry. Auguries were taken from the flight of birds, from beasts, and the appearance of clouds. Prodigies were not always perceived but by favoured parties. Thus we read in one poem, " The King alone beheld the terrible sight, and he foresaw the death of his people." Showers of blood were thus beheld. Bards at times recognized the sounds of approaching death on the strings of their harps.

Miracles were of ordinary occurrence, and of varied character. Tales were told of early saints crossing the Irish Sea by standing upon their garments laid upon the water. They are similar to what is noted in Hucher's *Le Saint Graal,* where a number of Christians came to Britain upon Joseph of Arimathea's shirt, which grew in size with the number mounting upon it.

Transformations, especially into animal forms, have been implicitly believed in by the peasantry. Some perceive in this the system of Totemism. Prof. Rhys was led to recognize a Dog-totem in Ireland from the number of dog-names. Conaire, son-of-bird, must not eat bird ; and Cuchulainn, the hero, named after a dog, was told not to eat of dog ; he was ruined by breaking the order. " The descendants of the wolf in Ossory," we are told in *Wonders of Erin,* " could then transform themselves into wolves." The wolf was the totem of Ossory.

Druids, as tradition relates, could change men into animals or trees. Dalyell's *Darker Superstitions of Scotland* gives a number of such transforming stories. Thus Minerva changed Ulysses, for fear of his enemies :—

> " She spake, then touched him with her powerful wand ;
> The skin shrunk up, and withered at her hand :
> A swift old age o'er all his members spread,
> A sudden frost was sprinkled on his head."

An Indian changed himself to a mouse to catch a fairy dancer. So many Irish tales relate to transformations, though more for war stratagem than love beguilements.

Andrew Lang, referring to Cupid and Psyche, equally applicable to other superstitions, observes, "We explain the separation of the lovers as the result of breaking a taboo, or one of etiquette, binding among men and women as well as between men and fairies."

Witchcraft—the conscious or unconscious exercise of a power peculiar to some persons, in greater or lesser degree, of controlling little-heeded or understood laws of nature—was ever common in Ireland. Witches were *Pitags*, *Buitseachs*, or *Taut-ags*. These had the *mark*, or "Seal of the Devil," in reddening skin, which would retain for hours an indentation upon it. Recently, it has been ascertained by a philosopher, that a sensitiveness in certain individuals exists even beyond their bodies, so that they suffer without being actually touched.

In a tradition respecting Conn of the Hundred Battles, the hero Eogan was told by three women that he should be slain in the coming fight. Upon his asking their names, they replied, "Our names are *Ah*, *Lann*, and *Leana*; we are daughters of Trodan the Magician." A witch, who sought to rescue a hero surrounded by foes, induced the tribesmen to leave him and attack some rocks, which they were hypnotized to believe were armed soldiery. The witches tied knots in a string, and breathed on them with a curse upon the object of their hateful incantation. Some persons, however, were clever enough, when finding such a charmed string, to undo the knots, and so prevent the calamity. The Koran contains a prayer for delivery "from the mischief of women blowing on knots."

Incantations were common in Ireland. A story in Erse —*Pandyeen O'Kelly*—has a man riding aloft on a besom. A giant blew a young man to a distant Rath, and sent him into a heavy sleep. A giant got from a little green man a black cap — like Jack-the-Giant-Killer's Cap of

Darkness, and gave it to the King of Ireland's son, that he might be invisible at his leisure.

Other superstitious traditions, more or less hypnotic, may be mentioned. A thimble was given by a fairy to a young man to serve as a boat. A large white cat declared herself a woman three hundred years old. Riding on fairy horses, carrying off princesses through the air, using swords that gave light, sending weasels to bring money, turning into flying beetles, forcing into magic sleep, and even restoring youth, were some of the wonders. A black dog was said to be a hag's father. Adepts could turn into vultures, swans, wolves, &c. But, according to Hyde's *Folk Lore*, witches could be released by masses. A hag or witch was a *gwrack* in Celtic Welsh.

Sir George Grey, in his New Zealand narratives, has several instances of enchantment, like those of Irish times. One old woman, by her spells, held a boat so that it could not be launched. Again, "Early in the morning Kua performed incantations, by which he kept all the people in the cave in a profound sleep." A sorcerer baked food in an enchanted oven to kill a party. Of another, "He smote his hands on the threshold of the house, and every soul in it was dead."

This was an Irish charm for the toothache :—

> "May the thumb of chosen Thomas
> in the side of guileless Christ
> heal my teeth without lamentation
> from worms and from pangs."

Charms of a peculiar kind were employed to ward off evil. Of these—more potent than the feminine sign of the horseshoe over the threshold—was the celebrated *Shelah-na-Gig.* The writer, many years ago, was shown one of these strange figures in the reserved depositaries of the British Museum. It was the squatting figure of an exposed naked female, rudely sculptured, not unlike, except in size, the singular colossi under the Museum porch brought from Easter Isle. This figure was taken down from over the doorway of an ancient church in Ireland, and was, without doubt, a relic of pagan days, used during many Christian centuries to ward off evil from the incoming congregation. Another stood by the moat of Howth.

In the *Stone Chips* of E. T. Steven we have the following—" The horse-shoe is still the conventional figure for the Yoni in Hindoo temples, and although its original import was lost, until lately the horse-shoe was held to be a charm against witchcraft and the evil eye amongst ourselves, precisely as was the case with the more unmistakable *Shelah-na-Gig* at certain churches in Ireland."

The Dublin Museum contains an extraordinary bone-pin representing the *Shelah-na-Gig*, and evidently a charm to shield the wearer. It was found alongside a skull in a field. Wilde declared that a Roscommon child was taken from the grave to obtain its arms for charm purposes.

Popular holidays are still associated with the ideas of former heathen festivals.

May-day in some parts of Ireland has its female mummers, who dance and hurl, wearing a holly-bush. A masked clown carries a pail of water with a mop for spreading its contents abroad. Boys then sing carols, as in France. In the south-east of Ireland a girl is chosen as May Queen, presiding at all May-makings till she is married. May Eve, having its dangers from fairies, &c., is spent in making cattle safe from the milk-thieving *little people*, by causing the cows to leap over fires. Dairy-maids prudently drive their cows along with the mystical rowan stick.

Of the phallic May-pole, set up for St. John's Eve or Midsummer-day, N. O'Kearney remarks, "The pole was evidently used in the Druidical ceremonies." Yule cakes were *Nur* cakes. Hogmanay was observed, as in Scotland. Hog was a Chaldæan festival. Irish pagan feasts were announced by the blowing of long horns, two or three yards in length, some of which are to be seen in Dublin Museum. The Christmas Candle of south-west Ireland was burnt till midnight on Christmas Eve, and the remnant kept as a preservative against evil spirits till the next year's candle was set up. Magic ointment revealed the invisible.

All Saints' Day perpetuated the pagan *Samhain* of November Eve. Holy cakes, known sometimes as triangular bannocks, were then eaten as Soul-Mass cakes.

"November Eve," says Mrs. Bryant's *Celtic Ireland,* "is sacred to the Spirits of the Dead. In the western islands the old superstition is dying very hard, and tradition is still well alive. It is *dangerous* to be out on November Eve, because it is the one night in the year when the dead come out of their graves to dance with the fairies on the hills, and as it is their night, they do not like to be disturbed."— " Funeral games are held in their houses." In olden times it was thought their dead heroes could help in distress.

> " Twice during the Treena of Tailten,
> Each day at sunrise I invoked Mac Eve
> To remove from me the pestilence."

The *Keens,* or lamentations for the dead, are connected with ancient and heathenish practices. Professional howlers had charge of the corpse. Rich, who wrote in 1610 of a Keen, remarked, "A stranger at the first encounter would beleeve that a quantity of hags or hellish fiendes were carrying a dead body to some infernell mansion." But some of the Death Songs have great beauty of composition. Shelah Lea's *Lament* is a fine example. It is thus translated from the Erse :—

" Sing the wild Keen of my country, ye whose heads

bend in sorrow, in the house of the dead! Lay aside the wheel and flax, and sing not in joy, for there's a spare loft in my cabin! Owenecn, the pride of my heart, is not here! Did you not hear the cry of the Banshee crossing the lovely Kilcrumper? Or, was there a voice from the tomb, far sweeter than song, that whistled in the mountain wind, and told you that the young oak was fallen? Yes, he is gone! He has gone off in the spring of life, like the blossom of the prickly hawthorn, scattered by the merciless wind, on the cold clammy earth.—Raise the Keen, ye whose notes are well known, tell your beads, ye young women who grieve; lie down on his narrow house in mourning, and his spirit will sleep and be at rest! Plant the shamrock and wild firs near his head, that strangers may know who is fallen! Soon again will your Keen be heard on the mountain, for before the cold sod is sodded over the breast of my Oweneen, Shelah, the mother of Keeners, will be there. The voice, which before was loud and plaintive, will be still and silent, like the ancient harp of her country," &c.

Another exclaimed:—" My sunshine you were. I loved you better than the sun itself; and when I see the sun going down in the west, I think of my boy, and my black night of sorrow. Like the rising sun, he had a red glow on his cheek. He was as bright as the sun at mid-day; but a dark storm came on, and my sunshine was lost to me for ever."

No one would claim for the Keens a Christian origin. The Rev. John Wesley saw a funeral in 1750, and wrote:—" I was exceedingly shocked at the Irish howl which followed. It was not a song, but a dismal, inarticulate yell, set up at the grave by four shrill-voiced women who were hired for the purpose; but I saw not one that shed a tear, for that it seems was not in the bargain."

Mrs. Harrington, in 1818, had this account of a professional Keener, a descendant of pagan performers :— " Before she began to repeat, she usually mumbled for a short time, with her eyes closed, rocking her body backward and forward, as if keeping time to the measure of the verse. She then commenced in a kind of whining recitative ; but, as she proceeded, and as the composition required it, her voice assumed a variety of deep and fine tones." Her eyes continued shut while repeating, with some variations, it may be, the ancient poem.

It is said of Curran, that he derived his earliest ideas of eloquence from the hired mourners' lamentations over the dead. Dryden refers to the ancient practice :—

> " The women mix their cries, and clamour fills the fields.
> The warlike wakes continued all the night,
> And funeral games were played at new returning light."

With so imaginative and ignorant a people, a supposed spiritual set of creatures played a great part in daily life, and those ancient ideas are not entirely driven off by the march of the school-master. Scotland, with its centuries of parish schools, retained many superstitions to a very late date, as the clergyman of Kirkmichael, Perthshire, declared he found there in 1795.

Some spirits answered to those described by Plato, as— " Between God and man are the *daimones*, or spirits, who are always near us, though commonly invisible to us, and know our thoughts." The Rev. R. Kirk left on record, in 1691, that "the very devils, conjured in any country, do answer to the language of the place ;" and yet he ascertained that when the Celt left his northern home, they lost power over him, as they were *Demones Loci*. In some cases they were ghouls, feeding on human flesh, causing the man or woman gradually to waste away, unless exorcism were practised in time.

Would that men had found as much comfort in the belief of good spirits, as they have suffered fears from the belief in evil ones ! There is still, alas ! in this world, more thought of a jealous and an avenging Deity than of one benevolent and paternal.

Subterranean spirits might dwell in burning mountains, or occupy themselves in mining, and the storing of treasure. Many Irish legends relate to such. They may appear as *Daome-Shi*, dressed in green, with mischievous intent. Others presented themselves restlessly moving over water. Not a few sought amusement by destroying at night what parts of a church had been constructed in the day. Hence the need, in certain cases, to bury alive a man, woman, or child under the foundations. Tradition says that St. Columba, thus tormented, buried St. Oran, at his own request, under the monastery of Iona.

The *Phookas*, or *Pookas*, have left some marks in Ireland. There is *Castle Pookah*, or *Carrig-a-Phooka*, Cork co., and a Phook cavern in Wicklow co. Pope calls it—

> " A dusky, melancholy sprite
> As ever sullied the fair face of night."

Phookas have been seen running from hill to hill. Their shapes vary, like the *Boduchs* of the Hebrides.

The *Cluricaune*, or *Leprechaune*, is a mischievous old fellow, dressing in a green coat, but without brogues :—

> " That sottish elf,
> Who quaffs with swollen lips the ruby wine,
> Draining the cellar with as free a hand
> As if it were his purse which ne'er lack'd coin."

In the *Religious Beliefs of the Pagan Irish*, by O'Beirne Crowe, is a reference to the *Morrigan*, which once appeared in the shape of a bird " addressing the famous bull *Dond* in dark mysterious language."—" On another occasion she appears to Cu, in the form of a beautiful lady, and tells him she is in love with him, and has brought him her gems and her cattle. Cu said he had something else than love to attend to at that time. She said when he would next engage in single combat, she would, in the shape of a serpent, coil herself around his feet, and hold him fast for his adversary."

Of the mysterious *Banshee* much has been said and sung. She is often attached to certain families, or even septs, and gives notice of coming calamities. She is the *Ben-sidhe* of Irish ; and *Cyveraeth*, or *Tyloethod*, of Welsh, whom it is fatal to meet, or to listen to her shrieks. As an old woman, she is the *White* or *House* fairy. In this sense she is said to " draw nigh at the time of death, and bear the soul to its fairy home." The White Lady of Avenel was a Banshee.

There is a curious old Irish legend about a lady whose father shut her up in a tower on Tory Isle, with twelve matrons in charge, who were to keep her from the sight of a man. All went well till McKineely consulted the Banshee of the mountain. Telling him to dress in women's garments, 'she ferried him to the island, asking shelter for a noble lady chased by an enemy. Landing the young man, she threw the dozen guardians into a Druidic sleep, and left the couple together awhile, afterwards rowing the man ashore. Serious results ensued.

Fairies are more pronounced in Irish than in English traditions. They are fairly represented in the west of Scotland, in Wales, Lancashire, and Cornwall, parts frequented by Irish friends and foes.

They are *Sides, Sighe, Sith, Duine Matha*, or *Good People. Fear-sig* of the supernatural world are Irish forms of the Welsh *Tylwyth teg*, the fair family ; Swedish, *Nissen ;*

Danish, *Damhest;* Polish, *Rotri;* the Russian, *Domavoi;*
English, *Puck*, Elf, Fay, or *Robin Goodfellow;* Cornish,
Pixie; Burmese, *Nats;* Breton, *Korigan*, or *Koril;* Scotch,
Brownie; Norwegian, *Trolls*, or *Nyss;* Oriental, *Jin;*
Jewish, *Schedim;* Italian, *Fata;* Greek, *Parcæ*, or *Eume-
nides.*

> " That which is neither ill nor well,
> That which belongs not to heaven or hell."

Because many are represented as little men, writers have
fancied the idea was but a tradition of pre-existing races,
small in stature, who were improved off by visitors or
marauders of larger growth.　Dwarfs or *Duzes* are thought
in Brittany to haunt the dolmens, or ancient graves, though
in some manner they are known as the ghosts of Druids.
Certainly Africa bears evidence of a wide-spread pigmy
race.　There are *Dokos* of South Abyssina, *Obongo* of
West Africa, *Akka* of Central Africa, *Batua* living in trees
like monkeys, and others in Congo, &c.

The Fairies are associated with mankind at present,
though they may carry off their children, replacing them
by changelings.　The mannikins may be white, brown,
grey, or yellow.　Some are small enough to sit in ears of
corn, while others fly about on magic horses.　It is sad to
know that these little people indulge in faction fights, and
pinch those who dance with them.　Giants figure less often.
The *Book of Leinster* tells of giant Luter, with fourteen
heads, wooing Gobal, whose charms extended over fifty
cubits.

Occasionally these little people are not content with
stealing babies, but would run off with men ; as Nea, of
the golden hair, did the Irish Fenian warrior.　The busy
Maakiset, who worked underground, were more worthy of
offerings than the *Kapeet*, who caused eclipses by catching
hold of the moon.　It is discreet always to speak well of

fairies, as they listen without being seen. Their females look after men, as their males look after women.

They have kings and queens. Oberon or Elberich was a king, and Titania a queen. The Irish say that Don, the Milesian leader, drowned in a storm raised by the Tuaths, became a King of the Fays. Inis Mananain, now Isle of Man, was so called from Mananan, an ancient chief transformed to a royal Sidhe. Mab, daughter of King Eochaidh Faidhleach, became Queen of the Fairies, being more than immortalized in Spenser's *Fairy Queen.* Another King of the Fairies was the Tuath Fionnbharr. The Welsh Fairy King was Gwyh ab Nudd.

As these spirits of air, earth, and water are numerous, it is a comfort to learn from the Talmud that, while the bad ones are exactly 7,405,926, the good ones number, in the rougher estimate, 1,064,340,000,000,000.

Black fairies are not conspicuous, unless in the mines. The Maories of New Zealand assure us that their merry little fays are not of their dark colour, but fair like Englishmen. They love the hills of Waikato. A chief, frightened of them, took off his ornaments, and gave them away. As soon as they finished their song, as he told the tale, they took the shadows of the Maori's earrings, and handed them about from one to the other.

As all know, the Fairies, or Peris, are suffering from some misconduct in happier climes. Christian tradition holds to their final redemption.

Irish fairies are thus mourned for by D. F. McCarthy :—

"Ah ! the pleasant time hath vanished ere our wretched doubtings banished
All the graceful spirit people, children of the earth and sea—
Whom in days now dim and olden, when the world was fresh and golden,
Every mortal could behold in haunted rath and tower and tree—
They have vanished, they are banished. Ah ! how sad the loss for thee."

Some were not so pleasant :—

> " While the Phooka horse holds his frantic course
> O'er wood and mountain fall,
> And the Banshee's croon, a rhythmic rime
> From the crumbling, ivied wall."

As elsewhere noted, the Irish fairies are intimately associated with the Druidical, ghostly, or magical Tuaths. When these were conquered by the Milesians, they betook themselves to the hills, and survived as fairies. The *Good People* have been also thought to be Druidesses. The English *Lubberfiend* of Milton is doubtless the Irish *Lurigadan*.

The *Sighe, Shee*, or *Sith* were of many varieties. As the *Farr-shee* was the man of the Sidhs, so was the *Bannshee* the woman of the Sidhs. They were magical deceivers; they built fine halls, and interfered in battles.

> " Behold the Sidh before your eyes,
> It is manifest to you that it is a king's. mansion,
> Which was built by the firm Daghda ;
> It was a wonder, a court, an admirable hill."

They might have been deified mortals. Lug Mac Ethlend had been a thousand years a Sidh. He would sometimes sojourn awhile on earth. Once he had a son by the fair Decture, and thus Cuchulainn became a hero. Carolan, the Irish bard, celebrates the fairy hills of Sith Beag and Sith More in Leitrim. Troops of them on horses followed their King Donn and Queen Cliodhna, or Cleena.

The *Daoine Shee*, or men of peace, referred to in the *Book of Armagh*, were peevish rather than malevolent. Dressing in green, they resented the appearance of human beings in green. They who wanted to see them must select Hallow-eve, walk *round* their hill nine times, when a door would open, revealing the dancing throng. It is dangerous to accept their invitation to come in for a dance, as the tripper never returns again to his home.

Fairy-inspired bards were liable to be spirited away by their muse, the *Leannan Sighe*. If she helped them in composition, they were bound to follow her throughout eternity.

"Were it not better thou shouldst dwell awhile with a young maiden
   of golden locks,
Than that the country should be laughing at thy doggrel rhyme?"

The Mermaids, or sea-fairies, were *Moruodh*, or *Moruogh*. Their hair and teeth were green. We have no record of their pugnacious qualities, as of the denizens of land. Ailne, whose lay is in old Irish, lamenting the death of her husband and two sons, knew—" by the mighty fairy host, That were in conflict over the Dun, Fighting each other "— that evil would befall her three beloved. They did not then play *Ceol-sidh*, or fairy music.

The word *Sidh* is said to be the Celtic root for a blast of wind. The whirlwind was certainly called a fairy wind. There is a *Sidh Thuim* on the Boyne, *Sidh Neanta* of Roscommon, *Sidh Meadha* near Tuam, *Sidh Aodha Ruaidh* a hill of Donegal. There are seventy Irish townships beginning with *Shee*.

Ireland abounds with localities having fairy associations. Joyce gives many. Finn and his Fenians are in *Sliabh-na-mban-fionn*, the mountain of the fair-haired women; *Rath Sithe*, the Fenian fortress, is in Antrim; the Fairy's wood is in Sligo. Then there are the *Sheegys*, fairy hills, in Donegal; the *Sheeauns*, fairy mounds; the haunted hills, *Shean*, *Sheena*, *Shane;* and *Knockna looricaim*, the hills of the Cluricane. In Lough Corrib the *Leprechauns* were said to have been provided with ground meal for supper by hospitable neighbours.

There was a Banshee's palace in South Munster, and another in a rock near Mallow. The Banshee *Aeibhell* had a fine palace in a rock by Killaloe; it was she who threw

her cloak round the hero O'Hartigan at the battle of
Clontarf, so rendering him invisible.   In fact, Joyce is led
to exclaim, "Some parts of Connaught must have been
more thickly populated with fairies than with men."

Were the fairies in Ireland of great antiquity?

One has written of the fancy, "that the tales of mortals
abiding with the Fays in their Sighe palaces are founded
on the tender preferences shown by the Druidic priestesses
of old to favourite worshippers of the Celtic divinities."
N. O'Kearney is of opinion that "our fairy traditions are
relics of paganism."   Kennedy says, "In borrowing these
fictions from their heathen predecessors, the Christian
story-tellers did not take much trouble to correct their
laxity on the subject of moral obligations."   Andrew Lang
sees that "the lower mythology—the elemental beliefs of
a people—do service beneath a thin covering of Christian
uniformity."

At least, we may admit, with Prof. Stokes, that "much
of the narrative element in the classic epics is to be found
in a popular or childish form in primitive Fairy tales."

Among the early and latter superstitions, *Ghosts* are
very prominent.

As so many ghost stories rest upon tradition, it is well to
bear in mind what the author of *The Golden Bough* says—
"The superstitious beliefs and practices which have been
handed down by word of mouth are generally of a far
more archaic type than the religions depicted in the most
ancient literature of the Aryan race."

It is not easy to laugh at Irish peasants for ghost yarns
when all nations, from the remotest antiquity, accepted
them, and philosophers like Dr. Johnson, preachers like
John Wesley, reformers like Luther, poets like Dante and
Tasso, recognized such spirits.   Some, like an author in
1729, may doubt souls returning from heaven—"Nor do

I know," said he, "whether it would be worth their shifting Hell, and coming back to this world in the wandering condition those things called Ghosts are understood to be." Others may exclaim with Dr. Johnson, "All argument is against it, but all belief is for it."

Thyræus, the Jesuit, thinks that they are but souls from purgatory, seeking rest. Earberg considered, "It is against no Scripture that souls should come from Hades." Henri Martin, the French Celtic scholar, said, "The intercourse between earth and heaven is a belief strongly accredited among the Bards." Gladstone recognizes that the recent Greek dead "are wanderers in the Shades, without fixed doom or occupation." Homer's *Odyssey* has this reference—

> " But swarms of spectres rose from deepest hell,
> With bloodless visage and with hideous yell.
> They scream, they shriek, and groans and dismal sounds
> Stun my scared ears and pierce hell's utmost bounds."

Virgil shows to Æneas his father Anchises—

> " Then thrice around his neck his arms he threw ;
> And thrice the flitting shadow slipp'd away,
> Like wind or empty dreams that fly the day."

Suetonius tells us that the ghost of Caligula walked in Lavinia's garden, where his body was buried, until the house was burnt down. Ecclesiasticus (chap. xlvi.) speaks of Samuel thus : "And after his death he prophesied, and showed the king his end." In the archives of the Royal Society is a MS. paper, read November 16, 1698, on some "Apparitions in ye N. of Scotland," in which we are informed that Mr. Mackeney, A.M., Oxford, "said that they saw apparitions allmost every week ; and upon his knowledge they did very frequently foretell the death of Persons, wch always succeeded accordingly."

Were all these mistaken ? Were they under the influence of Herbert Spencer's *Organ of Reviviscence*, or Wonder-

Organ, which "affords a tangible explanation of mental illusions"?

The Irish, like the ancient Jews, held that bad men, especially, could walk this earth after death; and the English law, almost to our day, allowed a stake to be driven through the body of suicides and murderers, to prevent their spirit troubling the living.

The Church has had its say in the matter. The Council of Elvira, A.D. 300, forbade the lighting of tapers in cemeteries, as that was apt to disturb the souls of Saints; so said the Council of Iliberit. St. Basil was told by a ghost that he had killed Julian. Both Ignatius and Ambrose were said to have appeared to their disciples. No Church has ever denied the existence and appearance of ghosts, and none opposed exorcism in some form or other.

"Irish pagans," observes Nicolas O'Kearney, "never dreamed of spirits after death having assumed such forms (misty ghosts). The spirits from Elysium always appeared in their proper shape, and spoke and acted as if they were still in the enjoyment of mortal life."

In this respect he differs from Macpherson's *Ossian.* The opinion is, also, opposed to other descriptions in recognized Irish poems of antiquity. In the poem *Cathluina*, as translated in *Ireland's Mirror*, is this:—" Ferarma, bring me my shield and spear; bring me my sword, that stream of light. What mean these two angry ghosts that fight in air? The thin blood runs down their robes of mist; and their half-formed swords, like faint meteors, fall on sky-blue shields. Now they embrace like friends. The sweeping blast pipes through their airy limbs. They vanish. I do not like the sight, but I do not fear it."

The Inverness *Gaelic Society* had a paper by Donald Ross on this subject, saying, "Spectres hovered gloomily over the reedy marsh or the moor, or arrayed themselves on the blasts of the wind ; and pale ghosts, messengers of the unseen world, brought back the secrets of the grave." A Gaelic song has the following —" In a blast comes cloudy death, and lays his grey head low. His ghost is rolled on the vapours of the fenny field." Henri Martin speaks of " harps of bards, untouched, sound mournful over the hill."

Some ghosts were material enough. That of St. Kieran, of Clonmacnoise, managed to strike King Felim, the plunderer of his church, so effectually, with his ghostly crozier, as to give an internal wound, of which the chief died. When Finn or Fionn appeared to Osgar, on the battle-field of Gabhra, it is affirmed that " his words were not murmurs of distant streams," but loud and clear.

But the *Fetch*, as recognized in the scattered poems collected, or revised, in Macpherson's *Ossian*, is more a spirit of the air. Some of the descriptions, relating to the ghosts of Erin and Argyle, are striking :—

" She was like the new moon seen through the gathering mist—like a watery beam of feeble light, when the moon rushes sudden from between two clouds, and the midnight shower is on the heath.—Clouds, the robe of ghosts,—rolled their gathered forms on the wind—with robes of light.— Soon shall our cold pale ghosts meet in a cloud, on Cona's eddying winds.—Tell her that in a cloud I may meet the lovely maid of Toscar."

Again—" Faint light gleams over the heath. The ghosts of Arden pass through, and show their dim and distant forms.—The misty Loda, the house of the spirits of men.— Ghosts vanish, like mists on the sunny hill.—His soul came forth to his fathers, to their stormy isle. There they pursued boars of mist along the skirts of winds.—I move like the shadow of mist.—The ghost of Crugal came from his cave. The stars dim—twinkled through his form. His voice was like the sound of a distant stream."

Of one it is said, " His eyes are like two decaying flames. Dark is the wound of his breast."—Caugal, who appeared in dress and form as living, but pale, is made by the poet to say, " My ghost is on my native hills, but my corse is on the sands of Ullin. Thou shalt never talk with Caugal, nor find his lone steps on the heath.—Like the darkened moon, he retired in the midst of the whistling blast."

Of another—" A cloud, like the steed of the stranger, supported his airy limbs. His robe is of the mist of Lano, that brings death to the people. His sword is the green meteor, half-extinguished, his face is without form and void." Some "show their dark forms from the chinky rocks." Others " fled on every side, and rolled their gathered forms on the wind." One comforts himself, dying, with, " My fathers shall meet me at the gates of their airy halls, tall, with robes of light, with mildly kindled eyes."

A hero cried out, " I never feared the ghosts of night. Small is their knowledge, weak their hands." A poet murmurs, " I hear at times the ghosts of bards, and learn their pleasant song." Of a great warrior, it is said, " A thousand ghosts are on the beams of his steel, the *ghosts of those who are to fall* by the King of resounding Morven." Or, " Let Carril (*a bard*) pour his songs, that the chiefs may rejoice in their mist." Of a beautiful woman, it is written—" She is fair as the ghost of the hill, when it moves in a sunbeam at noon over the silence of Morven."

A ghost may warn of danger, foretell disaster, foresee death, communicate intelligence. Whatever may be thought of Macpherson's *Ossian*, there can be no doubt that all the poetical representations of Irish ghosts bear pagan, and not Christian, characteristics. The traditions, coming through Christian centuries, have a distinct pagan colouring. The ghosts of Christian times would seem to have left their Christianity in this life, becoming heathen on the other side.

Other illustrations of Irish superstitions occur in the course of this work, though noted under various heads. The Irish were not more superstitious by nature than their neighbours ; but, in changing less their abodes, and retaining faith in the religion of their fathers, they have clung to old traditions more than those who were subject to greater transitions of place and ideas.

After all, as some of these Irish superstitions are the heritage from the past in all lands, can the scientific mind afford to treat them as irrational and absurd ? Is experience of all times and all nations utterly worthless ? If the photographer's sensitive plate can *see* more than the human eye, and exhibit stars which no telescope can show, are we so sure that nothing exists but what is revealed by our senses ? May we not hinder our own mental vision by a studied resolution to reject what we cannot explain ?

IRISH MAGIC, AND TUATHA DE DANAANS.

By far the most interesting of the peoples that formerly inhabited Ireland were the *Tuaths*, or *Tuatha de Danaans*, or *Dananns*. There is much mystery about them in Irish traditions. They were men, gods, or fairies. They came, of course, from the East, calling in at Greece on the way, so as to increase their stock of magic and wisdom. Some trace them to the tribes of Dan, and note Dedan in Ezek. xxv. 13. Mrs. Wilkins identifies them with the Dedanim of Isa. xxi. 13, "a nomad, yet semi-civilized, people." Isaiah calls them " travelling companies of Dedanim."

The credulous *Four Masters* have wonderful tales of Tuath doings. In their invasion of Ireland, Tuaths had to deal with the dark aborigines, known as the Firbo'gs, and are said to have slain 100,000 at the battle of Magh-Tuireadh Conga.   Driven off the island by their foes, they travelled in the East, returning from their exile as finished magicians and genuine Druids.   Mr. Gladstone, in *Juventus Mundi*, contends that *Danaan* is of Phœnician extraction, that a district near Tripoli, of Syria, is known as Danniè. He adds, " Pausanias says that at the landing-place of Danaos, on the Argive coast, was a temple of Poseidon Genesios, of Phœnician origin."

After reigning in Ireland two hundred years, the Tuatha were, it is narrated, invaded by the children of Gail Glas, who had come from Egypt to Spain, and sailed thence to Erin under Milesius, the leader of the Milesians.   When their fleet was observed, the Danaans caused a Druidic fog to arise, so that the land assumed the shape of a black pig, whence arose another name for Ireland—" *Inis na illuic*, or Isle of the Pig."   The Milesians, however, employed their enchantments in return, and defeated the Tuatha at Tailteine, now Teltown, on the Blackwater, and at Druim-Lighean, now Drumleene, Donegal.

The Tuatha have been improperly confounded with the Danes.   Others give them a German origin, or a Nemedian one.   Wilde describes them as large and fair-complexioned, carrying long, bronze, leaf-shaped swords, of a Grecian style, and he thinks them the builders of the so-called Danish forts, duns, or cashels, but not of the stone circles. McFirbis, 200 years ago, wrote—" Every one who is fair-haired, revengeful, large, and every plunderer, professors of musical and entertaining performances, who are adepts of druidical and magical arts, they are the descendants of the Tuatha-de-Danaans."

" The Danans," O'Flanagan wrote in 1808, " are said to have been well acquainted with Athens ; and the memory of their kings, poets, and poetesses, or female philosophers, of highest repute for wisdom and learning, is still preserved with reverential regret in some of our old manuscripts of the best authority." Referring to these persons, as Kings Dagad, Agamon and Dalboeth, to Brig, daughter of Dagad, to Edina and Danana, he exclaimed, " Such are the lights that burst through the gloom of ages." The Tuatha, G. W. Atkinson supposes, " must be the highly intellectual race that imported into Ireland our Oghams, round towers, architecture, metal work, and, above all, the exquisite art which has come down to us in our wonderful illuminated Irish MSS." The polished Tuatha were certainly contrasted with the rude Celts. Arthur Clive declares that civilization came in with an earlier race than the Celts, and retired with their conquest by the latter.

" The bards and Seanachies," remarks R. J. Duffy, " fancifully attributed to each of the Tuath-de-Danaan chiefs some particular art or department over which they held him to preside ; " as, Abhortach, to music. The author of *Old Celtic Romances* writes—" By the Milesians and their descendants they were regarded as gods, and ultimately, in the imagination of the people, they became what are now in Ireland called ' Fairies.' " They conquered the Firbolgs, an Iberian or a Belgic people, at the battle of Moytura.

There is a strong suspicion of their connection with the old idolatry. Their last King was *Mac-grene*, which bears a verbal relation to the Sun. The Rev. R. Smiddy assumes them descendants of *Dia-tene-ion*, the Fire-god or Sun. In the *Chronicles of Columba* we read of a priest who built in Tyrconnel a temple of great beauty, with an altar of fine glass, adorned with the representation of the sun and moon. Under their King Dagda the Great, the Sun-god, and his wife, the goddess *Boann*, the Tuaths were once pursued by the river Boyne. This Dagda became King of the Fairies, when his people were defeated by the warlike Milesians ; and the Tuatha, as Professor Rhys says, "formed an invisible world of their own," in hills and mounds.

In the *Book of Ballimote*, Fintan, who lived before the Flood, describing his adventures, said—

> "After them the Tuatha De arrived
> Concealed in their dark clouds—
> I ate my food with them,
> Though at such a remote period."

Mrs. Bryant, in *Celtic Ireland*, observes :—"Tradition assigns to the Tuatha generally an immortal life in the midst of the hills, and beneath the seas. Thence they issue to mingle freely with the mortal sons of men, practising those individual arts in which they were great of yore, when they won Erin from the Firbolgs by 'science,' and when the Milesians won Erin from them by valour. That there really was a people whom the legends of the Tuatha shadow forth is probable, but it is almost certain that all the tales about them are poetical myths."

Elsewhere we note the Tuath Crosses, with illustrations ; as that Cross at Monasterboice, of processions, doves, gods, snakes, &c. One Irish author, Vallencey, has said, "The Church Festivals themselves, in our Christian Calendar, are but the direct transfers from the Tuath de Danaan ritual. Their very names in Irish are identically the same as those by which they were distinguished by that earlier race." That writer assuredly did not regard the Tuatha as myths. Fiech, St. Patrick's disciple, sang—

> "That Tuaths of Erin prophesied
> That new times of peace would come."

Magic—*Draoideachta*—was attributed to the Irish Tuatha, and gave them the traditional reputation for wisdom.

" Wise as the Tuatha de Danaans," observes A. G. Geoghegan, " is a saying that still can be heard in the highlands
of Donegal, in the glens of Connaught, and on the seaboard
of the south-west of Ireland." In *Celtic Ireland* we read—
" The Irish worshipped the Sidhe, and the bards identify
the Sidhe with the Tuath de Danaan.—The identity of the
Tuath de Danaan with the degenerate fairy of Christian
times appears plainly in the fact, that while Sidhes are the
halls of Tuatha, the fairies are the people of the Sidhe, and
sometimes called the Sidhe simply."

The old Irish literature abounds with magic. Druidic
spells were sometimes in this form—" I impose upon thee
that thou mayst wander to and fro along a river," &c.

In the chase, a hero found the lost golden ring of a
maiden :—

" But scarce to the shore the prize could bring,
    When by some blasting ban—
Ah ! piteous tale—the Fenian King
    Grew a withered, grey old man.

Of Cumhal's son then Cavolte sought
What wizard Danaan foe had wrought
    Such piteous change, and Finn replied—
'Twas Guillin's daughter—me she bound
    By a sacred spell to search the tide
Till the ring she lost was found.

Search and find her. She gave him a cup—
Feeble he drinks— the potion speeds
    Through every joint and pore ;
To palsied age fresh youth succeeds—
Finn, of the swift and slender steeds,
    Becomes himself once more."

Druidic sleeps are frequently mentioned, as—

" Or that small dwarf, whose power could steep
The Fenian host in death-like sleep."

Kennedy's *Fictions of the Irish Celts* relates a number
of magical tales. The *Lianan* might well be feared when

we are told of the revenge one took upon a woman—"Being safe from the eyes of the household, she muttered some words, and, drawing a Druidic wand from under her mantle, she struck her with it, and changed her into a most beautiful wolf-hound." The *Lianan* reminds one of the classical Incubi and Succubi. Yet Kennedy admits that "in the stories found among the native Irish, there is always evident more of the Christian element than among the Norse or German collections."

The story about Fintan's adventures, from the days of the Flood to the coming of St. Patrick, "has been regarded as a Pagan myth," says one, "in keeping with the doctrine of Transmigration."

In the *Annals of Clonmacnoise* we hear of seven magicians working against the breaker of an agreement. Bruga of the Boyne was a great De Danaan magician. Jocelin assures us that one prophesied the coming of St. Patrick a year before his arrival. Angus the Tuath had a mystic palace on the Boyne. The healing stone of St. Conall has been supposed to be a remnant of Tuath magic ; it is shaped like a dumb-bell, and is still believed in by many.

In spite of the Lectures of the learned O'Curry, declaring the story to be " nothing but the most vague and general assertions," Irish tradition supports the opinion of Pliny that, as to magic, there were those in the British Isles "capable of instructing even the Persians themselves in these arts." But O'Curry admits that "the European Druidical system was but the offspring of the eastern augurs " ; and the Tuaths came from the East. They wrote or repeated charms, as the *Hawasjilars* of Turkey still write *Nushas*. Adder-stones were used to repel evil spirits, not less than to cure diseases. One, writing in 1699, speaks of seeing a stone suspended from the neck of a child as a remedy for whooping-cough. Monuments ascribed to the

Tuatha are to be seen near the Boyne, and at Drogheda, Dowth, Knowth, &c.

According to tradition, this people brought into Ireland the magic glaive from Gorias, the magic cauldron from Murias, the magic spear from Finias, and the magic *Lia Fail* or talking coronation stone from Falias ; though the last is, also, said to have been introduced by the Milesians when they came with Pharaoh's daughter.

Enthusiastic Freemasons believe the Tuatha were members of the mystic body, their supposed magic being but the superior learning they imported from the East. If not spiritualists in the modern sense of that term, they may have been skilled in Hypnotism, inducing others to see or hear what their masters wished them to see or hear.

When the Tuatha were contending with the Firbolgs, the Druids on both sides prepared to exercise their enchantments. Being a fair match in magical powers, the warriors concluded not to employ them at all, but have a fair fight between themselves. This is, however, but one of the tales of poetic chronicles ; of whom Kennedy's *Irish Fiction* reports—" The minstrels were plain, pious, and very ignorant Christians, who believed in nothing worse than a little magic and witchcraft."

It was surely a comfort to Christians that magic-working Druids were often checkmated by the Saints. When St. Columba, in answer to an inquiry by Brochan the magician, said he should be sailing away in three days, the other replied that he would not be able to do so, as a contrary wind and a dark mist should be raised to prevent the departure. Yet the Culdee ventured forth in the teeth of the opposing breeze, sailing against it and the mist. In like manner Druid often counteracted Druid. Thus, three Tuatha Druidessess,—Bodhbh, Macha, and Mor Kegan,— brought down darkness and showers of blood and fire upon

Firbolgs at Tara for three days, until the spell was broken by the Firbolg magic bearers—Cesara, Gnathach, and Ingnathach. Spells or charms were always uttered in verse or song. Another mode of bringing a curse was through the chewing of thumbs by enchantresses. Fal the Tuath made use of the *Wheel of Light*, which, somehow, got connected with Simon Magus by the Bards, and which enabled the professor to ride through the air, and perform other wonders. We hear, also, of a *Sword of Light*. The magic cauldron was known as the *Brudins.*

Some of the Tuath Druids had special powers,—as the gift of knowledge in Fionn; a drink, too, given from his hands would heal any wound, or cure any disease. Angus had the power of travelling on the wings of the cool east wind. Credne, the Tuath smith, made a silver hand for Nuadhat, which was properly fitted on his wrist by Dianceht, the Irish Æsculapius. To complete the operation, Miach, son of Dianceht, took the hand and infused feeling and motion in every joint and vein, as if it were a natural hand. It is right to observe, however, that, according to Cormac's *Glossary*, Dianceht meant " The god of curing."

Finn as elsewhere said, acquired his special privilege by accidentally sucking his thumb after it had rested upon the mysterious *Salmon of Knowledge*. He thus acquired the power of Divination. Whenever he desired to know any particular thing, he had only to suck his thumb, and the whole chain of circumstances would be present to his mind. The *Magic Rod* is well known to have been the means of transforming objects or persons. The children of Lir were changed by a magic wand into four swans, that flew to Loch Derg for 300 years, and subsequently removed to the sea of Moyle between Erin and Alba.

Transformation stories are numerous in the ancient legends of Ireland. A specimen is given in the *Genealogy of Corea*

Laidhe. A hag, " ugly and bald, uncouth and loathesome to behold," the subject of some previous transformation, seeks deliverance from her enchanted condition by some one marrying her ; when " she suddenly passed into another form, she assumed a form of wondrous beauty."

Some enchanters assumed the appearance of giants. The Fenians of old dared not hunt in a certain quarter from fear of one of these monsters. Cam has been thus described in the story of *Diarmuid*—" whom neither weapon wounds, nor water drowns, so great is his magic. He has but one eye only, in the fair middle of his black forehead, and there is a thick collar of iron round that giant's body, and he is fated not to die until there be struck upon him three strokes of the iron club that he has. He sleeps in the top of that Quicken tree by night, and he remains at its foot by day to watch it." The berries of that tree had the exhilarating quality of wine, and he who tasted them, though he were one hundred years old, would renew the strength of thirty years.

The *Fate of the Children of Tuireann,* in an Irish MS., gave a curious narrative of Tuath days and magic. It was published by the " Society for the Preservation of the Irish Language." The sons had to pay heavy *eric,* or damages, on account of a murder. One failed, and died of his wounds. Lugh got helped by Brian the Druid against the Fomorians, who were then cruelly oppressing the Tuaths, exacting an ounce of gold from each, under penalty of cutting their noses off. Druidical spells were freely used by Lugh, the hero of the story.

The *eric* in question required the three sons to procure the three apples from the garden of the Hesperides,—the skin of the pig, belonging to the King of Greece, which could cure diseases and wounds,—two magic horses from the King of Sicily,—seven pigs from the King of the Golden Pillars, &c.

Once on their adventures, Brian changed them with his
wand into three hawks, that they might seize the apples ;
but the King's daughters, by magic, changed themselves
into griffins, and chased them away, though the Druid, by
superior power, then turned them into harmless swans. One
son gained the pig's skin as a reward for reciting a poem.
A search for the Island of Fianchaire beneath the sea was
a difficulty. But we are told, "Brian put on his water-
dress." Securing a head-dress of glass, he plunged into
the water. He was a fortnight walking in the salt sea
seeking for the land.

Lugh came in contact with a fairy cavalcade, from the
Land of Promise. His adventure with Cian illustrated
ideas of transformation. Cian, when pursued, "saw a great
herd of swine near him, and he struck himself with a
Druidical wand into the shape of one of the swine.". Lugh
was puzzled to know which was the Druidical pig. But
striking his two brothers with a wand, he turned them into
two slender, fleet hounds, that "gave tongue ravenously"
upon the trail of the Druidical pig, into which a spear was
thrust. The pig cried out that he was Cian, and wanted to
return to his human shape, but the brothers completed their
deed of blood.

Not only the pig, but brown bulls and red cows figure
in stories of Irish magic. We read of straw thrown into
a man's face, with the utterance of a charm, and the poor
fellow suddenly going mad. Prince Comgan was struck
with a wand, and boils and ulcers came over him, until he
gradually sunk into a state of idiocy. A blind Druid
carried about him the secret of power in a straw placed
in his shoe, which another sharp fellow managed to
steal.

Illumination, by the palms of the hands on the cheek of
one thrown into a magical sleep, was another mode of

procuring answers to questions. Ciothruadh, Druid to Cormac, of Cashel, sought information concerning a foe after making a Druidical fire of the mystical mountain ash. But he was beaten in his enchantments by Mogh Ruith, the King of Munster's Druid, who even transformed, by a breath, the three wise men of Cashel into stones, which may be seen to this day. That he accomplished with charms and a fire of the rowan tree. The virtues of rowan wood are appreciated to this day in Munster, where provident wives secure better butter by putting a hoop of it round their churns.

Tuaths had a reputation for their ability in the interpretation of dreams and omens, and their skill in auguries. Some Druids, like Mogh Ruith, could fly by the aid of magical wings. It was, however, no Irishman, but Math, the divine Druid, who brought his magic to Gwydron ab Dom, and was clever enough to form a woman out of flowers, deemed by poetic natures a more romantic origin than from the rib of a man. Manannan, son of a Tuath chieftain, he who gave name to the Isle of Man, rolled on three legs, as a wheel, through a Druidic mist. He subsequently became King of the Fairies.

Professor Rhys speaks of the Tuatha as Tribes of the goddess Danu ; though the term, he says, " is somewhat vague, as are also others of the same import, such as *Tuath Dea*, the Tribes of the goddess—and Fir Dea, the men of the goddess." He further remarks—" The Tuatha de Danann contain among them light and dark divinities, and those standing sometimes in the relation of parents and offspring to one another."

Massey has the following philological argument for the Tuatha, saying :—" The *Tuaut* (Egy.), founded on the underworld, denotes the gate of worship, adoration ; the worshippers, *Tuaut ta tauan*, would signify the place of worship within the mound of earth, the underground sanctuary. The Babylonian temple of Bit-Saggdhu was in the gate of the deep. The *Tuaut* or portal of Ptah's temple faced the north wind, and the Irish Tievetory is the hill-side north. The Tuaut entrance is also glossed by the English *Twat.* The Egyptian *Tuantii* are the people of the lower hemisphere, the north, which was the type of the earth-temple. The Tuatha are still known in Ireland by the name of the Divine Folk ; an equivalent to Tuantii for the worshippers."

The Rev. R. Smiddy fancies the people, as *Denan* or Dene-ion, were descendants of *Dene*, the fire-god. An old MS. calls them the people of the god Dana. Clive, therefore, asks, if they were simply the old gods of the country. Joyce, in *Irish Names* says, ' This mysterious race, having undergone a gradual deification, became confounded and identified with the original local gods, and ultimately superseded them altogether." He recalls the Kerry mountain's name of Da-chich-Danainne. He considers the Tuatha " a people of superior intelligence and artistic skill, and that they were conquered, and driven into remote districts, by the less intelligent but more warlike Milesian tribes who succeeded them."

Lady Ferguson, in her *Story of the Irish before the Conquest*, has the idea of the Danaans being kinsmen to the Firbolgs, that they came from the region of the Don and Vistula, under Nuad of the Silver Hand, defeating Eochaid, King of the Firbolgs, at Moytura, and ruling Ireland two hundred years.

They were certainly workers in metal, and have therefore been confounded by monkish writers with smiths. St. Patrick's prayer against smiths, and the traditional connection between smiths and magic, can thus be understood. They—according to the *Book of Invasions*—

" By the force of potent spells and wicked magic
    And conjurations horrible to hear,
    Could set the ministry of hell at work,
    And raise a slaughtered army from the earth,
    And make them live, and breathe, and fight again.
    Few could their arts withstand, or charms unbind."

They were notorious in Sligo, a county so full of so-
called Druidical remains. In Carrowmore, with its sixty-
four stone circles, there must once have been a large
population. "Why," asks Wood-Martin, "is that narrow
strip of country so thickly strewn with monuments of the
Dead ?" But he learned that the Fomorian pirates, possibly
from the Baltic, swarmed on that wild coast. He especially
notes the tales of Indech, a mighty Fomorian Druid,
grandfather of the dreaded Balor, of the Evil Eye.

The mythic *Grey Cow* belonged to Lon mac Liomhtha,
the first smith among the Tuaths who succeeded in making
an iron sword. At the battle of Moytura, Uaithne was
the Druid harper of the Tuatha. Of Torna, last of Pagan
Bards, it was declared he was

" Sprung of the Tualtha de Danans, far renown'd
    For dire enchanting arts and magic power."

But, as Miss Brooke tells us, " most of the Irish romances
are filled with Dananian enchantments, as wild as the
wildest of Ariosto's fictions, and not at all behind them
in beauty." It was Dr. Barnard, Bishop of Killaloe, who
traced the race to visitors from South Britain ; saying,
"The Belgæ and Danmonii, whose posterity in Ireland
were called Firbolghs and Tuatha de Danan."

In the destructive battle between the "manly, bloody,
robust Fenians of Fionn," and "the white-toothed, handsome Tuatha Dedaans," when the latter saw a fresh corps
of Fenians advancing, it is recorded that "having enveloped
themselves in the Feigh Fiadh, they made a precipitate
retreat."

Jubainville's *Cours de la littérature Celtique* does not omit mention of these wonder-workers. He calls to mind the fact that, like the Greeks of the Golden Age, they became invisible, but continued their relations with men; that the Christian writers changed them into mortal kings in chronicles; that their migrations and deities resemble those of Hesiod; that they continue to appear in animal or human forms, though more commonly as birds; that ancient legends record their descent to earth from the blue heavens.

He brings forward a number of the old Irish stories about the Tuaths. When defeated by the sons of Milé, they sought refuge in subterranean palaces. One Dagan, a word variant of the god Dagdé, exercised such influence, that the sons of Milé were forced, for peace' sake, to make a treaty with him. His palace retreat below was at Brug na Boinné, the castle of the Boyne. The burial-place of Crimtham Nia Nair, at Brug na Boinné, was chosen because his wife was a fairy of the race of Tuatha. In the *Tain bô Cuailnge* there is much about the *Sid*, or enchanted palace. Dagdé had his harp stolen by the Fomorians, though it was recovered later on.

The son of Dagdé was Oengus. When the distribution of subterranean palaces took place, somehow or other, this young fellow was forgotten. Asking to be allowed to spend the night at one, he was unwilling to change his quarters, and stayed the next day. He then absolutely refused to depart, since time was only night and day; thus retaining possession. The same Tuath hero fell in love with a fair harper, who appeared to him in a dream. The search, aided by the fairies, was successful in finding the lady, after a year and a day.

It was in his second battle that Ogmé carried off the sword of Tethra, King of the Fomorians. This sword had

the gift of speech; or, rather, said Jubainville, it seemed
to speak, for the voice which was heard was, according to
a Christian historian, only that of a demon hidden in the
blade. Still, the writer of this Irish epic remarked, that
in that ancient time men adored weapons of war, and
considered them as supernatural protectors.

The *Book of Conquests* allows that the Tuatha were
descended from Japhet, though in some way *demons;* or,
in Christian language, heathen deities. One Irish word
was often applied to them, viz. *Liabra,* or phantoms. It
is believed that at least one Tuath warrior, named
Breas, could speak in native Irish to the aboriginal
Firbolgs.

A writer in *Anecdota Oxon* is of opinion that very
different notions and accounts exist at the different
periods of Irish epic literature concerning them. He
declares that, excepting their names, no very particular
traces of them have come down to us. The most distinct
of the utterances about the race points to the existence of
war-goddesses.

Wilde gives a definite reason why we know so little about
the Tuatha de Danaans. It was because "those who
took down the legends from the mouths of the bards and
annalists, or those who subsequently transcribed them, were
Christian missionaries, whose object was to obliterate every
vestige of the ancient forms of faith." The distortion of
truth about these singular, foreign people makes it so
difficult to understand who or what they were; to us they
seem always enveloped in a sort of Druidic fog, so that
we may class them with men, heroic demi-gods, or gods
themselves, according to our fancy.

IRISH GODS.

SOME writers, from a jealous regard to the reputation of their ancestors, have been unwilling to acknowledge the idolatry of ancient Erin. They reject the testimony as to images, and decline to accept the record as to heathen deities. Yet it is surely a satisfaction to know that the *Highest* and *Unseen* was worshipped at all, though under rude and material symbolism, instead of being unknown and unfelt.

If claiming to be, in some degree, at least, of Celtic heritage, the Irish may conceivably be esteemed of kindred faith with Celtic Gauls and Celtic Germans, whose divinities were recognized by the Romans, though called, from certain supposed similitudes, by more familiar Italian names.

The Irish, from their geographical position, were a mixture of many peoples, forming a succession of human layers, so to speak, according to the number of the newcomers, and the period of local supremacy. The tendency of populations northward and westward, from wars or migrations, was to carry to Erin various races from the Continent of Europe, with their different customs and their gods, having more permanent influence than the visitation of their coasts by Oriental seamen.

Thus we perceive, in fragmentary traditions and superstitions, the adoration of the Elements, and the fanciful embodiment of divine attributes in their phases and their apparent contradictions. In some way or other, the Islanders failed not to see, with Aristotle, that "the principle of life is in God." Yet J. S. Mill thought that religion may exist without belief in a God.

In our investigations, we need bear in mind what the

learned Professor Rhys asserts, that—"most of the myths of the modern Celts are to be found manipulated, so as to form the opening chapters of what has been usually regarded as the early history of the British Isles." So we know of other lands, that their chronicles may be a disguised form of faith, clad in the mysticism fostered by all priests.

As ancient mythologies, apparently so idle and meaning-less, are now perceived to embody truths, scientific and religious, so the seemingly foolish traditions of nations, descriptive of their early history, are recognized to convey ideas more or less astronomical and theological.

NATURE WORSHIP has been regarded as the foundation of all religions. Aristotle left this remarkable saying, "When we try to reach the Infinite and the Divine by means of mere abstract terms, are we even now better than children trying to place a ladder against the sky?" Early man could not avoid anthropomorphizing the Deity. The god could show himself. He could walk, talk, come down, go up. Earlier still, man saw the reflection of the godhead in the sun, the storm, or the productive forces.

Boscawen writes—"The religion of Assyria was in con-stitution essentially a Nature worship; its Pantheon was composed of deifications of Nature powers. In this opinion I know I differ considerably from other Assyriologists, Mr. Sayce, M. Lenormant and others being of opinion that the system was one of solar worship." An author speaks of "one great surge of voluptuous Nature worship that swept into Europe."

According to Pliny—"The world and sky, in whose embrace all things are enclosed, must be deemed a god, eternal, immense, never begotten, and never to perish.

To seek things beyond this is of no profit to man, and they transcend the limits of his faculties." Not a few learned men of our day are satisfied with Pliny's principles.

That Nature worship is a natural impulse, has been well illustrated in a pretty story told of a little English girl, whose father was expected home from sea, and who was seen to take up some water from a basin near her, and say, "Beautiful water! send home my father here."

We have a right to assume that our island races, existing in the country long before the arrival of Celts in the west, did indulge in Nature worship, and continued to do so long after they came to these shores. Even Canute, at the end of a thousand years after Christ, found occasion to say, that "they worship heathen gods, and the sun or the moon, fire or rivers, water, wells or stones, or forest trees of any kind."

Baron d'Holbach said, "The word *Gods* has been used to express the concealed, remote, unknown causes of the effects he (man) witnessed." And Dormer's *Origin of Primitive Superstitions* declared that, "If monotheism had been an original doctrine, traces of such a belief would have remained among all peoples." Lubbock considered the Andaman Islanders "have no idea of a Supreme Being." Professor Jodl talks of "the day on which man began to become God." Dr. Carus, while affirming that "the anthropomorphic idol is doomed before the tribunal of science," says, "The idea of God is and always has been a moral idea."

Pictet observes, "There existed very anciently in Ireland a particular worship, which, by the nature of its doctrines, by the character of its symbols, by the names even of its gods, lies near to that religion of the Cabirs of Samothracia, emanating probably from Phœnicia." He thought the

Phœnicians introduced it into Erin, the *Muc Innis*, or Holy
Isle. Of this system, *Bryant's Antient Mythology* has much
to relate.

A French author held that the Celtic religion was based
upon a belief in the dual powers of good and evil in
perpetual strife ; and that the Irish associated with this a
contradictory pantheism and naturalism, as in the Theogony
of Hesiod.

Certainly the Irish called sea, land, or trees to witness
to their oaths. The *Four Masters* had this passage—
" Laeghaire took oaths by the sun, and the wind, and all
the elements, to the Leinster men, that he would never
come against them, after setting him at liberty." The
version in the *Leabhar-na-h-Uidhri* is that " Laeghaire
swore by the sun and moon, the water and the air, day
and night, sea and land, that he would never again,
during life, demand the Borumean tribute of the Leinster
men."

O'Beirne Crowe, at the Archæological Association, 1869,
declared the poem *Faeth Fiada* pre-Christian ; adding,
" That the pagan Irish worshipped and invoked, as did
all other pagan people, the personified powers of Nature,
as well as certain natural objects, is quite true."

The Irish prayer, in the *Faeth Fiada*, runs thus—" I
beseech the waters to assist me. I beseech Heaven and
Earth, and Cronn (a river) especially. Take you hard
warfare against them. May sea-pouring not abandon them
till the work of Fene crushes them on the north mountain
Ochaine." And then we are told that the water rose, and
drowned many. This prayer was said to have been used
by Cuchulainn, when pressed hard by the forces of Medb,
Queen of the Connachta.

If the Palæolithic man be allowed to have been susceptible to the impressions of Nature, the mixture of many

races, driven one upon another in the western corner of Europe, and so coming in contact with some higher influences, could not be imagined without impulses of devotion to the mighty and mysterious forces of Nature.

Our knowledge of so-called Celtic religion has been largely derived from Cæsar and other Roman authorities. These, imbued with Italian ideas, were not very reliable observers. They saw Jupiter in one Celtic deity; Mars, Minerva, Apollo, and Mercury in others. They knew the people after relations, more or less intimate, with visitors or traders from more enlightened lands. They were acquainted with Iberians, Germans, and Celts in Gaul, but only partially with those across the Channel, until Christianity had made some way. The wilder men of those nationalities, in Ireland and Northern Scotland, were little known; these, at any rate, had not quite the same mythology as Romans saw in Gaul.

It may be granted that the traditional opinions of the Irish would be more safely conveyed to us through their early literature, rude as that might be, and capable of conflicting interpretations,—historical or mythological. In spite of the obscurity of Fenian and other poets of that remote age, their writings do furnish a better key to the religion of Erin, than theories founded upon the remarks of Roman writers respecting Gaulish divinities. It must, however, be conceded that, in the main, Ireland consisted of varieties of the three great ethnological divisions of Gaul, commonly classed as Iberian, German, and Celtic, and inherited something from each.

A difficulty springs up from the language in which the early poets wrote. Like our English tongue, the Irish passed through many phases, and the reading thereof has occasioned much contention among translators. The early introduction of Latin, Norman-French, and English increased the obscurity, and hampered the labours of copyists in the Middle Ages, as was the case with that composite language known now as Welsh.

The god most prominently set forth in early Irish missionary records, in the Lives of the Saints, and in the ancient Bards, is *Crom, Cromm Cruach* or *Cenn Crûach*, the bleeding head ; or *Cromm Cruaich,* the Crooked or Bent One of the Mound. As *Crom-cruaghair*, the great Creator, he has, by some writers, been identified with the Persian *Kerum Kerugher. Crom* has been rendered *great ;* and *Cruin*, the *thunderer.* One considers *Cromleac* as the altar of the Great God. He is also known as *Ceancroithi*, and the head of all gods. Cromduff-Sunday, kept early in August, was the festival of *Black Crom.*

He figures in the several Lives of St. Patrick. At the touch of the Saint's sacred staff of Jesus, his image fell to the ground. He is associated with Mag Slecht, a mound near Ballymagauran, of Tullyhead Barony, County Cavan. The Welsh god *Pen Crug* or *Cruc*, Chief of the Mound, answered to the Irish deity.

He was certainly the Sun-god, for his image was surrounded by the fixed representations of twelve lesser divinities. Irish imagination pictured the first of gold, the others of silver. They were certainly stones ; and, as Andrew Lang remarks, "All Greek temples had their fetish stone, and each stone had its legend." The one surrounded with the twelve would readily suggest the Sun and the twelve Signs of the Zodiac.

An old reference to Crom has been recorded in Ogham letters, thus translated, " In it Cruach was and twelve idols of stone around him, and himself of gold." In the old book *Dinseanchus* we read thus of Crom Cruach—" To whom they sacrificed the first-born of every offspring,

and the first-born of their children." This record of
their heathen fathers must have been, doubtless, a libel
in the excess of zeal. The priests of Crom were the
Cruim-thearigh.

Instead of gold, one story declares the image was ornamented with bronze, and that it faced the South, or Sun.
It was set up in the open air on the Mag Slechta, says
Colgan, the *Field of Adoration.* They who are not Irish
or Welsh scholars have to submit to a great variety of
readings and meanings in translators.

The mythology has been thus put into verse by T. D.
McGee :—

> " Their ocean god was Menanan Mac Lir,
>   Whose angry lips
> In their white foam full often would inter
>   Whole fleets of ships.
>
> Crom was their Day god, and their Thunderer,
>   Made morning and eclipse ;
> Bride was their queen of song, and unto her
>   They prayed with fire-touched lips."

Professor Rhys has an explanation of Cromm Cruaich
as the *Crooked* or *Bent* one of the Mound ; saying—" The
pagan sanctuary had been so long falling into decay, that
of the lesser idols only their heads were to be seen above
ground, and that the idol of Cenn Cruaich, which meant
the *Head* or *Chief* of the Mound, was slowly hastening to
its fall, whence the story of its having had an invisible
blow dealt it by St. Patrick."

The Mother of the Irish gods,—the *Bona Dea* of Romans
—appears to have been the *Morrigan*, to whom the white-
horned bull was sacred. She was the *Great Queen.* Some
old poet had sung, " Anu is her name ; and it is from her
is called the two paps above Luachair." From her paps
she was believed to feed the other deities, and hence
became Mother of the gods. According to another, she

was the goddess of battle with the Tuatha, and one of the wives of the Great Dagda. She was thought to have her home in the *Sighi*, or fairy palaces.

The *Bona Dea* of Rome is said to have been Hyperborean. Hence, observes Crowe, it may have been Ireland that gave the goddess and her worship to the Romans. As *Anu*, she may have been the goddess of wealth. *Rea* or *Reagh* was, also, Queen of Heaven. Not a few crescents have been found in the neighbourhood of Castle-reagh. Dr. Keating calls the Moriagan, Badha, and Macha the three chief goddesses of the Tuath de Danaans.

Her white-horned bull of Cruachan, Find-bennach, was in direct opposition to the brown bull of Cualnge. She was the goddess of prosperity. She occasionally appeared in the shape of a bird and addressed the bull *Dond.* She is the *Mor Riogan*, and identified with Cybele.

The Female Principle was adored by the old Irish in various forms. As the *Black Virgin*, she is the dark mould, or matter, from whose virgin material all things proceed. She is the *Ana-Perema*, of the Phœnicians, and the queen of women. She may be the Brid, *Bride* or *Bridget*, goddess of wisdom, but daughter of the Druid Dubhthach. Several goddesses are like the Indian Dawn goddesses. *Aine*, or circle, was mother of all gods. Ri, or Roi, says Rhys, was "the mother of the gods of the non-Celtic race."

The Celtic *Heus* or *Esus* was a mysterious god of Gaul. The Irish form was *Aesar*, meaning, *he who kindles a fire*, and the Creator. In this we are reminded of the Etruscan *Aesar*, the Egyptian sun bull *Asi*, the Persian *Aser*, the Scandinavian *Aesir*, and the Hindoo *Aeswar.* The Bhagavat-Gita says of the last that "he resides in every mortal."

Hesus was acknowledged in the British Isles. In one

place he is represented with a hatchet, cutting down a tree. As the Breton Euzus, the figure is not attractive looking. Dom Martin styles Esus or Hesus "the Jehovah of the Gauls." He was, perhaps, the Aesar, or *Living One*, of the Etruscans. Leflocq declares, "Esus is the true god of the Gauls, and stands for them the Supreme Being, absolute and free." The name occurs on an altar erected in the time of the Emperor Tiberius, which was found in 1711 under the choir of Notre Dame, Paris.

Sun-gods were as common in Ireland as in other lands. Under the head of "Sun-worship" the subject is discussed; but some other references may be made in this place.

The Irish sun-gods, naturally enough, fought successfully in summer, and the Bards give many illustrations of their weakness in winter. Sun heroes were not precisely deities, as they were able to go down to Hades. Aengus, the young sun, whose foster-father was Mider, King of the Fairies, was the protector of the Dawn goddess *Etàin*, whom he discreetly kept in a glass grianan or sun-bower, where he sustained her being most delicately on the fragrance and bloom of flowers. His father was the great god Dagda.

Sun-gods have usually golden hair, and are given to shooting off arrows (sunbeams), like Chaldæan ones. As a rule, they are not brought up by their mothers; one, in fact, was first discovered in a pig-sty. They grow very rapidly, are helpers and friends of mankind, but are engaged everywhere in ceaseless conflicts with the gods or demons of darkness.

The Irish sun-gods had chariots, like those of the East. They indulged in the pleasures of the chase, and of fighting, but were more given to the pursuit of Erin's fairest daughters. Occasionally they made improper acquaintance with darker beings, and were led into trouble thereby.

Grian was the appellation of the sun, and *Carneach* for the priest of the solar deity. Strabo mentions a temple in Cappadocia to Apollo *Grynæus*. Ovid notes a goddess called by the ancients *Grane*. The Phrygians had a god *Grynæus*. *Grane* and Baal both refer to the sun. J. T. O'Flaherty regarded the Irish word *Grian* as pure Phœnician. The *Four Masters* inform their readers that "the monarch Laogaire had sworn ratha-Greine agus Gavithe"; that is, by the sun and wind. Breaking his oath, he was killed by those divinities. Eusebius held that Usous, King of Tyre, erected two pillars for worship to the sun and wind.

It has been affirmed by an Erse scholar, that the Irish Coté worshipped the sun under forty different names. *Dal-greine*, or *sun standard*, was the banner of the reputed Fingal. *Daghda* was an Apollo, or the sun. He was also the god of fire.

The Phœnicians have been credited as the introducers of Irish solar deities. Sir S. Rush Meyrick held their origin in these Islands from Arkite sun-worship: Tydain was the Arkite god, the Lord of Mystery. H. O'Brien, in *Phœnician Ireland*, Dublin, 1822, spoke of the Irish word *Sibbol* as " a name by which the Irish, as well as almost all other nations, designated and worshipped Cybele ; " *sibola*, an ear of corn, being a symbol of Ceres and Cybele of the Phœnicians. Several supposed Phœnician relics, especially swords, have been discovered in Ireland.

The Gaulish *Belenus* was known over these Islands. In his temples at Bayeux and at Bath there were images of the Solar god. He was adored, too, at Mont St. Michel. A remnant of his worship is seen in the custom of maids washing their faces in May-morn dew, and then mounting a hill to see the sunrise. According to Schedius, the word may be rendered $2 + 8 + 30 + 5 + 50 + 70 + 200$ or 365, the period in days of the sun's annual round. The solar Hercules was represented in Irish by *Ogmian* or *Ogham.* The god of light was ever god of the Heavens.

Belenus was Belus or Belis, from *belos*, an arrow, or ray, and therefore a form of Apollo. As Apollo-Belinus, he was the young Sun, armed with arrows or rays, and was exhibited as a young man without beard, and rays round his head. As Apollo-Abelios, he was the old or winter sun, having no rays. The Breton god was Beletucadrus —Mars and Apollo being identical. The votive altar at St. Lizier bears the names of Minerva and Belisana. Baron Chaudruc-de-Crazannes, writing upon *Belisana,* goddess of the Gauls, observes that Cæsar "had found in Esus, Taranis, Teutates, Camulus, Belisana, an identity with Jupiter, Mercury, Apollo, Mars, and Minerva, of Greeks and Romans." Belisana, without lance or shield, was called the Queen of Arrows, *i. e.* the solar rays. She was represented as thinking profoundly.

Samhan, literally servant, is derived from *Sam*, the sun ; so, *samh-an,* like the sun. As the Irish Pluto, he is guardian of the Dead. As such, he would receive the prayers for souls on Hallow Eve. The Arab *schams* is the sun. *Cearas,* god of fire, has a feminine equivalent in *Ceara*, goddess of Nature. As the horse was a symbol of the sun, we are not surprised to see it associated with the god *Cunobelin* of Gaul, who had the sun's face, with locks of hair. The Gaulish *Cernunnos* appeared as an old man with horns on his head.

Le Blanc, in *Etude sur le Symbolisme Druidique,* asserts that the name of Bal-Sab proves that Bâl, Bel, or Beal is the same as the Irish Samhan. Bâl is the personification of the sacred fire become visible. The year, the work of

Samhan, the Sun, was known as the Harmony of Beal.
Samhan, adds Le Blanc, "was that idol which the King of
Ireland adored after the name of head of all the gods."
In the Psalms we read, "They join themselves to Baal-
Peor, and eat the sacrifice of the dead." This was true of
many ancient countries, and may, perhaps, be applied to
Ireland.

A Hymn to Apollo, appearing in the ably conducted
Stonyhurst Magazine, is so beautiful, and so truly descriptive of the sun and fire worship of ancient Erin, that a verse
of it may be transcribed :—

> " Pile up the altar with faggots afresh,
>   The head be off severed—strew wheat and rye,
> Pouring libations of wine on the flesh,
>   That odorous incense ascend the sky !
>   Ward against evil,
>   Guard of the byre—
>   Glorious sun-god—
>   Prince of the lyre !
>   Olympus compelling
>   With harmonious swelling—
>   Apollo aeidon !
>   Worshipped with fire ! "

There was an Irish fish god, associated with caves and
storms, with the attributes of Dagon in the land of the
Philistines. *Neith*, a god of war, had two wives, Nemain
and Fea ; these were also styled goddesses of war. The
Book of Leinster names *Brian*, *Tuchar*, and *Sucharba* as
gods of the Tuaths. The Irish *Badb* is but the Gaulish
Badna, and yet not a goddess of war. *Deuc* or *Ducius* was
known to St. Austin as "a libidinous demon." *Aou* was
another Celtic god.

Camulus, the Gaulish Mercury, whose image was on the
Puy de Dome, was the Irish Cumall, father of the mythical
Finn, and said to be the same as the Welsh Gwyn, son of
Nûd. The Irish *Toth* was probably a copy of *Thoth*, or
the Gaulish *Teut*, god of war. Canobalinos, the Welsh

Conbelin, was adored in both isles. *Decete* is named in Devon, Anglesey, and South-west Ireland.

Dormer supposed the deities were first of place, then of peoples. Rhys saw minor gods as *genii locorum;* and asked what race it was that gave the Celtic lands its population of spirits. He regarded the mass of divinities as "very possibly creations of the people here long before the Celts." The non-Aryan mythology had doubtless great influence on the religion of the Goiedels.

When St. Patrick tried conversion upon the King's daughters, Eithne and Finola, they inquired if his god lived in the hills, valleys, fountains, or rivers. Seeing his party in white, the princesses concluded they were men of Sidhe, or earth divinities.

Some imagine the popular Mithraic faith of the East reached Ireland. It did gain the shores of Gaul; for, in 1598, a stone cist was dug up near Dijon, enclosing a glass vessel. Upon the stone was this Greek inscription—" In the sacred wood of Mithras, this tumulus covers the body of Chyndonax, high priest. Return, thou ungodly person, for the protecting gods preserve my ashes."

Chaldæan influence may have been carried to Erin by Tyrian traders. Very many terms of divination used there are like those employed in Chaldaic. A Chaldæan record on physic or divination was found in India in 1765. The Tuaths, so associated with Irish deities, have been thought to be wandering Chaldees. It is singular that the Irish Venus was recognized under the names of *Bidhgoe, Nanu,* and *Mathar*, which in Persian would be *Biducht, Nanea,* and *Metra*.

The circle may represent the universe. The Irish god *Ti-mor* means the *great circle.* He was Alpha and Omega, A Ω, the perfect Decad or 10, of Pythagoras. *Much* was another name for the Great God.

In comparing Irish gods with others, Neit has been identified with the *Naat* of India and *Neith* of Egypt ; *Creeshna*, the sun, with the Indian *Christna : Prith*, lord of the air, with *Pritha*, a title of Vishnu ; *Ner*, latinized to *Nereus*, with the *Naros* of India ; *Cau*, with *Caudra ; Omti* with the Buddhist *Om ; Esar* with *Eswara*, &c. Comhdhia —the middle and end—reminds one of the Orphic hymn— " Zeus is the first, Zeus is the last : Zeus is the head, Zeus is the middle."

" The god of the Gael," writes Donald Ross, " was outside of him, and draped awfully by his imagination." The Deity everywhere has been regarded with awe, and even terror, in all religious systems. Pantheism, however, in some mystical form, entered the mind of the Gael, as well as that of the Greek and Hindoo. While Orpheus sang, " All has come from the bosom of Zeus," Finlanders held that their god Kawe was in the bosom of K-unattaris (Nature).

Some fancy the butterfly—Dealbhaude—was in Ireland a symbol of God, from its changes of being. *Be'al* was the source of all being, as the Scandinavian *Tuisco*, after whom our *Tuesday* is named, was the Father of all beings.

Dr. Todd affirmed—" The Irish had no knowledge of the *Dei Gentium*, Saturn, Apollo, Mars, &c., or of the feminine deities Juno, Venus, Minerva, &c., under any Celtic name or designation." Crowe answered, " Now, this is not true. The *Dei Gentium*, under the ancient Gaulish or Iberno-Celtic names, are often met with in Irish story." But Crowe held with Cæsar and Tacitus, that the Celts of Gaul and our Isles had similar gods to those of Rome and Greece.

Though the transcribers of the *Book of Leinster*, during the fifteenth, sixteenth, and seventeenth centuries, corrupted the MS., from ignorance more than design, yet not a few learned men trace in that book the most ancient Irish mythological treatise.

With so fighting a race as that of Erin, war-gods were common. Some were battle furies, as *Nemon*, the *Neme-tona* of Gaul. Others were like Cairbre, whose exploits are narrated by the *Four Masters*, and who, as a hero, was, as Prof. Rhys says, "placed on a level with the gods." It is not easy, however, to discover there those ancient legends which, as Cory's *Ancient Fragments* supposes, "recognize as the primary element of all things, two independent principles, of the nature of male and female ; and those in mystic union, as the soul and body, constitute the Great Hermaphrodite Deity." There was scarcely that refinement in ancient Ireland.

Dr. Kenealy's *Book of God* perceives in the Irish *Oun* or *Ain* the cycle, or seasons' course ; as in *Bel-ain*, the year of Baal, the sun. The Irish *anius* is the astrologer, surveying the cycle. *Bay* is regarded as circle or cycle in Irish and Sanscrit. The Irish *Cnainh* was, in Kenealy's view, the Phœnician *great-winged one*, or *Cneph* of Egypt. He speaks of "their more ancient manner of invocation being Ain treidhe Dia ainm Tau-lac, Fan, Mollac or Ain, triple God, whose name is Tau-lac, Fan, Mollac. This third person was the Destroyer." *Fan* he places with *Pan* or *Phanes*.

Another fanciful author sees the source of an Irish religious festival in the *Charistia* of Romans, a feast sacred to *Concord* and the *Loves* at the end of the year—whence the word Eu—charist. Lenoir is more correct in saying, "Astronomy is truly the fruitful source from which the Mages and the priests have drawn ancient and modern fables."

The Rev. R. Smiddy writes of the Celtic *Ceal*, the heaven ; and *Cealtach*, a heavenly person. Church, a circle,

is *swreal*, or swrealleacht, the pillared temple of the Druids.
He derives *teampul* from *tiomchal*, round, as the sun.
Taking *Dia* as both *god* and *day*, he gets Dia Sol, Dia
Luan, Dia Moirt (death), Dia Ceadion (the first god), Dia
Ardion (the high God), Dia Beanion (the woman god),
Dia Satharn (Saturn). After all, we may perceive, with
Max Müller, that "the whole dictionary of ancient religion
is made up of metaphor."

The French author of *Sirius*, who perceives in that
star the origin of all thundering or barking gods, has a
god of thunder in the Celtic *T-aran*, which is *T* affix to
the sound made by a dog.

"The Celtic priests, or Druids," says he, "who, like the
Egyptian priests, had adopted the *Chien-Levrier* for a
symbol, called themselves the ministers of an Unknown
God, descended, it is said, upon earth, as Thoth, under a
human form, and having all the characteristics of that
Egyptian god, with the head of a dog; benefactor of
Humanity, Supreme—civilizing Legislator, Poet and Mu-
sician, King of Bards, Inventor and Protector of Agriculture,
Regulator of Waters, Protector in Darkness, raised to the
Presidency in a circle of stones, Founder of sacred cere-
mony, Model-priest, invoked under the name of Father."

All that is very Welsh, and cannot be applied to Ireland.
The Welsh Triads have had claimed for them a greater
age than modern critics are disposed to allow. Many of
the Welsh gods therein recorded are of doubtful pagan
origin, and belonged rather to the mysticism that crept into
Europe from the East during the early Middle Ages.

The Irish—except where their Bards came under the
influence of the same wave of oriental or Gnostic learning—
of olden time knew little of *Addon*, the seed-bearer in himself; *Ammon*, without beginning; *Celi*, the mystery; *Deon*,
the just; *Duv*, he is; *Dovydd*, regulator; *Deon*, separate

One ; *Dwyv*, I am ; *Daw*, being ; *Gwawr*, dawn of day ;
Gwerthevin, supreme ; *Ton*, source ; *Tor*, one of yore ;
Nudd, manifest ; *Perydd*, cause ; *Rhen*, pervader ; *Rhwyf*,
overlooker, &c.

There is no mention of their recognition of the Three
Attributes—*Plennydd, Alawn*, and *Gwron*, indicated by
the three divergent rays. They had no *Circle of Ceugant*
as the infinite space ; nor did they look upon the cromlech
as representing, in three stones upholding the cap-stone,
the doctrine of Trinity in Unity.

We cannot conceive of an Irish bard writing, as did a
Welsh bard, of Ceridwen—" Her complexion is formed of
the mild light in the evening hour, the splendid, graceful,
bright, and gentle Lady of the Mystic Song." But we
do know that the early Crusaders brought home much of
this mystic talk from the East, and that ecclesiastics of
an imaginative turn were charmed with pseudo-Christian
gnosticism. The Irish pagan, as the Welsh pagan, was
ignorant of such refinement of speech or ideas. The
Welsh Archdruid assured the writer of his belief that so-
called pagan philosophy was the source of Bardism, that
the teaching of the Triads was but the continuation of a
far older faith in his fathers.

Ossian more properly pictures the opinions of his race
in Ireland and Scotland, though they are rather negative
than affirmative. He, doubtless, never entered the esoteric
circle of Druidism, and is very far from displaying any
tincture of mysticism in his verses.

His gods were hardly spiritual, but vulnerable ; as, when
Fingal fought the Scandinavian Deity, that shrieked when
wounded, " as rolled into himself, he rose upon the wind."
Yet the gods could disturb the winds and waves, bring
storms on foes, and so destroy them. Dr. Blair was struck
with the almost total absence of religious ideas in Ossian.

Even at the funeral, in *Temora*, we have only, "Loud at once from the hundred bards rose the song of the tomb."

He lived in the age of Christianity. Hear the challenge of the wild Northmen—"Are the gods of the Christians as great as Loda (Odin) of the Lochlins?" Dr. Donald Clark fancied that in Ossian's day the people had lost faith in their old Druidic religion, but had not then embraced Christianity.

The remarks of Dr. H. Waddell are entitled to careful attention. Referring to Ossian, he says—

"All local gods, to him, were objects of ridicule. He recognized the Deity, if he could be said to recognize Him at all, as an omnipresent vital essence, everywhere diffused in the world, or centred for a lifetime in heroes. He himself, his kindred, his forefathers, and the human race at large, were dependent solely on the atmosphere; their souls were identified with the air, heaven was their natural home, earth their temporary residence, and fire the element of purification, or the bright path to immortality for them when the hour of dissolution came.—The incremation of Malvina's remains, on the principle of transmutation, and escape from dark, perishable clay to luminous and immortal ether, is a beautiful illustration of this."

After all, one is constrained to admit with Ernest Rhys— "I for one am quite prepared to believe in a Druidic residue, after you have stripped all that is mediæval and Biblical from the poems of Taliesin." So it is with Ossian, or other bards of Irish origin. With all that has been accumulating of a mediæval character, from the hands of supposed transcribers and translators, there yet remains something of the primeval barbaric conception of religion in the grand old tales of Erin.

In the Bardic story of the *Battle of Gabhra* we read— "I return my thanks to the gods."

This led N. O'Kearney to observe—" From this passage it is evident that the pure monotheism of the Druids had dwindled down into a vulgar polytheism, previous to the date of the Fenian era. Historians assert that Tighernmas was the first monarch who introduced polytheism, and that a great multitude of people were struck dead. on the worship of strange gods. The sun, moon, stars, elements, and many animals that were adored by the Egyptians, were introduced as deities."

Jocelin, an interesting romancer, speaking of Legasius, son of King Neal, tells the reader that "he swore by an idol called *Ceaneroithi*, or the head of all the gods, because he was believed by the foolish people to give answers."

A periodical called the *Harp of Erin*, which appeared in 1818, has the following argument from an old tradition :—

"That the Ancient Irish were not idolaters, we have sufficient evidence to convince any person who is possessed of common understanding. We are informed that Tighernmas, the King, was the first who paid divine honors to an idol, and that having been struck by lightning, his death was considered as a judgment. Surely, if idolatry had been a common practice of the people, their bards and history would neither have represented the act of the monarch as a crime, nor his death punishment from heaven for the offence."

The quotations from Bardic chronicles and poems, made by Prof. Rhys and others, would not sanction the views of the *Harp of Erin*. Their Nuada, Diarmait, Conchobar, &c., were assuredly sun-deities. Rhys says of the last-named, " Conchobar was doubtless not a man ; his sister Dechtere, the mother of Cuchulainn, is called a goddess." He was known in the *Book of the Dun* as *Diaalmaide*, or terrestrial god. The river Boyne may have had its name from the goddess *Boann*, wife of the Irish Neptune, Nodens.

Adolphe Pictet was formerly regarded as the most learned Celtic scholar in France. He is very precise in his belief of Irish polytheism, though influenced too strongly by the Cabiric theory. " The double Cabiric Irish chain," says he, " is only the ascending development of the two primitive principles."

Ordinary people may fail to follow this philosopher in his metaphysical views concerning the early Irish. They may doubt his progression of six degrees in Irish masculine and feminine divinities.

He held that Eire, Eo-anu, and Ceara were only the same being in three degrees of development; that Por-saibhean, daughter of Ceara, was the Greek Persephone, the Roman Proserpine ; that Cearas and Ceara were Koros and his sister Kore ; that Cearas was Dagh-dae, god of fire, and that he was a sort of demiurgus ; that Aesar and Eire or Aeire, as fundamental duality, give birth to two chains of progressive parallels,—masculine and feminine, fire and water, sun and moon ; that the goddess Lute or Lufe is power and desire, but Luth is force ; that the Midr, children of Daghdae, were rays of God ; that Aesar was god of intelligible fire ; that Brighit was goddess of wisdom and poetry, like Nath, while Aedh was goddess of vital fire.

Much of this might be esteemed by some readers as a pleasing or romantic philosophy of Irish mythology.

———

It may be useful to look at the religion of the Manx, or people of the Isle of Man, who were, if not Irish, close kinsmen of the same. We take the following from a Manx poem, first printed in 1778, as dealing with the divinities.

> " Mananan beg, hight Mac of Lerr,
>   Was he the first that ruled the land ;
> A pagan, and a sorcerer,
>   He was, at least I understand."

This *Mananan*, a deity of the Tuath de Danaans, was god
of waters ; but *Mac of Lir* was styled son of the sea.
Neid and *Bad* were gods of the wind. We are informed
by the author that " By the name *Gubh* or *Gobh*, a blaze,
fire, &c., the pagan Irish meant to insinuate that *Sam-
Gubha* were particularly inspired by the solar heat." The
motto of old was, " Let the altar for ever blaze to
Daghdae."

Easc was the new moon to Manx and Irish. The Irish
still say Paternoster at the new moon, and, crossing themselves, add, " May you leave us as safe as you found us ! "
Ce-Aehd was a goddess of Nature. An old poem says,
" There was weeping in the day of Saman Bache." *Ceara*
was the sun ; and Badhh-Be-bad, the god of wind. *Brid*,
daughter of Daghdae, was the goddess of wisdom and
poets ; *An*, the *mater dea ; Aodh*, goddess of fire. Manx
traditions and customs are similar to the Irish.

Sword-worship, in some respects, figured in the past, as
with the Huns, &c. Famous heroes or deities have had
the names of their swords preserved, as in the case of
Arthur and Fingal.

Speaking swords occur in the *Leb na huidre*, as recorded
in the *Revue Celtique*. Noticing the custom of bringing in
the tongues of the slain as trophies, the Irish MS. says—
" And it is thus they ought tò do that, and their swords on
their thighs when they used to make the trophy, for their
swords used to turn against them when they made a false
trophy—for demons used to speak to them from their
arms."

Spenser gives this narrative on the fabled power of the

sword ; saying, " So do the Irish at this day, when they go
to battle, say certain prayers or charms to their swords,
making a cross therewith upon the earth, and thrusting
the points of their blades into the ground, thinking thereby
to have the better success in fight. Also they use commonly to swear by their swords."

The Fairies or *Sides* are often presented as deities. As
the Tuatha were largely supernatural, and their spirits
haunted the old spots, it is not surprising that these *ar-
rachta* or spectres were reverenced by the Irish. Though
St. Patrick drove many of them away, a number fled
across Donegal Bay to the pagans of Senghleann. In St.
Fiacc's Story of the Saint we are assured that the Irish
used to worship the Sides.

" This *Side* worship," wrote Beirne Crowe, " had nothing
to do with Druidism ; in fact, was opposed to it, and must
have preceded it in Ireland." They were deified mortals,
anyhow, and capable, by intercourse with women, of producing heroes. But one was hardly justified in declaring
that " the worship of these deities reaches back to the
remotest antiquity, to at least a thousand years before the
Druid appeared."

The Sides and the Druids are curiously opposed to each
other in legends. The Side goddess, in the adventures of
Condla Ruad, told Coud's Druid that Druidism had the
grades conferred on it in the Great Land or Elysium.
It was thought that their temples were the so-called
Druidical monuments, especially New Grange. They
were scattered all over Ireland.

By the Irish *Mac Oc*, King of the Fairies, living in a
glass structure, is meant the young Sun. Rhys said the
story " doubtless belonged originally to Irish mythology
before any Celts had settled in Ireland."

This Mac Oc, or Aengus, is regarded as the Irish counterpart of Merlin or Emrys. He is associated with a fairy maiden, in the form of a Swan. He was the son of the divine King of the Tuaths, and usurped his father's crown, as Zeus did that of his father Chronos. As in other lands, the domains of heroes and gods continually encroach upon each other ; as divine attributes are bestowed upon departed chiefs, and divine honours, after the *tapu* order, are often paid to living heads of Septs. In no country, perhaps, was there more reverence given to chiefs, and in none more rigorous obedience exacted from the people by those who then controlled the very tribal lands.

It may be that this peculiarity of native character would account for the devotion to Saints in Irish Christian times. Still, it has been pointed out how tradition has converted honoured heroes or divinities of former days into modern Saints. This is, at least, a very curious coincidence, and by no means confined to Ireland, being witnessed in Scotland, Wales, Cornwall, and Brittany.

The great age to which some of these lived, according to such authorities as *The Four Masters*, &c., excites attention. St. Diarerca and St. Fechin continued on earth 180 years ; but St. Ciaran, 300 ; St. Mochta, 300 ; St. Sincheall, 330. Their ubiquity is suspicious. Thus, there are 25 St. Shanauns or Shannons, 37 Moluans, 43 Molaises, 58 Mochuans, 200 Colmans, and a number called St. Dagan, St. Molach, St. Duil, &c. It is odd to perceive so many provided with an alias.

" If the ancient Irish," observes Marcus Keane, " belonged to one great system of mythology, we would naturally expect to find traditions of different gods of the same system preserved in the same locality. This accordingly we find to be the case."

Mrs. Wilkes, in *Ur of the Chaldees*, remarked that many

of the Saints of Ireland bear Aryan and Semitic names. Again, " They (the missionaries) found it necessary, in many cases, to preserve to the Christian faith the names of many of the gods and heroes of their forefathers." She instances St. Molach, St. Dagan, St. Duil, St. Satan, St. Di(ch)ul, St. Cronan, &c. Another points out that St. *Luan* is derived from Lune or Lugedus ; St. *Bolcain* from Vulcan ; St. *Ciaran* from the Centaur Chiron ; and St. *Declan* from Declain, the Irish god of generation. M. Sonnerat held that St. Shannon was the god Dearg.

The author of *Towers and Temples of Ancient Ireland* derives St. *Diul* from *Dia-Baal ;* St. *Maedog* from *Mae-deog* of Virginity ; and St. *Earc* from *Earch,* the sun. He found 24 with the name of Colomb, 12 of Bridget, 25 of Senan, 12 of Dichul, and 30 of Cronan.

He contended that Irish Hagiology " began to be committed to writing about the tenth century "; that " in after times when it was thought desirable to ascribe ancient legends to Christian Saints, all were without distinction referred to the fifth and sixth centuries, as of course no celebrated Saint could have been ascribed to a period before St. Patrick, and that "the ancient literature seems to have been destroyed by the early Christians."

Although every one cannot be expected to follow Marcus Keane in opinion, there is much plausibility, if not reason, in the assumption that some of the Irish Saints were baptized deities of the Island.

Prof. Bevan, in a recent lecture at the Gresham College, showed how the Celtic gods were Romanized. Ogmius became Mercury ; Grannos, Apollo ; Caturix or Camulos, Mars ; Bridgit, Minerva ; Esas, Jupiter. He thought the Irish religion was partly of aboriginal forms of belief, and partly Druidic. He considered the transition from Druidism to Christianity a very gradual one. Lud or Llud, whose temple was on the site of St. Paul's Cathedral, he recognized as the Irish Nodens.

As the *Revue Celtique* contains a wealth of learning pertaining to the mythology of Ireland, some information from that work may be here placed before the reader.

Badb, one of the Irish goddesses of war, had three sisters, Neman, Macha, and Morrigan or Morrigu. These are described as Furies, able to confound armies ; even though assuming but the form of a crow. Hennessey thought these three were separate beings : "the attributes of *Neman* being those of a being who confounded her victims with madness, whilst *Morrigu* incited to deeds of valour, or planned strife and battle, and *Macha* revelled amidst the bodies of the slain." *Badb* was the daughter, also, of the mythical Tuatha King Ernmas. She inspired fear, so as to produce lunacy.

Standish O'Grady, in his critical and philosophical *History of Ireland*, adduces evidence of the useful labours of the early Irish gods, whom he detects under the assumed names of heroes. Parthalon was he who cleared from forest the plain of the Liffey. The Dagda Mor drove back the sea from Murthemney, forming the district now known as the Louth. Lu taught men first to ride on horses. Creidené first discovered and smelted gold in Ireland.

When the old original gods of Ireland were driven out by a younger and more vigorous set of divinities, they retired to Tir-na-n-og, the land of the young ; or to Tir-na-m-beo, land of life ; or to Tir-na-Fomorah.

The temple of Ned, the war god, was near the Foyle. According to O'Grady, "The *Dagda Mor* was a divine title given to a hero named Eocaidh, who lived many centuries before the birth of Christ, and in the depths of the pre-historic ages he was the mortal scion or ward of an elder god, *Elathan.*" He considered the *Mor Reega*, or great Queen, even more important than the Dagda Mor. She was connected with wealth, fertility, and war. She could transform herself into a water serpent, &c.

Then there is *Dana*, who became Brigit, mother of the three gods, Brian, Inchar or Incharba, and Inchair. Though the daughter of Dagda or good god, King of the Tuatha, she was wife to Bress, King of the Fomoré. As goddess of literature, it was fitting that *Ecné*, poetry or knowledge, should be her descendant.

The old form of the goddess *Brigit* is thought to have been *Brigentis.* Four inscriptions to her have been found on the east of Ireland. The god *Brian* was formerly *Brénos.*

The writings of Arbois de Jubainville, in the *Cours de la littérature Celtique*, have been justly admired. As he regarded the stories concerning the migration of early races, and the narratives of heroes and heroines, as having a mythological side, his views of Irish gods are interesting.

When Parthalon arrived in Ireland, the country was far from complete in form. At Mag Itha he had a battle with Cichol Gri-cenchos. The word *cenchos, without feet*, suggested Vitra, the Vedic god of evil, who possessed neither feet nor hands. He was assisted by men with only one foot and one hand, like *Aja Ekapad*, the one-footed, and Vyamsa, the shoulderless demon, of the Hindoo Vedas. Parthalon, by that victory, freed Ireland from foreign Fomoré. All his race, 5000, were struck dead by the gods in one day. So was the Silver Age destroyed by the anger of Jupiter against Niobe.

The chronicler had no record of years, but of days. Parthalon arrived on the first of May, the festival of the god of death, *Beltené*, ancestor of the human race. In older Erse MSS. he is described as the son of that deity. He gained the shore in Kenmare river, opposite the setting sun, where dead Celts recovered their lives.

The god *Dagda*, *Dago-devo-s*, the good god, yet King of the Tuatha de Danaans, was the Zeus or Ormazd of Irish mythology. The Danaans, or people of God, were, like the *Devas* of India, gods of the day, light, and life. The Fomoré, their enemies, represent the Titans of Greek story, whose chief Bress, Balar, or Tethra, was identical with the Persian Ahriman, the Vedic Yama, or even Varuna.

The Fomoré are, says Jubainville, " the gods of the dead, of night, and of storms." On the other hand, the Tuatha " are the gods of life, of day, and of the sun, constituting another group, the less ancient of the gods, if we believe the doctrine of Celts ; for, following the Celtic theory, night preceded day."

The Fomorian gods of earth and night were spoken of by the Christian chroniclers as pirates ravaging the coast. But the *Book of Invasions* simply mentions their arrival by sea. They must have been monsters, for a work treating of them had for its title the *History of Monsters*. Even Geraldus Cambrensis translated *Fomoré* by *Gigantibus*.

Among the stories told of them was the one giving some Fomorians but one foot and one hand, while others were goat-headed. The tale told of their Kings exacting the tribute of two-thirds of corn and milk, and two out of three children born in a family, reminds us of the Greek Minotaur. The Fomoré seem to belong to the beginning of all things, since no Irish legend knows of anything before their coming.

Our French author, who had much to report on solar gods, has the following remarks upon the lunar deity :—

" The queen of night is the moon, which, among the

stars, is distinguished by the crescent form, under which she usually presents herself to our notice. The god of night is distinguished from other gods by a crescent placed upon his forehead, and this crescent is transformed into the horns of the calf, the bull, or the goat. Hence, in the *Prometheus* of Æschylus, *Io*, the horned virgin, becomes, later on, a heifer; hence, in the Athenian fable, the conception of the Minotaur with the head of a bull; hence, in the Irish fable, the conception of the Fomoré with the goat's head;—and, upon the continent of Gaul, the numerous horned gods which now ornament the Salle of St. Germain Museum. For to render to these gods of the dead the worship they exact, it was necessary to immolate to them human lives."

We are told that Greeks poets and painters gave distinct characteristics to gods, as Phæton, Apollo, and Hercules, originally the same. The ancient literature of Ireland lacks these well-defined contours.

The dual idea of good and bad gods, with good and bad tribes, corresponds with the *Dasyu* of India, who were both demons and the hostile tribes preceding the Aryans in that peninsula. The Irish *triad* is produced by the habit of using three synonyms to express the same mythological thought.

Lug, one of the Tuatha gods, nursed by the Queen of the Fir-Bolgs, is supposed to have introduced games, races, &c. His festival was August 1. It has been suggested that the festival on the same day, in honour of Augustus, was only a new form of a more ancient custom. Lug's mother was Ethniu, daughter of Balar, but his father was the god Dagda.

Balar Balebeimnech, "Balar of the strong blows," was said to have been killed by his grandson. He carried off the cow of the three brothers, smiths of the Tuatha. Balar was killed by Lug. He is sometimes called the son of the bull-faced god. Lug and he may be compared with Bellerophon and the Chimæra. A doublet of Balar is seen in Tigernmas.

Cûchulainn, the son of Lug, was a deified hero. His remarkable adventures formed the subject of many bardic songs. Labraid, of the *swift hand on the sword*, was then King of Hades, the Irish Pluto. Being assisted against his foes by the mighty Cûchulainn, he presented the hero with his sister-in-law, Fand, for a wife; and she returned with the warrior from Hades. But Cûchulainn paid other visits to the world of spirits, with a view of rescuing friends from Hades, and returning to Erin. He had the deity Lug for his father, and the goddess Dechtere for his mother. As an Apollo, he was beardless; yet, when re-born, he appeared with long hair (rays). He released a maiden changed into a swan, being the goddess of Dawn. N. O'Kearney, translator of the Conn-eda story, found that the Irish hero was so beloved, that people would not "swear an oath either by the sun, stars, or elements, except by the head of Conneda."

Nuada, the Welsh Nudd or Lludd, must not be confounded with Net, god of war. He is declared by Rhys "of the non-Celtic race in both Britain and Ireland; for an old inscription in the county of Kerry gives the name without a case-ending, and so marks it as a probably non-Celtic word." In his *Celtic Britons* the same writer notes another deity; speaking of "the sea god *Nodens*, who was of sufficient importance during the Roman occupation to have a temple built for him at Lydney, on the western side of the Severn, while the Irish formerly called the goddess of the Boyne his wife."

The Feast of Goibniu, which assured immortality to the Tuatha, consisted principally of beer, a more common

drink· than nectar or ambrosia, but which had a similar
power of raising the consumer in his own estimation.
Goibniu, the smith, was the brewer of this magical drink
for the gods. Ogmé, founder of oghamic writing, was
called the *sun-faced*. He was the son of Elada, whose
name means poetic composition, or knowledge. His
brother Dian-cecht, the god of rapid power, was long the
Tuath god of medicine.

The deities, when they desired to make themselves
visible, appeared as birds. The Fomoré gods were seen as
crows or ravens. As Chronos was King of the world at
the time of the Golden Age, so Bress, King of the Fomoré
ruled awhile even over the Tuatha, who represent the Greek
golden race.

It is well to conclude with M. Jubainville, that "the gods
of the Gauls (*or Irish*), like those of the Romans, are, to
our eyes, a creation of the human mind." It may be also
added that usually the gods rise from low types to higher.
Still, Lubbock assures us that "religion, as understood by
the lower savage races, differs essentially from ours; nay,
it is not only different, but even opposite." Some may
be disposed to fancy the same of the more ignorant in
Christian lands.

In connection with Irish idolatry, the question of sacrifices
to the gods needs some consideration.

We may assume that the lower animals may have been
so offered; as, black sheep to Samhan on November 1,
and firstlings to the god Crom. But whether the Irish
ever had human sacrifices has been much debated. Such
a practice we know existed in both civilized and uncivilized
countries. It prevailed with worshippers of Baal, with
American Indians, with Khonds, and other tribes of India,
&c. In Deut. xii. 30, we read, "Their sons and their

daughters have they burnt in the fire to their gods." The animal sacrifice may be but a survival of the human.

Cæsar was positive as to the Gauls and Britons doing so. Strabo, Plutarch, and others said the same. Augustus, Tiberius, and Claudius opposed the Druids on account of that cruelty. Yet the Archdruid Myfyr exclaimed—"They never wrought an atonement for sin by the sacrifice of bloody carcases of any kind." The writer has heard the learned Welsh Druid affirm this in most earnest tones. He would not admit so degrading a practice for his Druids.

Yet Nennius tells how Vortigern, seeking to build a fort, was constantly annoyed by spirits running off with the stones ; and how he was told by his Druids to get a father-less boy, kill him, and sprinkle his blood upon the foundation of the buildings. Similar stories are mentioned in relation to Jericho, and to the erection of even Christian ecclesiastical edifices.

O'Curry affirms that there is "no instance of human sacrifices at any time in Erin." There is only one known text referring to the custom in Ireland, which occurs in the *Dinnsenchus.* Both men and women were liable to be burnt to ashes for certain crimes, but not in worship. The Lives of St. Patrick do not mention such offerings, though the *Book of Leinster* and Lucan's verses note their ancient service. Elton thought that some of the penalties of the ancient laws seemed to have originated in an age when criminals were offered to the gods.

Some old poem upon the *Fair of Tailté*, a pagan cemetery, has it—

> " The three forbidden bloods—
> Patrick preached therein (*i. e.* the fair)
> Yoke oxen, and slaying milch cows,
> Also by (against the) burning of the firstborn."

There was, however, in Leitrim a *Plain of Shrieking*, and Magh-sleacht was the place of slaughter.

In an article, contributed to an antiquarian periodical, in 1785, concerning the Irish mountain *Sliabh Croobh*, we find the following :—

" On its summit still remain the vestiges of Druid worship, the rude altar, and the sacred well, and that during the era of Druidical government, their priests were not only the judges, but executioners of those who were doomed to death either as delinquents, or victims of sacrifice. I am inclined to suspect that it was anciently styled *Sliabh cro abh ; cro* signifying death, and *abh* the point of a weapon,—and as a spot destined for human slaughter, might bear the appellation of the mountains of final death. A stone hatchet, and undoubtedly a sacrificial one, belonging to the Druids, was dug up at the foot of this mountain a few years ago, and is in Lord Moira's possession."

To show how wide-spread was the custom of human sacrifices, we may quote the list of nations adopting it, as given in the work *Indo-Aryans*, by Rajendralala Mitra. This includes the " Phœnicians, Carthaginians, Druids, Scythians, Greeks, Trojans, Romans, Cyclops, Lamiæ, Sestrygons, Syrens, Cretans, Cyprians, Assyrians, Egyptians, Jews, Aztecs, Khonds, Toltecs, Tezcaucans, Sucas, Peruvians, Africans, Mongols, Dyaks, Chinese, Japanese, Ashantis, Yucatans, Hindus." He adds—" The Persians were, perhaps, the only nation of ancient times that did not indulge in human sacrifices."

If, then, O'Curry, and other Irish writers, object to such a charge being made against their rude forefathers, it must be allowed that the latter would have been in, at least, respectable and numerous company.

The astronomical side of idolatry should not be passed over. It has been maintained, with much learning, that all tales of gods and goddesses, in all lands, can be traced to ideas connected with the heavenly bodies, and their several movements. The writer's old colonial friend, Henry Melville, nearly half a century ago, read Lemprière's stories of the deities on astronomical lines. Upon the Celestial Atlas he moved his cardboard masonic tools, bringing the figures of various constellations together, so as to explain the particular story. Later on, he discovered a system of interpretation, as certain and infallible, which he called the *Laws of the Medes and Persians*, as they were unalterable.

Melville had no opportunity of explaining the stories of Irish bards upon his plan. Vallencey, Jubainville and others have attempted it on other and theological lines. But if the stories could be treated at all astronomically, the interest in them would be increased, as showing their derivation from other and more enlightened lands. The great puzzle is, however, how several and such different keys manage to turn the same lock. But, as remarked by the Rev. Geo. St. Clair, "time will make the secret things plain and patent."

It may not be wrong, therefore, to trace in those Irish legends the existence of ancient and Oriental learning of a more or less astronomical character.

The Irish had a notion of the week, or seven days' period. That may have come from the East, meaning the sun, the moon, and the five then known planets. One has supposed that five were named after the Romans, and two from the Belgæ. But the *Woden* day was changed to *Gaden ;* and Thursday to *Tordain*, or *Torneach*, thunder, or the spirit of *Tor* or *Thor*. Schlegel says—"Among the Greeks and Romans, the observation of the days of the week was introduced very late." And yet they were well known long before in Babylon. The Phœnician, characterized by Sayce as the link between Chaldæan and Hebrew, may have been the means of introducing the week to Ireland.

The twelve signs of the zodiac were not unknown to the Irish. They were ever like the ladder, with six steps upward, and six downward. *Mazzaroth*, the twelve, is in the Arabic *manzeel*, a house or dwelling. The Targumists and Rabbins employed the words *tereysar mazzalaya* for the Signs. Philo called the dodecahedron a perfect number. " It is to honour that sign," adds Philo, " that Moses divided his nation into twelve tribes, established the twelve cakes of the shewbread, and placed twelve precious stones around the ephod of the pontiffs."

On the Irish zodiac, above the figures representing the Signs, the Irish letters were placed. The figure in the *Sagittarius* was a deer's body with a man's head. That in the *Scales* had legs, but no feet. The *Virgin* was standing, apparently spinning, being fully clothed, even to shoes. *Aquarius* was seen with a very long body, but short, thin legs and feet.

The Phœnician presence was to be, also, traced in Ireland by the remarkable evidences of Baal worship. Of this the Irish language and Irish customs bear witness.

Thus,—we have *Beal-agh*, fire of Baal, in the Giant Ring at Belaugh, Co. Down, four miles from Belfast, 579 ft. in diameter. There is *Bal-Kiste*, or Baal, Lord of the chest or ark ; *Meur-Bheil*, the finger of Be'il; *Bell*, god of fire ; *Baal Tinne*, for the summer solstice ; *Suil-Beal*, oracle of Druids ; *Bealtime*, the Baal month.

Four miles north of Cork is *Beal-atha-magh-adhoir*,— the field for the worship of Baal. *Sliabh-bulteine* was the hill of Bel. The *ark-Breith*, a covered coracle, was drawn by oxen. The old Irish name for the year was *Bealaine* or *Bliadhain*, the circle of Baal.

The *Bel-tor* of Dartmoor, the *Belenus* of Gaul, the *Beal* of the Gaedhil, the *Bali* of India, the *Belus* obelisk of Pomona in Orkney, the *Bealtien* cake of Scotland, the *Bel-eg*, priest or learned one of Brittany, the Punic *Bal*— all take us outside of Ireland. But Camden declared the cromlech on Sliabh Greine, hill of the sun, was to Beli. As reported by J. J. Thomas—" The Irish expression ' *Bal mhaith art* '—May Bel be propitious to thee ! or *Bal dhia dhuit*, the god Bal .to you ! were deemed complimentary addresses to a stranger along the sequestered banks of the Suir, in the South of Ireland, about twenty-two years ago."

There can be no doubt about this Baal worship being connected with Phallicism. Devotion to generative powers preceded, perhaps, that to the sun, as the main cause of production in Nature ; but the Baal development appeared later on in the so-called march of civilization. An increased fondness for ritual is generally taken for an evidence of refinement.

This Phallic exponent has been conspicuous in the *Bal-fargha*, or *Bud*, of the Island of Muidhr, off the coast of Sligo, represented as similar to the *Mabody* of Elephanta in India, where the *argha* was an especial object of worship, and which was seen by the writer, in Bombay, as still an object of religious devotion. Thére was on the Irish island a wall of large unmortared stones, some ten feet high, and of a rude circular form, having a low entrance. The *Bud*, or Linga, was surrounded by a parapet wall.

Innis Murra, an islet about three miles from the Sligo coast, has always been held sacred. In that, the area of this *Bal-fargha*, or argha, of rough stone-work, is 180 feet by 100, in its oval shape. To preserve its devotional character, three Roman Catholic chapels have been erected on the Isle. The holy ground is used as a cemetery; but the males are buried apart from the females. For some reason, a wooden image of St. Molos is placed there for the regard of worshippers.

As is well known, the snake has been associated with amatory sentiments in nearly all countries, and has for thousands of years. been a favourite form of ornament with women. Now, opposite this island, once given up to sexual worship, the limestone coast has been worn into shapes often tortuous or serpentine. Tradition asserts that this is the spot where St. Patrick cast the snakes of Ireland into the sea; that is to say, in other words, that Christianity extirpated the libidinous deities.

Irish literature notices the presence of two religious sects once existing in the country; viz. those who adored fire, and those who adored water. The first were *Baalites;* the second *Lirites.* The *Samhaisgs* were of the one, and *Swans* of the other. O'Kearney, in his observations upon this peculiarity of the past, incidentally shows the antiquity of faction fights in Ireland; saying, " It is probable that very violent contentions were once carried on in the Island by the partizans of the rival religions, who were accustomed to meet, and decide their quarrels, at the place set apart for battles." In later and Christian times, when Ireland had a multitude of independent bishops, under no ecclesiastical supervision, disputes of a more or less theological kind are said by the ancient historians to have been settled by their followers in the same fashion.

As the population of Ireland is, perhaps, the most mixed, in racial descent, of any in the world, it is not surprising that this Island should exhibit a greater variety of religions, several of which have left their traces in the traditions and superstitions of out-of-the-way localities.

That Buddhism should have found a foothold there is not surprising, since Buddhist missionaries at one era had spread over much of the Northern hemisphere. Though the reader may find in this work, under the heading of " Round Towers," references to this Oriental faith, some other information may be here required.

Whenever it came, and however introduced, Buddhism, as it was taught in its early purity, was a distinct advance upon previously existing dogmas of belief. It was a vast improvement upon Baal worship, Hero worship, or Nature worship, as it carried with it a lofty ethical tone, and the principle of universal brotherhood. Though there is linguistic as well as other evidence of its presence in Ireland, it may be doubted if the labours of the foreign missionaries had much acceptance with the rude Islanders.

Cnox Buidhbh, Budh's hill, is in Tyrone. A goddess of the Tuatha was called *Badhha. Budhbh,* the Red, was a chief of the Danaans. Buddhist symbols are found upon stones in Ireland. There are Hills of Budh in Mayo and Roscommon. Fergus Budh or Bod was a prince of Brejea. He was Fergus of the fire of Budh. Budh or Fiodh was the sacred tree.

Vallencey, the fanciful Irish philologist, was a believer in the story of Buddhist visitations. He found that *Budh* in Irish and Sanscrit was *wise ;* that *Dia Tait* was Thursday, and the day between the fasts (Wednesday and Friday), Wednesday being a sacred day in ʰonour of Budh in India, showing that "they observed Budhday after Christianity was introduced." *La Nollad Aois,* or *La Nollad Mithr,* December 24th, was sacred to Mithras the Sun ; to which he quotes Ezek. iv. 14. *Eire aros a Niorgul* alluded to the crowing of *Nargal,* the cock of Aurora, which was sacrificed on December 25th, in honour of the birth of Mithras, the Sun.

He further shows that the *Oin-id* lamentation for the Dead was kept in Ireland on the eve of *La Saman*, the day of Saman, the Pluto or Judge of Hell, November 1st (All Saints), as in several other heathen lands of antiquity. He sees a new reckoning on *Mathair Oidhehe*, the eve before *La Nollah Mithr*. The *Sab-oide,* or festival of *Sab*, the Sun, was held on the 1st, 8th, 15th, and 23rd of the month, as with the Sabbaths of the Persian Magi. He was not then aware that *Sabbath,* day of rest, was an old Chaldæan word. He recognizes Christmas Eve in *Madra nect*, or *Mother* night.

Buddhism abolished caste and sacrifices. The *Tripitaka*, or Bible, contains 592,000 verses. The last Buddhist council was held 251 B.C.

Dr. Kenealy observes, in his *Book of God,* " The Irish hieratic language was called *Ogham* (pronounced *owm*), which is the same as the Buddhist and the Brahmin *Aum*, and the Magian and Mexican *hom*, or ineffable name of God. This last, the Greek changed into A O M, A Ω, or Alpha and Omega." W. Anderson Smith, in *Lewisiana*, reluctantly acknowledges, " We must accept the possibility of a Buddhist race passing north from Ireland." Thus he and others must trace the relics of Buddhism in Scotland and the Hebrides through Ireland. Truly, as Fergusson writes, " Buddhism, in some shape or other, or under some name that may be lost, did exist in Britain before the conversion of the inhabitants to Christianity."

Hanloy, Chinese interpreter at San Francisco, who claims the discovery of America for his countrymen, that left written descriptions of the strange land, has this additional information—" About 500 years *before* Christ, Buddhist priests repaired there, and brought back the news that they had met with Buddhist idols and religious writings in the country already. Their descriptions, in many respects, resemble those of the Spaniards a thousand years after."

In the vaulted stone building at Knockmoy, Galway Co., assumed by some to have been a temple of the Tuatha, and next which sacred spot an abbey was subsequently erected, is a figure, taken for Apollo, bound to a tree, pierced with arrows, yet slaying the Python with his dart. Other three figures represent, in their crowns and costume, Eastern divinities, before whom another person is approaching. These have been conjectured to be the three, Chanchasm, Gonagom, and Gaspa, who obtained the perfect state of Nirvana before the birth of Godama, founder of Buddhism.

The mythological figures to be seen at the chapel of Cormac, the King and Bishop of Cashel, are not less strange in a Christian edifice than the heathen *argha* witnessed on a banner in some English churches. They are, to say the least, in a novel situation.

The *Lion of Cashel*, with its tail over its back, and a head partly human, is confronted by a centaur shooting an arrow. The figure's helmet is said to be like that of an Irish warrior in the tenth century. The two mythological hares, devouring foliage of the shamrock appearance, present a more striking character. Anna Wilkes was led to exclaim— " The supposed Cuthite remains at Cashel bear striking resemblance to some of the Ninevite sculptures ; Nergal or Nimrod, the winged lion, as exhibited in the British Museum, is a remarkable imitation of the winged lion of Cashel."

Were these, and similar sculptures, survivals of older faiths in the minds of the artists ? They were not fancies of their own, but they reflect past phases of heathenism. Superstitions ever indicate former beliefs.

It is not a little surprising to notice, in the ancient

writings of Irish Churchmen, so few references to the idolatrous practices of their countrymen. In the catalogues of the Dublin Museum of the Irish Academy one finds expression of the same wonder in these words : " The eccle-siastical chroniclers of the period, in their zeal for the establishment of Christianity, would appear to have alto-gether ignored the subject of pagan worship." It is this silence which has led so many persons to doubt the idolatrous customs of the early Irish, or to be very scep-tical as to the nature of the gods they worshipped.

The Akkadian religion of Assyria throws some light upon Irish faiths. Major Conder, referring to the inscrip-tions of Tell Loh, thought they proved " the piety of those ancient Akkadian rulers, and showing that the deities adored represented the sun and moon, the dawn and sunset, with the spirits of the mountains, the sea, the earth, and of hell." Elsewhere he says, " As regards the deities adored, they evidently include heaven, hell, the ocean, the sun and moon, the dawn, and the sunset." This was in Ur of the Chaldees, but long before Abraham's time.

The Major was struck with another inscription—" I have made the Pyramid temple to the Lord of the heavenly region. To Tammuz, Lord of the Land of Darkness, I have built a Pyramid temple." He further adds—" The Akkadians and Babylonians believed in pairs of deities inhabiting the various kingdoms of the gods." Others have detected the same duality in the divinities of Ireland. The Druidical three rods, or rays of light, have been compared to a Phœnician Trinity—the three sons of *Il*, and called *Elohim*. Morien contends that Jehovah is represented in Druidism by the three letters, I A O.

It is curious to note the remains of a very ancient building on the Hebridean Harris Island, known locally as the temple of Annait, and a similar one at Skye, afterwards becoming the Church of the Trianade, or Trinity. We are reminded of the Tanat or Tanath of the Phœnicians, the Anaietis of the Lydians, the Aphrodite Tanais of the Babylonians. How such mysteries got to the Hebrides need not surprise us. Two races left their descendants in those Islands—the Norwegian and the Irish; the latter spread over the islets and coastline of Western Scotland, and carried thither the popular creed of the migration era.

Sir W. Jones considered that "the whole crowd of gods and goddesses meant only the powers of Nature." Adolphe Pietet proceeds on the following lines—" From a primitive duality, constituting the fundamental force of the Universe, there arises a double progression of cosmical powers, which, after having crossed each other by a mutual transition, at last proceed to blend in one Supreme Unity, as in their essential principles ; such, in a few words, is the distinctive character of the mythological doctrines of the ancient Irish."

As elsewhere mentioned, the Irish Saints are traditionally mixed up with matters connected with former deities. Thus, Ledwich, in his *Antiquities of Ireland*, is induced to exclaim, " Very few of the Saints who adorn our legends ever had existence, but are personifications of inanimate things, and even of passions or qualities." St. Thenew or Mungo, patron Saint of Glasgow, was but a metamorphosed divinity of the same race. He was born of a virgin, a proof of her goddess-ship. His miraculous powers were like those of Irish gods, being exerted over Nature's laws. His rod was the Druidical hazel-branch, which burst into flame after his breathing upon it. Thus we see the river Shannon, once an object of worship, remembered under the name of St. Senanus ; and the mountain Kevn of Glendalough, also adored, become the Saint Kevin.

The strange mixture of heathenism and Scripture has

struck many inquirers. Meyrick's *Druidical Religion during the residence of the Romans*, points to this strange union in Britain. It was his opinion that "at the commencement of the fourth century, the Druids felt a common cause with the Roman priests in the extermination of Christianity." Bergmann detected the same influence in Snorre's Scandinavian *Fascination of Gulfi*. He separated the two elements for us. Leflocq remarked the mixture in the "transferring the gods themselves, and placing in the mouth of Odin an echo of the language of Moses." He might well say, "We are surprised to find the teaching of Genesis, and the morals of the Evangelists, in a book of the Eddas." Many may be equally surprised at the same in the MSS. of Erin.

"The Druids and Bards of these far-reaching bardic times," says Mrs. Bryant, "were practically heretics with respect to the more ancient forms of religious idea, which linger without meaning in the Irish peasants' tenacious memory, or adhere to his habits by the same persistence of conservative instinct."

While the cultured Egyptians, Assyrians, Hindoos, Jews, and Greeks, bowed to other gods than the *First Cause*, no Irishman need be astonished at a similar weakness in his half civilized ancestors. It might be that the moral infirmities of the former were greater than those in the men and women of old Erin.

IDOL-WORSHIP.

SOME Irish writers, from a spirit of patriotism, have expressed the opinion that, though English, French, Germans, &c. may have bowed before idols. their countrymen had never been subject to that error.

While professing a derivation from Spain, they have ignored the fact that Iberian idolatry was well known. They equally ignore the testimony of St. Patrick and other missionaries in Erin, the writings of Irish Saints, and the evidence of objects which are substantial witnesses.

Roman authors had no doubt of the presence of idols among the Celtic inhabitants of Gaul ; and any visitor to Hôtel Cluny, in Paris, can soon satisfy himself as to the truth, by a glance at the images stored in that noble museum of French history.

Vallencey said, " The Irish Druids were not idolaters, had no graven images." O'Kearney admits that " the pure monotheism of the Druids had dwindled down into a vulgar polytheism, previous to the date of the Fenian era." But O'Curry denies alike images, human sacrifices, and sun-worship. Arthur Clive could write—" There is abundant reason to suppose that there were no idols in use among the ancient Irish, no carved representations of the gods."

In the Museum Catalogue of the Irish Academy, it is written—" The ecclesiastical chroniclers of the period, in their zeal for the establishment of Christianity, would appear to have altogether ignored the subject of pagan worship." But Ennius distinctly records that when Patrick went to Cashel, " all the idols fell prostrate."

In St. Patrick's *Confession* we read—" Whence is it that in Ireland, those who never had the knowledge of a God, but worshipped even filthy idols," &c. Petrie declares it was " not unusual for St. Patrick to dedicate pagan monuments to the true God." In the Fiacc Hymn it is said— " There was darkness over Erin, they adored things of Faery." The Tripartite Life speaks of this adoration ; the *Confession* says the adorers " shall unhappily fall into eternal punishment."

Dr. E. B. Tylor says, " The idol answers to the savage, in one province of thought, the same purpose that its analogue the doll does to the child. It enables him to give a definite existence and a personality to the vague ideas of higher beings." Elsewhere he declares that idols " belong to a period of transition and growth."

It was not possible that, while Celts and Iberians in Great Britain and Gaul should have idols, the same races in Erin should be without them.

Gaul had Hesus, Belenus, and other deities in images. Mên, the Bayeux god, had horns. Cæsar called the chief Gaulish divinity by the name of Mars, whose shrine was on the Isle of Paris. Another, described as a Mercury, stood on the summit of Puy de Dome. Cernunnos was represented holding a bag of acorns. Belenus was declared, by Montfaucon, to be the same as a British Island idol. Lucan exclaimed, " Hesus, with cruel altars, horrid god." At Arles was found an idol, with a serpent twined about its legs. Elsewhere, it was a female in Gaul, with a serpent round the legs. Lucan left the following account of another :—

" The Gauls," said he, " call Hercules in their country language *Ogmius.* But they represent the appearance of their god in a very unusual manner. With them he is a decrepid old man, bald before, his beard extremely grey, as are the few other hairs he has remaining.—I was of opinion that all these things were perversely done, in dishonour of the Grecian gods.—This old Hercules draws after him a vast multitude of men, all tied by their ears. The cords by which he does this are small fine chains, artificially made of gold and electrum, like the most beautiful bracelets. And though the men are drawn by such slender bonds, yet none of them thinks of breaking loose, when they might easily do it.—The painter, to fix the extreme ends of the chains, made a hole in the god's tongue, who looks smiling towards those he leads."

The foreigner turned for explanation to a Gaul, who said, "We Gauls do not suppose, as you Greeks, that Mercury is speech or language, but we attribute it to Hercules, because he is far superior in strength." They thought Hercules, as speech, should draw men after him, with their ears tied to his tongue.

As to Wales—though some patriotic Welsh will not allow that their people ever were so degraded—there were idols, like that of Darvell-gadarn at St. Asaph. From a report on the Welsh, in 1538, we learn that they "come daily a pilgrimage unto him, some with kine, others with oxen or horses, and the rest with money." The old writer shows the respect paid to this idolatrous survival : remarking, "A common saying amongst them, that whosoever will offer anything to the said images of Darvell-gadarn, he hath power to fetch him or them that so offer out of hell when they are damned."

Scotland, too, had its idols. In a letter from Mr. Donald Clark to the author, several years ago, that gentleman added—"Since the above was written, an image of a female has been dug up from a moss in North Lochaber, of black oak, in good preservation, and about five feet long, which goes far to show that they had deity houses with images in North Britain also." Yet, as a linguist, he declared, "But there is nothing in their language to show that they worshipped those images—only venerating them." Apologists of other nations might say as much of their own ancestors' veneration of images.

King Laoghaire, contemporary with St. Patrick, was the worshipper of Crom Cruach, described as a pillar of stone. The Tripartite Life of the Saint called it "a crooked stone of adoration." As Magh-Sleacht meant *field of slaughter*, many supposed sacrifices were offered to the idol.

The Patron Saint made war against Crom. An old writer in 1695 said—"No sooner did he then eleuate his pure handes in prayer for the subuersion of the Idol, and had after a threatening manner lifted up the Rod of Jesus against it, but it fell downe upon the left side, and all the gold and silver dissolved into dust, the little gods were swallowed vp by the earth, euen to their neckes."

In the *Four Masters* is this version—"Crom Cruach stood near a river called Gathard, and St. Patrick erected a church near at Domhnachmor." Then they added, "According to Dinnsenchus (the geographer), this was the principal idol of all the colonies that settled in Ireland, from the earliest period to the time of St. Patrick, and they were wont to offer to it the firstlings of animals, and other offerings."

An inscription in Ogham tells that "in it Cruach was, and twelve idols of stone around him, and himself of gold." Another testimony is that it had much gold and silver, with twelve brass idols round it, as if in reference to the zodiac.

We are informed, that, when struck by St. Patrick, with his staff of Jesus, the image fell to the *west*, with the impression of the rod on its side, the twelve stone gods sinking into the ground. When the Saint called aloud for the Devil to come forth from the image, an ugly black fellow appeared, upon whom the Saint threw himself in anger. In the struggle, he lost a button from his coat. Though found soon after on the heath, nothing could grow on the spot ever after.

Toland, in 1728, had this account:—

"The chiefest in all Ireland was Crom Cruach, which stood in the midst of a circle of twelve obliscs on a hill in

Brefin, a district of the county of Cavan, formerly belonging to Leitrim. It was all over covered with gold and silver, the lesser figures on the twelve stones about it being onely of brass ; which mettals, both of the stones and the statues they bore, became everywhere the prey of the Christian priests upon the conversion of that kingdom." The legendary writers of Patrick's *Life* tell many things, not less ridiculous than incredible, about the destruction of this temple of Moysleet (Magh-Sleucht), or the Field of Adoration, in Brefin ; where the stumps of the circular obliscs are yet to be seen.—" The Bishop's See of Clogher has its name from one of these stones, all covered with gold (*Clogher* signifying the *Golden Stone*), on which stood *Kermand Kelstach*, the chief Idol of Ulster. The stone is still in being." He continued, " Kermand Kelstach was not the only Mercury of rude stone, since the Mercury of the Greeks was not portray'd antiently in the shape of a youth, with wings to his heels and a caduceus in his hand, but without hands or feet, being a *square stone*, says Phurnutus, and I say without any sculpture."

Vallencey maintained the same ; observing, " The ancient records of Ireland assert that the Irish Pagans worshipped no images ; the rough unhewn stone, capped with gold and silver, representing the sun and moon, and round these were twelve others, showing the number of the Signs of the Zodiac." Herodian has a similar view of the sun temple of Emasa, near Tyre—" There is no image, as among the Greeks and Romans, to represent the God, but an exceeding large stone, round at the bottom, and terminating in a point, of a conical form, and black color."

An old MS. says—" Magh-sleacht was so called from an idol of the Irish, named Crom-cruaith, a stone capped with gold, about which stood twelve other rough stones."

It is curious that the last Sunday in summer was known

as *Domnach Crumdnibh,* or Sunday of Black Crom ; it was afterwards changed to St. Patrick's Sunday.

O'Beirne Crowe thinks it absurd to suppose that the golden idol of Mag Slecht was only a stone pillar ; but "that the most ancient Irish idols, however, were of wood and stone is most probable, and that some of these ancient idols would be continued through pure veneration, even after the introduction of metallurgy, is also not improbable."

In Richardson's *Folly of Pilgrimage* is the record of a wooden image, carved and painted like a woman, kept in the house of the O'Herlebys, in Ballyvourney, Cork Co. The sick sent for it as a means of cure, and sometimes sheep were offered to it with peculiar ceremonies.

The *Gentleman's Magazine* for 1742, notes "two silver images found under the ruins of an old tower." They were described as being three inches high, in armour, with an Osirian helmet and neck covering.

Hindoo-like images of brass have been several times dug up. They appear in Oriental garb, or in a short petticoat or kilt, with the fingers touching a forked beard. One of such, now in the Dublin Museum, was taken from beneath the root of a large tree in Roscommon. In that instance, the arms were crossed. The height of this brazen idol was five inches. It had once been gilt. A metal idol, weighing twenty-four lbs., and fifteen inches high, was recovered from the soil at Clonmel, near the spot where another was seen, with a similar expression of face, and the hand holding something round.

A letter written to Pownall by the Rev. Mr. Armstrong, about 1750, has the story of an image found sixty years previously, in the bog of Cullen, Tipperary. It was a large wooden image. Mention is made that "little pins or pegs were stuck in different parts of it ; and that Mr.

Damer imagined that the little gold plates found there (four inches by three each), one of which I saw with him, were suspended by these pegs in different parts of that image." Subsequently the god was converted into a gate-post, and lost sight of after.

A bronze one, from Clonmacnoise, had a waved pattern on its eastern kilt and sleeves, with a conical head-dress ornamented with figures, a waving beard, and long prominent nose.

A Phallic image of Fro or Friceo, like the Priapus guardian of Brussels, was useful in driving disease from the Irish cattle. Feminine figures were employed down to quite modern times to remove evil ; like that female deity found in December, 1880, in the moss bed, north of Lochaber, which was of black oak, and five feet in height.

King Cormac is mentioned as refusing to worship the Golden Calf set up by the Druids. As, however, he met his death shortly after, through a salmon-bone sticking in his throat, the priests concluded he suffered through the vengeance of the god Crom Cruach. Later bards made him declare—" I will offer no adoration to any stock or image shaped by my own mechanic. It were more rational to offer adoration to the mechanic himself."

In the *Lays of the Western Gael* we have the bardic story of King Cormac, who lived 300 years before St. Patrick, refusing a burial after the heathen custom :—

> " For all the Kings who lie in Brugh
>   Put trust in gods of wood and stone ;
> And 'twas at Ross that first I knew
>   One, unseen, who is God alone.
>
> His glory lightens from the East,
>   His message soon shall reach our shore ;
> And idol god and cursing priest
>   Shall plague us from Moy Slaught no more."

The *Winged Lion* of Cashel may remind scholars of the

like looking creature of the Assyrian Nergal. The tail, which has a Phallic termination, was curled round the hind-leg and over the back. The hair was composed of curved lines. The animal was, apparently, to be attacked by a Centaur with a Norman helmet. These, perhaps, were not idols, but figures with a Freemasonic meaning, by some mystic architect of the Middle Ages.

Very different were the petticoated images, as the brass one of Roscommon, resembling those still to be observed in India, and recognized among the figures on pre-Christian crosses in Ireland. These bear evident traces of being brought to Erin by a people from the Mediterranean shores, and whose blood is yet mingled with that of the many varied races of the Western Island.

The old Tuath, vaulted, stone temple at Knockmoy, in Galway, which was afterwards turned into an abbey, had a remarkable figure, like Apollo, bound to a tree, pierced by arrows, yet slaying the Python by a shaft. This was congenial to a land with such strong serpent reminiscences.

A curious bronze instrument, extricated from the bog of Ballymoney, Antrim, was found to be of three parts, and may have held liquor. The figures about it were suggestive of ancient idolatry. Four birds were attached to it by pins passing through the tube, with rings outside. These may have been the two swans of Apollo, and the two bulbul of Iran. As Aristotle speaks of the brass appendage of Dodona, through which the oracles were announced, some regard this remarkable Irish ornament as pertaining to that ancient heathen superstition.

By far the most remarkable idol known to the author was that shown him at Cashel many years ago, but which may have been since discreetly hidden away. The guardian of the ruins, who was somewhat excited by the national drink, perceiving an extra inquisitiveness on the part of his visitor, who had been entranced by a splendid illustration of serpent worship, loudly exclaimed, "I will show you something." He soon returned with a stone image, some two feet high, bearing the rough lineaments of a female, but with the legs being serpents crossed.

Epiphanius vehemently attacked a Gnostic idol of his day ; saying, "Yea, even his legs are an imitation of the serpent, through which the Evil One spake and deceived Eve."

Governor Pownall, last century, traced Irish idols to Carthaginian intercourse ; "rather," said he, "than to the Celtic Druidical theology of the more ancient Irish ; for though their symbolic idols are said to be covered with gold and silver, yet they were but unhewn stones, and not images containing any organized form." His account of the find in the Tipperary Bog of Cullen was addressed to the Society of Antiquaries in 1774.

"The fragment," said he, "which is said to be part of an image found at the same time, is of a black wood, entirely covered and plated with thin gold, and seems to have been part of the breasts, the tet or nipple of which is radiated in hammered or chased work, in lines radiating from a centre, as is usual in the images of the sun ; and round the periphery, or setting on of the breast, there are like radiations in a specific number, with other linear ornaments. There is another fragment of the same kind of wood, which seems to be a fragment of an Ammonian horn ; there are in it the golden studs or rivets by which it may be supposed to have been plated with gold. The first account I had of this image was that it was of a human form, with a lion's face ; then, that it was indeed biform, but of what sort not specified. I have since been informed that the image, whatever it was, was of a size sufficient to make a gate-post."

The lion's face he regarded as "the symbolic image of Mithras, as used by the Gadetani (of Spain), for which I will refer to the Saturnalia of Macrobius, when he quotes a historical passage to show that the Hercules of Gades (Cadiz) and of the sun were one and the same *numen*, represented by biform figures with heads of lions, radiating like the sun." As Pownall found the sword, recovered from the same bog, to be of Carthaginian work, he was disposed, as he says, to refer the image "to this line of later theology, rather than to the Celtic Druid theology of the more ancient Irish." He means that of the Carthaginian colony of Spain, which he thought held commerce with Ireland. The idol might be that of the foreign visitors. "I feel persuaded," he added, "to refer the idol, and the various vessels and instruments of religious ceremonies, found in the same part, to the ritual of this later idolatry used in these particular settlements, but never in general use amongst the people of Ireland at large."

An image was found on Innis Mura, Sligo, being called after St. Molas,—known as the *Bal fargha*, a Phallic emblem. It has a singular likeness to the Phallic Mahoody of the Isle of Elephanta. It is an erect stone in a sort of basin (masculine and feminine emblems), and being, like the Mahoody, enclosed by a wall. The like symbol is still an object of worship in India.

Two rude stones were discovered in Neale Park, Mayo Co. One had the appearance of a goat, and the other of a lion. There was the inscription of *Dié na feile*.

Jean Reynaud held that the Gauls had no image of any sort. Henri Martin affirmed that "no idols recovered upon our soil belong to the age of independence"—that is, before the Roman Conquest. Herodotus bears testimony to one ancient people free from idols. The Persians he observed to have none—"because," said he, "they do not believe that the gods partake of our human nature."

Before the day when teraphim idols were known in the family tent of Jacob, men were accustomed to symbolize by images the attributes of the Deity ; and it is no great reflection upon the Irish character that Erin should once have bowed to idols.

We are told by the *Wisdom of Solomon*, 14th chap., that "graven images were worshipped by the commandment of Kings." Froude reminds us that, now, "in place of the old material idolatry, we erect a new idolatry of words and phrases." It might be added, that many of the political, religious, and social sentiments of the day are bowed to as fetishes, in defiance alike of reason and common sense. There are more forms of idolatry than the old Irish worship of *Black Crom*. In kneeling to that image, the man had doubtless in his mind and heart the real God whom it but symbolized.

SERPENT FAITH.

No country in Europe is so associated with the Serpent as Ireland, and none has so many myths and legends connected with the same. As that creature has furnished so many religious stories in the East, and as the ancient faiths of Asia and Egypt abound in references to it, we may reasonably look for some remote similarity in the ideas of worship between Orientals and the sons of Erin.

That one of the ancient military symbols of Ireland should be a serpent, need not occasion surprise in us. The Druidical serpent of Ireland is perceived in the Tara brooch, popularized to the present day. Irish crosses, so to speak, were alive with serpents.

Although tradition declares that all the serpent tribe have ceased to exist in Ireland, "yet," as Mrs. Anna Wilkes writes, "it is curious to observe how the remains of the serpent *form* lingered in the minds of the cloistered monks, who have given us such unparalleled specimens of ornamental initial letters as are preserved in the *Books of Kells, Ballymote*, &c." A singular charm did the reptile possess over the imagination of the older inhabitants. Keating assures his readers that "the Milesians, from the time they first conquered Ireland, down to the reign of Ollamh Fodhla, made use of no other arms of distinction in their banners than a serpent twisted round a rod, after the example of their Gadelian ancestors."

And, still, we recognize the impression that Ireland never had any snakes. Solinus was informed that the island had neither snakes nor bees, and that dust from that country would drive them off from any other land. But the same authority avers that no snakes could be found in the Kentish Isle of Thanet, nor in Crete. Moryson, in 1617, went further, in declaring, "Ireland had neither singing nightingall, nor chattering *pye*, nor undermining *moule*."

Bishop Donat of Tuscany, an Irishman by birth, said—

> "No poison there infects, nor scaly snake
> Creeps thro' the grass, nor frog annoys the lake."

As to frogs, they were known there after the Irish visit of William III., being called *Dutch Nightingales*. Even Bede sanctioned the legend about the virtues of wood from the forests of Ireland resisting poison ; and some affirm that, for that reason, the roof of Westminster Hall was made of Irish oak. Sir James Ware said, two centuries ago, that no snake would live in Ireland, even when brought there. Camden wrote, "Nullus hic anguis, nec venematum quicquam." Though adders might creep about, no one dreamed they were venomous.

While it was popularly believed that the serpent tribe once abounded there, some naturalists contend that Ireland was cut off from the continent of Europe before the troublers could travel so far to the north-west. An old tradition is held that Niul, the fortunate husband of Pharaoh's daughter Scota, had a son, Gaoidhial, who was bitten by a serpent in the wilderness. Brought before Moses, he was not only healed, but was graciously informed that no serpent should have power wherever he or his descendants should dwell. As this hero, of noble descent, subsequently removed to Erin, that would be sufficient reason for the absence of the venomous plague from the Isle of Saints.

But, granting that the reptiles once roamed at large there, how came they extirpated thence?

Universal tradition in Ireland declares that St. Patrick drove them all into the sea; and various, as well as often humorous, are the tales concerning that event. The Welsh monk, Jocelin, in 1185, told how this occurred at Cruachan Aickle, the mountain of West Connaught; for the Saint "gathered together the several tribes of serpents and venomous creatures, and drove them headlong into the Western Ocean." Others indicate the spot as the sacred isle near Sligo—Innis Mura. St. Patrick's mountain, Croagh Phadrig, shares this honour.

Giraldus Cambrensis, who went over the Irish Sea with Henry II. in the twelfth century, having some doubt of the story, mildly records that " St. Patrick, according to common report, expelled the venomous reptiles from it by the *Baculum Jesu*"—the historical staff or rod. The Saint is said to have fasted forty days on a mount previous to the miracle, and so gained miraculous power. Elsewhere, Giraldus says, " Some indeed conjecture, with what seems a *flattering fiction*, that St. Patrick and the other Saints of that country cleared the island of all pestiferous animals."

As, however, there was the notion that there never were any but symbolical snakes, it was held sufficient to assert, that the Apostle absolutely prohibited any such vermin coming near his converts. An Irish historian of 1743 gives the following differences of belief about the affair:—" But the earlier writers of St. Patrick's Life have not mentioned it. Solinus, who wrote some hundreds of years before St. Patrick's arrival in Ireland, takes notice of this exemption ; and St. Isidore, Bishop of Seville, in the seventh century, copies after him. The Venerable Bede, in the eighth century, mentions this quality, but is silent as to the cause."

The non-residence of snakes in the Isle of Thanet was accounted for by the special blessing of St. Augustine, who landed there on his mission to the Saxons. So also tradition ascribed the Irish deliverance to the blessing of St. Patrick. Yet, while Giraldus evidently treats the story as a fable, St. Colgan felt compelled to "give it up." Ancient naturalists relate that Crete was preserved from snakes by the herb Dittany driving them away.

In a work by Denis, Paris, 1843—*Le Monde Enchante Cosmographie et Histoire Naturelle Fantastiques du Moyen Age*—the following remarks occur—" Erin the green, the emerald of the sea, the country of the Tuatha Dedan, counts for little at that time, nor arrests the attention of the rapid historian. Yet there happened a wonder which ought not to be ignored by the rest of Europe, and Messire Brunetto relates it with a simple faith, which forbids any brevity in the narration. Now, you must know, that the land of magical traditions, this Ireland, is a region fatal to serpents ; should some evil spirit carry them thither, all the reptiles of the world would perish on its shores. Even the stones of Ireland become a happy talisman which one can employ against these animal nuisances, and the soil upon which they are thrown will not be able to nourish the serpents."

But there are competitors for the glory of reptile expulsion. St. Kevin, the hero of the *Seven Churches* of Wicklow, is stated to have caused the death of the last Irish serpent, by setting his dog Lupus to kill it. This event was commemorated by a carved stone placed under the east window of Glendalough Cathedral, delineating the struggle between Lupus and the snake. This stone was stolen by a visitor on the 28th of August, 1839.

Again, the gallant conqueror of, or conquered by, the Irish Danes, King Brian Boroimhe, we are assured by an ancient MS., had a famous son, Murchadh, who destroyed all serpents to be found in Ireland. This is mentioned in the Erse story of the *Battle of Clontarf.*

St. Cado, of Brittany, was an expeller of serpents from Gaul ; and Doué de Gozon expelled them from Malta. Even Colomba did the same good service for Iona, as others of his disciples did for Donegal. On the tombstone of the Grand Master of Malta, 1342, are the words, *Draconis Extinctor.* Among the heroes of serpent-destroyers were also St. Clement, the vanquisher of the Dragon of Metz ; St. Marcel, the deliverer of Paris from the monster ; and St. Romain, whose exploits were immortalized over the gargouille of Paris, not to speak of German, Spanish, Russian, and other Saints—Michael. The serpent is the Divine Wisdom of several lands.

One meaning, however, for these revelations of a miracle, has been found. Keating, the Irish historian, fancies the whole must be taken in a figurative sense, referring to the expelling from the converts of the old Serpent, the Devil. O'Neill, also, observes—" The conquest which the Irish

Apostle of Christianity is said to have gained over the serpents of Ireland has been doubted, but if it means that he gained a victory over the serpent-worship, the story seems entitled to credit."

Ancient Ireland was certainly given to serpent-worship.

Allowing for the pre-Christian origin of some Irish crosses, we may understand why these were accompanied by twining serpents. " Is it not a singular circumstance," asks Keane, " that in Ireland where no living serpent exists, such numerous legends of serpents should abound, and that figures of serpents should be so profusely used to ornament Irish sculptures ? There is scarcely a cross, or a handsome piece of ancient Irish ornamental work, which has not got its serpent or dragon."

The singular cross of Killamery, Kilkenny Co., exhibits thereon two Irish serpents. The font of Cashel illustrates the same mystery. The writer saw several stones at Cashel cathedral with sculptured snakes, one large specimen ornamenting a sarcophagus. The Crozier, or Pastoral Staff of Cashel, which was found last century, bears a serpent springing out of a sheath or vagina. The end of the sheath is adorned with wreathing serpents. In the handle a man stands on a serpent's head with a staff, at which the reptile bites. This staff was like that of a Roman augur, or of an Etruscan and Babylonian priest.

Brash's *Sculptured Crosses of Ireland* refers to one cross, at Clonmel, having four serpents at the centre, coiled round a spherical boss. Several instances were known in which the serpents have been more or less chipped away from off such crosses.

A serpent occupies a large space on the beautiful Irish sculptured stone, *Clwyn Macnos*, or Clon Macnois. Not long ago, a stone serpent was discovered, with twelve divisions, marked as for the twelve astronomical signs, reminding one of the Babylonian serpent encircling the zodiac. Several ancient Irish fonts have upon them sculptured serpents. Glass snakes of various colours have also been frequently turned up.

When the author was at Cashel some years since, he saw, among a lot of fragments of the ancient church, a remarkable stone, bearing a nearly defaced sculpture of a female—head and bust—but whose legs were snakes. This object of former worship was not very unlike the image of the Gauls, that was to be seen in Paris, though that goddess had two serpents twisted round her legs, with their heads reposing on her breasts. The Caribs of Guadaloupe were noticed by the Spaniards worshipping a wooden statue, the legs of which were enwreathed by serpents. Auriga is sometimes represented with legs like serpents. The Abraxis of the Christian Gnostics of the early centuries had serpents for legs.

———————

Rude carvings of snakes adorn the pyramidal stones overlooking the plains of Dundalk in Louth County. This is on Killing Hill. The marvellous megalithic temple of New Grange, one of the finest antiquities of Ireland, has its curled serpentine monument.

The legends still floating about among the peasantry of the country parts of Ireland have frequent reference to the *Piastra*, *Piastha*, *Worm*, or Serpent. This creature is always in some lake, or deep pond. The Fenian heroes are recorded in ancient songs to have killed many of them. Fionn, in particular, was the traditional dragon-killer of Ireland. Of one monster in a lake, it said :—

> " It resembled a great mound—
> Its jaws were yawning wide ;
> There might lie concealed, though great its fury,
> A hundred champions in its eye-pits.

> Taller in height than eight men,
> Was its tail, which was erect above its back ;
> Thicker was the most slender part of its tail,
> Than the forest oak which was sunk by the flood."

Fionn was inquisitive as to the country from which the reptile had come, and what was the occasion of the visit to Erin. He was answered—

> "From Greece, to demand battle from the Fenians."

It seems that it had already swallowed up a number of Fenian warriors, and finished by gulping down Fionn ; but the Hero cleverly opened the side of the Piast, and released himself and the imprisoned men, and then killed it. After this the poet added—

> "Of all the Piasts that fell by Fionn,
> The number never can be told."

Fionn elsewhere figures in *The Chase of Sliabh Guilleann,* being after one in Lough Cuan.

> "We found a serpent in that lake.
> His being there was no gain to us ;
> On looking at it as we approached,
> Its head was larger than a hill.
>
> Larger than any tree in the forest,
> Were its tusks of the ugliest shape ;
> Wider than the portals of a city
> Were the ears of the serpent as we approached."

He destroyed serpents in Lough Cuilinn, Lough Neagh, Lough Rea, as well as the blue serpent of Eirne, and one at Howth. He killed two at Glen Inny, one in the murmuring Bann, another at Lough Carra, and beheaded a fearful creature which cast fire at him from Lough Leary.

> "Fionn banished from the Raths
> Each serpent he went to meet."

Another poet left this version—

"A serpent there was in the Lough of the mountain,
Which caused the slaughter of the Fianna ;
Twenty hundred or more
It put to death in one day."

It demanded a ration of fifty horses a day for meals.

Croker, in his *Legend of the Lakes*, gives a modern allusion to the myth, which relates to Lough Kittane of Killarney. A boy is asked—

"Did you ever hear of a big worm in the lake?

"The worm is it, fakes then, sure enough, there is a big worm in the lake.

"How large is it?

"Why, then, it's as big as a horse, and has a great mane upon it, so it has.

"Did you ever see it?

"No, myself never seed the sarpint, but it's all one, for sure Padrig a Fineen did."

There is in Wexford County a *Lough-na-Piastha*. O'Flaherty calls one known in Lough Mask, the *Irish crocodile*. No one would dream of bathing in the lake of Glendalough (of the *Seven Churches*), as a fearful monster lived there. There was a *Lig-na-piaste* in Derry. The present *Knocknabaast* was formerly *Cnoc-na-bpiast* in Roscommon. Near Donegal is *Leenapaste*. A well of Kilkenny is *Tobernapeasta*. A piast was seen in Kilconly of Kerry. Some names have been changed more recently ; as, Lough-na-diabhail, or Lake of the Devil.

The Dragon of Wantley (in Yorkshire) was winged, and had forty-four iron teeth, "with a sting in his tail as long as a flail," says an old ballad.

Scotland, as the author of its *Sculptured Stones* shows, furnished a number of illustrations of the like Dracolatria. Among the score of megalithic-serpent Scotch monuments, some have crosses as well. There is, also, the well-known earthen serpent of Glen Feochan, Loch Nell, near Oban, in view of the triple cone of Ben Cruachan, being 300 feet long and 20 high.   Professor Blackie noted it thus :—

> "Why lies the mighty serpent here,
>   Let him who knoweth tell ;
> With its head to the land, and its huge tail near
>   The shore of the fair Loch Nell ?
>
> Why lies it here?   Not here alone—
>   But far to the East and West ;
> The wonder-working snake is known,
>   A mighty god, confessed.
>
> And here the mighty god was known
>   In Europe's early morn ;
> In view of Cruachan's triple cone,
>   Before John Bull was born.
>
> And worship knew, on Celtic ground,
>   With trumpets, drums, and bugles ;
> Before a trace in Lorn was found
>   Of Campbells and Macdougalls.
>
> And here the serpent lies in pride,
>   His hoary tale to tell ;
> And rears his mighty head beside
>   The shore of fair Loch Nell."

Visitors to Argyllshire and to Ireland cannot fail to recognize this old-time symbol.   The mound on the Clyde in Argyllshire, is the head remains of a serpent earthwork. A lithic temple in serpentine form is seen west of Bute. Some connect the cup and disc superstition with this worship.   Forlong, however, thinks of a relationship in the spectacle-ornament with the phallic, though one form of inscription is decidedly draconic.   Serpent stones put into water, were, until lately, used in the Hebrides to cure diseased cattle.

The Great Serpent mound of the North, at Ach-na-Goul, near Inverary, was opened by Mr. Skene. Serpent worship was common in Argyll, as that part of Scotland was Irish by contiguity and racial descent.   Keating tells us that the Gaedhal, derived from Gadelius, got the name of *Glas,* or *green*, from the green spot on his neck caused by the bite of the serpent in the days of Moses.

South Britain can still exhibit vestiges of serpent worship. Among English fonts bearing reminiscences are those of Stokes-Golding, Alplington, Fitzwarren, Tintagel, East Haddon, Locking in Somerset, and Avebury. The three first represent George and the Dragon, or, rather, Horus of Egypt piercing the monster. In the last case, the serpent's tail is round the font. The Vicar of Avebury remarks :—

"On the ancient Norman font in Abury Church there is a mutilated figure, dressed apparently in the Druidical priestly garb, holding a crozier in one hand, and clasping an open book to his breast with the other. Two winged dragons or serpents are attacking this figure on either side. May not this be designed to represent the triumph of Christianity over Druidism, in which there was much veneration entertained for this serpent and serpent worship ? "

In interviews with the late Archdruid of Wales, a man full of curious learning and traditional lore, the writer heard much of serpent adoration in Ancient Britain. Whatever the race or races might have been, the mystic creature had friends in the British Isles, though chiefly in Ireland. Long ago Bryant's *Mythology* taught that, " The chief deity of the Gentile world was almost universally worshipped under the form of the serpent."

———

A rapid glance may be taken over fields, ancient and modern, illustrating human respect for the serpent. This devotion is not confined to the Old World, being found in the New. It is not limited by time, ranging over all periods. It is not peculiar to any race or colour.

Aboriginal races, so called, have from remote antiquity

honoured the serpent. All over Africa, the vast regions of Tartary and China, the hills and plains of India, the whole extent of America, the Isles of the Pacific, alike in sweltering tropics and ice-bound coasts, is the same tale told.

Civilized man,—whether beside the Nile, the Euphrates, or the Indus,—on the deserts of Arabia, the highlands of Persia, the plains of Syria, or the Islands of Greece,—among the tribes of Canaan, the many named peoples of Asia Minor, the philosophers of Athens and Alexandria, the mariners of Phœnicia, or the warriors of Rome,—bowed to the serpent god. All religions, past and present, recognize the creature.

The Rev. Dr. D'Eremao, in the *Serpent of Eden*, sees direct serpent worship in " the worship of the serpent as a god, in himself, and for his own sake"; but indirect worship in "the use and veneration of the serpent, not for himself, but merely as the symbol or emblem of some one or more of the gods." He esteems the Egyptians indirect worshippers. The Greeks had it as a symbol of Apollo, Minerva, and Juno. The Ophites, of early Christendom, saw in it a symbol of Christ, or the mundane soul.

The creature spoke from under the tripod of Delphi ; it moved about the holy bread on the altar of the Gnostics ; it was a living and moving symbol in Egypt ; it had a place of honour in the temples of Tyre, Cyprus, Babylon, and India ; it crawled in the sacred cave of Triphonius, and its eyes glistened within the shadows of Elephanta.

As the *Apophis*, pierced by the god Horus, and as the emblem of Typhon, it was the evil spirit of Egypt ; but in the uræus of Oriris, it was the good one. The Egyptian faith several thousand years before Christ also included serpent worship. The serpent symbol distinguished Sabaism. It was in Egypt the illustration of a new birth, as it cast its skin, and thence gave to man a hope of the Resurrection. In the *Book of the Dead*, and other Egyptian

Scriptures, it is frequently mentioned. The great serpent
on human legs was a solemn mystery. The Agathadæmon
was the Guardian of the Dead.

Flinders Petrie, in *Ten Years Digging in Egypt*, when
referring to the fact that the oldest pyramid, Medum, was
erected on the principle of the Mastaba or tomb; declared
that in the architecture of that very ancient structure,
"there was the cornice of uræus serpents, which is familiar
in later times." This points to an era of, perhaps, seven
thousand years ago.

The neighbouring Assyrians paid no less devotion to it.
It is known that in the land of Canaan there was the same
Ophiolatreia, as the Hebrew Scriptures testify. Cyprus
and Rhodes, not less than all Phœnicia, abounded in it.
Christianity was early affected by it in Gnosticism. Epiphanius, relates that the Gnostics kept "a tame serpent in a
cista, or sacred ark, and when celebrating their mysteries
(the Eucharist), piled loaves on a table before it and then
invoked the serpent to come forth." The Ophites (serpent
worshippers) were derived from the Gnostics.

The Chinese for the lunar period represents a serpent.
The word for an hour, *Sse*, is the symbol of the serpent. The
dragon still presides in China. Persia, which supplanted
Assyria, copied thence much of its serpent ideas ; so did
the Semitic conquerors of Babylonia, at an earlier period,
receive their theology and letters from the Akkadians.
The Zendavesta three-headed serpent had to yield to the
Sun god. Ahi, the great serpent, was in opposition to the
Zoroastrian deities. Bel and the Dragon have a fixed
place in Oriental literature. Bel and the serpent may still
be discerned in excavated Pompeii. Clemens Alexandrinus
remarked, "If we pay attention to the strict sense of the
Hebrew, the name Evia (Eve) aspirated signifies a female
serpent."

India, however, is down to our time the high seat of Ophiolatreia.

The Maruts, Rudras, and Pitris are esteemed "Fiery dragons of wisdom," as magicians and Druids were of old. Abulfazl states that there are seven hundred localities where carved figures of snakes are objects of adoration. There are tribes in the Punjaub that will not kill a snake. Vishnu is associated with the reptile in various ways. Sesha, the serpent king, with one hundred heads, holds up the earth. The Nagas are given up to this peculiar worship. The Buddhist poem *Nagananda* relates the contest between Garuda, king of the birds, and the prince of the Naga or snake deities.

India beyond the Ganges has, as in Cambodia, magnificent temples in its honour. The soul of a tree in Siam may appear as a serpent. "In every ancient language," writes Madame Blavatski, "the word *Dragon* signified what it now does in Chinese, *i. e.* the being who excels in intelligence." The brazen serpent is in the East the Divine Healer. Æsculapius cannot do without his serpent. In the Hell of the Persians, says Hyde, "The snake ascends in vast rolls from this dark gulf, and the inside is full of scorpions and serpents." In the poem *Voluspa* of the *Edda* we read —"I know there is in Nastzande (Hell) an abode remote from the sun, the gates of which look towards the north.— It is built of the carcases of serpents."

The ancient Greeks borrowed their serpent notions from older lands through the medium of Phœnician traders. Hesiod's monster, the Echidna, was half "a speckled serpent, terrible and vast." The Atmedan of Constantinople, showing three brazen serpents interwined, was said to have been taken by the Greeks from the Persians at Platæa. Apollo, the Greek Horus, fights the Python of darkness, as a sun-god should do, but owns a serpent symbol. Euripides notes that in processions " The fire-born serpent leads the way."

Etruria, of which Rome was a colony, probably borrowed its serpent worship from Egypt. It was there, as elsewhere, a form of sun-worship, as the reptile hybernates to renew its strength, and casts off its slough to renew its youth, as the sun is renewed at spring. And yet Ruskin says, " The true worship must have taken a dark form, when associated with the Draconian one."

Africa is well known to be still under the cruel bondage of serpent worship, and that of the evil Apophis kind. The negro's forefathers appear to him as serpents. Over the Pacific Ocean, the serpent, carved in stone, was adored. Tales, in Fiji Isles, spoke of a monster dragon dwelling in a cave. Samoa had a serpent form for the god Dengie. Even in Australia, though in ruder style, the serpent was associated, as in Oceana, with some idea of a creator.

America astonished Spaniards of the sixteenth century with its parody of their own faith. The civilized Aztecs and Peruvians adored serpents. Vitzliputuli of Mexico held, like Osiris, a serpent staff. Cihuacohuatziti, wife of the Great Father, was an immense serpent. The name of the goddess Cihuacohuatl means the female serpent.

But the wilder North American Indians bowed to the serpent, as may be known from Squier's *Serpent Symbol.* A serpentine earthwork in Adam's County, Ohio, upon a hill, is 1000 ft. in length. Mounds in Iowa, arranged in serpentine form, extend over two miles. A coiled serpent mound by St. Peter's River, Iowa, is 2310 ft. long. In the desert of Colorado have been reported lately the remains of a temple. It is said that the capitals for the two remaining pillars are stone serpents' heads, the feet of the columns look like rattlesnakes. The pillars seem to be rattlesnakes standing on their tails.

Europe was, doubtless, indebted to travelling "dragons of wisdom" for this mystic lore; how, or under what circumstances, we know not. Whether the older, and long passed away, races were thus learned is a question; but that peoples, far removed from our era, or but survivals of remoter tribes, were acquainted with it may be believed, if only from serpentine mounds, or piles of stones in serpent form.

Rome carried forth the serpent in war, since one of its standards was the serpent on a pole. Long after, in the church processions on Palm Sunday, the serpent figured, mounted on a pole. Scandinavia had its Midgard, encircling the globe with its body. The Norse serpent Jormungandr had a giantess for mother, and the evil Loki for father. Muscovites and Lithuanians had serpent gods, while Livonia bowed to the dragon. Olaus Magnus records serpents being kept in sacred buildings of the North, and fed on milk. Thor was able to kill a serpentine embodiment of evil, by striking it with his *tau*, or hammer. In pagan Russia the serpent was the protector of brides. St. Hilarion, of Ragusa, got rid of the dangerous snake Boas by lighting a great fire, and commanding the reptile to go on the top to be burnt. One of the symbols of both Hercules and the Celtic *Hu* was a serpent. The German white serpent gave wisdom to the eater of it.

In Gaul it was reverenced. Nathair was a serpent god. Priests, Druidical or otherwise, had a caduceus of two serpents embracing one another. A Gaulish goddess had, in like manner, two snakes about its legs and body. Druids kept live serpents for pious purposes. A French writer notices one twisted round a lingam, as can be seen now, also, in Pompeii. Gaulish coins represent a serpent under or over a horse, the sun emblem.

As the Koran informs us, Eblis was brought to Eden

in the mouth of the serpent. The Pythia, or Serpent of Delphi, was the priestess. Snake offerings were made to Bacchus. The phallic character is exhibited in the serpent at Mayence, with the apple of love in its mouth, upon which creature the Virgin is represented as treading.

France was not without its snake destroyers. In Brittany, St. Suliac, watching the emergence of a great serpent from its cave, put his stole round its neck, and cast it into the sea. Up to 1793, a procession of the clergy of St. Suliac annually took place, when a silver cross was lowered into the serpent cavern of La Guivre.

M. About tells of a serpentine dance he witnessed in Greece. A number of women and children formed the tail of a serpent, which incessantly revolved round itself, without the extremities ever joining. In ancient ornaments, an egg is seen with a serpent coiled round it, as if to fertilize it.

All readers of Welsh Druidism are aware of the part played therein by this creeping creature. It was the Celtic dragon Draig. It was the gliding god. Ceridwen is associated with a car and serpent. Abury gives us the serpent of the sun. The *Glain neidr*, or serpent's egg, was a great mystery of the Druids.

Serpent worship has been taken up to the heavens. where constellations have been named after the creeping, silent creature. There is the Hydra, killed by Hercules, but not till it had poisoned him by its venom. There are the voluminous folds of Draco. There is that one held by Ophiuchus, which sought to devour the child of Virgo. There is the seven-headed Draco, each head forming a star in the Little Bear. Thus we may exclaim with Herschel, " The heavens are scribbled over with innumerable snakes."

Classical mythology tells of a Python, which sought to devour the offspring of Latona, whose child, Apollo, became the eternal foe of the would-be destroyer. Jupiter himself became a dragon to deceive Proserpine. Minerva carried a serpent on her breast. Medusa bore snakes for curls on her head.

What is the meaning of it all ?

Betham mentions the fact that the Celtic word for a serpent is expressive of its wisdom. The same meaning is in other languages, and the legends are of various nations. A knowing man, one versed in the mysteries, was called a *serpent*. Was it the silence which distinguished it in the animal creation that brought this reputation, and made it a fitting emblem of the esoteric system ?

It was the symbol of productive energy, and was ever associated with the egg, symbol of the progressive elements of nature. The male was the Great Father ; the female, the Great Mother.

O'Brien, and others, see a close connection between Solar, Phallic, and Serpent worship, the author of *The Round Towers of Ireland*, saying, " If all these be identical, where is the occasion of a surprise at our meeting the sun, phallus, and serpent, the constituent symbols of each, occurring in combination, embossed upon the same table, and grouped under the same architrave ? "

The connection of the serpent with the starry host has been observed. Its scales resemble revolving stars. Like them, it moves swiftly, but noiselessly. The zodiacal girdle appeared like a serpent devouring its own tail, and it was always deemed of a fiery nature.

Some have supposed the stories of monstrous reptiles —the object of dread and conflict—to have originated from traditional records of gigantic and fearful-looking Saurians or serpents that once lived on earth, and some lingering specimens of which might have been seen by early tribes of mankind. The *Atlanto-Saurus immanis* was a hundred feet long, with a femur two yards in diameter.

The serpent was certainly the token or symbol of an ancient race celebrated for wisdom, giving rise to the naming of the learned after dragons or serpents. The Druid of the Welsh Triads exclaims, " I am a serpent."

According to J. H. Baecker—" The three, five, seven, or nine-headed snake is the totem of a race of rulers, who presided over the Aryan Hindus.—The Snake race was that of the first primæval seafarers.—The faring-wise serpent race became at the earliest stage of tradition rulers and civilizers." And Ovid sang—

> " As an old serpent casts his scaly vest,
>   Wreaths in the sun, in youthful glory dress'd,
>   So when Alcides' mortal mould resigned,
>   His better part enlarged, and grew refined."

It must be remembered that even traditions bear testimony to a variety of races in the Island. The Celts were among the later visitors, coming, certainly, after the Iberian, whose type remains in south-west Ireland. One of these early tribes brought the knowledge from afar; or, what may rather be conjectured, some shipmen from the East found a temporary sojourn there.

Dr. Phené justly remarks—" The absence of such reptiles in Ireland is remarkable, but their *absence* could certainly not have originated a serpent worship through *terror;* while everything artistic or religious in old Irish designs, from the wonderful illuminations in the *Book of Kells* to the old Celtic gold ornaments, represent the serpent, and indicate, therefore, some very strong religious idea being always uppermost in connection with it."

A Cyprus amulet gives a goddess, nude and winged, having serpents for legs. A Typhon has been seen, with its extremities two twisted snakes. A Buddha has been indicated with two twisted snakes for appendages. The Greek poet also describes the "divine stubborn-hearted Echidna (mother of Cerberus) half nymph, with dark eyes and fair cheeks, and half a serpent." The mother of an ancient Scythian hero was a serpent maiden. A story was told, in 1520, of a Swiss man being in an enchanted cave, and meeting with a beautiful woman, whose lower part was a serpent, and who tempted him to kiss her.

As recently reported from France, a lady has there a familiar in the form of a serpent, able to answer her questions, and cleverly writing down replies with the point of its tail. There is no saying how this marvellous creature may enter into future theological controversies.

A book published in the reign of Charles I. had this story—"Ireland, since its first inhabitation, was pestered with a triple plague, to wit, with great abundance of venemous beastes, copious store of Diuells visiblely appearing, and infinit multitudes of magitians."

The Saint's share in the trouble is thus described— " Patrick, taking the staffe or wand of Jesus with his sacred hand, and eleuating it after a threatning manner, as also by the favourable assistance of Angels, he gathered together in one place all the venemous beastes that were in Ireland, after he draue them up before him to a most high mountaine hung ouer the sea, called then Cruach-anailge, and now Cruach Padraig, that is St. Patricks mountaine, and from thence he cast them downe in that steepe precipice to be swallowed up by the sea."

The Druids, or Tuaths, or other troublers, fared nearly as badly as the snakes ; as the author affirmed—" Of the magitians, he conuerted and reclaimed very many, and such as persisted incorrigible, he routed them out from the face of the earth."

From the *Book of Leinster* we gather the intelligence

that three serpents were found in the heart of Mechi, son of the great queen. After they had been killed by Diancecht, their bodies· were burnt, and the ashes were thrown into the river Barrow, "which so boiled that it dissolved every animal in it."

As tradition avows, St. Kevin, when he killed one of the remaining serpents, threw the creature into the lake at Glendalough, which got the name of Lochnapiast, or serpent loch. Among the sculptures on impost mouldings at Glendalough is one of a dog devouring a serpent. Snake-stones have been found, consisting of small rings of glass. The ammonite fossil is known as the snake stone.

Windele, of Kilkenny, shows the persistence of ancient ideas in the wilder parts of Ireland. " Even as late as the eleventh century," says he, "we· have evidence of the prevalence of the old religion in the remoter districts, and in many of the islands on our western coasts.—Many of the secondary doctrines of Druidism hold their ground at this very day as articles of faith.—Connected with these practices (belteine, &c.), is the vivid memory still retained of once universal *Ophiolatreia*, or serpent worship ; and the attributing of supernatural powers and virtues to particular animals, such as the bull, the white and red cow, the boar, the horse, the dog, &c., the memory of which has been perpetuated in our topographical denominations."

The Irish early Christians long continued the custom of entwining their old serpent god around the cross. One has said, " The ancient Irish crosses are alive with serpents." Their green god-snake was *Gad-el-glas*. The word *Tirdaglas* meant the tower of the green god. The old Milesian standard, of a snake twisted round a rod, may seem to indicate a Phallic connection with the *Sabh.*

The *Book of Lismore* asserts the same distinguished

power of serpent expulsion on behalf of St. Columba, as others have done for St. Patrick, or any other Saint; saying, " Then he turned his face westward, and said, ' May the Lord bless the Island, with its indwellers.' And he banished toads and snakes out of it."

Thus have we seen that Ireland, above most countries of the earth, retained a vivid conception of ancient serpent worship, though some of the myths were naturally and gratefully associated with the reputed founders of a purer faith.

"Search where we will," says Kennersley Lewis, "the nuptial tree, round which coils the serpent, is connected with time and with life as a necessary condition ; and with knowledge—the knowledge of a scientific priesthood, inheriting records and traditions hoary, perhaps, with the snows of a glacial epoch."

SUN-WORSHIP.

WHATEVER the earlier savage races may have thought of religion, if they thought at all about it, those who came after, with more or less touch of civilization, were led, in Ireland, as elsewhere, to contemplate Deity in the Sun. Sun-worship may have superseded other and grosser forms of Nature worship.

Stuart-Glennie has well expressed our thoughts thus— " We should be quite unable truly to understand how the central myths and poesies originated, if we cannot, in some degree at least, realize the wonder with which men saw the daily and yearly renewed sublime spectacle of the birth, the life course, and the death of the life-and-light-giving Creator actually visible in the Heavens.—A wonder of eternal Re-birth."

Dr. Tylor has reason when saying, " In early philosophy throughout the world, the sun and moon were alive, and, as it were, human in their nature." Professor Rhys refers to the tendency of the savage " to endow the sun, moon, the sky, or any feature of the physical world admitting of being readily acknowledged with a soul and body, with parts and passions, like their own."

In all ages, in all climes, and in all nations, the Sun, under various names and symbols, was regarded as the Creator and as sustainer of all things.

Egypt, the primeval seat of learning, was the high seat of Sun adoration. The Sphinx, with the face to the east, represents Harmachus, young Horus, or the rising Sun. The orb is Osiris, the ruling god of day. In its descent it is the dying deity, going below to the land of Shades; but only to be resurrected as the victorious Horus, piercing the head of the dragon of darkness. Twice a year did the bright rays enter the great hall of the Nile temple, to fall straight upon the shrine.

The ancient Persian bowed to Mithra as the Sun; for it was said—

> " May he come to us for protection, for joy,
> For mercy, for healing, for victory, for hallowing.
> Mithra will I honour with offerings,
> Will I draw near to us as a Friend with prayer."

The Assyrians, the Akkadians, the Phœnicians, the Greeks, the Romans, all alike worshipped the sun, as Merodach, Baal, Apollo, or Adonis. Rabbi Issaaki reads Tammuz of Ezek. ch. viii., as the *burning one* : i. e. Moloch.

India has down to this day reverenced the Sun. Its Vedic names grew into some sort of active personality. " We can follow," writes Max Müller, " in the Vedic hymns, step by step, the development which changes the sun from a mere luminary into a creator, preserver, ruler." " As the

sun sees everything, and knows everything, he is asked to
forgive and forget what he alone has seen and knows."
He may be Indra, Varuna, Savritri, or Dyaus, the shining
one. What to us is poetry was in India prose.

Even in Homer, Hyperion, the sun-god, was the father
of all gods. According to Plato, Zeu-pater, or Jupiter, was
the Father of Life. Minerva, or Pallas, the early dawn,
sprang from the head of Jove every morning, fully armed,
to fight the clouds of darkness. Baldur, the *white god*, or
sun, was killed, said our Norseman and Saxon forefathers,
by an arrow from the blind Höder, or night. Africa has
in all time been a centre of sun-worship. The Spaniards
found the cult both in Mexico and Peru.

There are survivals of the worship in the customs and
languages of Europe. Up to this century, a singular
ceremony took place in the church of the Carmine, Naples,
attended by civic officials in procession. The day after
Christmas Day, when the new sun of the year began then
first to move in position, there was a solemn cutting of the
hair of an image, symbol of the sun's rays, as in the old
heathen times.

A Scotch dance, the *Reel*, still keeps up the memory of
the old Celtic circular dance. There is, also, the *Deisol*, or
practice of turning sun-ways, to bless the sun. This was
from right to left, as with Dancing Dervishes now, or the
old Bacchic dance from east to west. Plautus wrote,
"When you worship the gods, do it turning to the right
hand." Poseidonius the Stoic, referring to the Celts, said,
" At their feasts, the servant carries round the wine from
right to left. Thus they worship their gods, turning to the
right." The Highland mother, with a choking child, cries
out, " *Deas-iul!* the way of the South." A *Dîsul* Sunday
is still kept up in Brittany.

A stone was dug up in the road from Glasgow to Edin-burgh, on which was an inscription to *Grannius*, the Latin form of *grian*, the sun.   Enclosures in the Highlands were called *Grianan*, the house of the sun.   On Harris Island is a stone circle, with a sfone in the centre, known as *Clack-na-Greine*, the stone of the sun.   At Elgin, the bride had to lead her husband to the church following the sun's course.

But did the Irish indulge in this form of idolatry?

Some writers, zealous for the honour of their country-men, have denied the impeachment.   Even the learned O'Curry was of that school, declaring—"There is no ground whatever for imputing to them human sacrifice—none whatever for believing that the early people of Erinn adored the sun, moon, or stars, nor that they worshipped fire."

But what was St. Patrick's teaching?

The Saint is recorded to have said of the sun, "All who adore him shall unhappily fall into eternal punish-ment."   In his *Confessio*, he exclaimed, "Woe to its unhappy worshippers, for punishment awaits them.   But we believe in and adore the true Sun, Christ!"

Morien, the modern and enthusiastic Welsh Bard, is equally desirous to remove from his sires the reproach of being sun-worshippers.   "One of the Welsh names of the sun," he remarks, "proves that they believed in a personal God, and that they believed He dwelt in the sun.   That name of the sun is *Huan*, the abode of *Hu*" (the Deity). Elsewhere he writes, "There was no such a being as a Sun-God in the religious systems of the Druids.   They named the sun the *House of God* (Huan-Annedd Hu)."   Again, "The Gwyddorr (*High Priest*), was emblematical of the Spirit of God in the sun.   The Gwyddon was clad in a robe of virgin white, symbolizing light and holiness.   His twelve disciples, representing the twelve constellations, formed the earthly zodiac. They too were robed in white." Morien is the ablest living advocate of Welsh Druidism, but his views on that subject are somewhat governed by his extensive reading, his love of symbolism, and his poetic temperament.

St. Patrick gives, according to an Erse poem, no such credit to the Irish; crying out, "O blasphemous Cumhal, that honour you pay to the sun, through ignorance of the omnipotent King, is no more perfect than if you worshipped your shield." The Milligans, in their learned story of the Irish under the Druids, say, " They worshipped the sun as their principal Deity, and the moon as their second Deity, like the Phœnicians."

Donald Ross, Scotch Inspector of Schools, writes in a similar way of his ancient northern kindred—" The noblest strains in all Gaelic literature are in praise of the sun, and which is also represented as the ultimately inexplicable factor in the universe. In the sun the Gaels found the two highest attributes of divinity, power, and purity."

There is a remarkable passage from St. Patrick's *Confession*, which refers to his being tempted by Satan in a dream —" It was suggested to me in the spirit that I should invoke *Helia* (*Elias* or *Eli*) ; and meanwhile I saw the sun rising in the heaven. And while I was calling out *Helia* with all my might, behold the splendour of that sun fell upon me, and immediately struck from me the oppressive weight." Probus had this version of the event, " When he had thrice invoked the true Sun, immediately the sun rose upon him."

The language of the country has much association with sun adoration. The mythical Simon Brek of Irish history may be *Samen*, the sun. Waterford was *Cuan-na-Grioth*, the harbour of the sun. One Irish name for the sun is

Chrishna, of Eastern origin; but the Welsh *Hu Gadarn,* the sun, was *Finn Mac Haul* in Erse.

Griann, Greine, Grianan, Greienham, have relations to the sun. The hill *Grianan Calry* is a sunny spot. The word *Grange* is from *Griann.* There is a *Grianoir* in Wexford Bay. The *Grange,* near Drogheda, is a huge cone of stones, piled in honour of the sun. Greane, of Ossory, was formerly *Grian Airbh.* As *Graine,* the word occurs in a feminine form. The beautiful story of Diarmuid, or Dermot, and Graine is clearly a solar myth. The runaway pair were pursued by the iráte husband, Finn Mac Coul, for a whole year, the lovers changing their resting-place every night. One bard sings of "Diarmuid with a fiery face." The last Danaan sovereign was *Mac Grene.* The cromlech on a hill of Kilkenny is known as the *Sleigh-Grian,* hill of the sun. The women's quarter of the dwelling, was the *Grianan,* so-called from its brightness.

The cromlech at Castle Mary, near Cloyne, is *Carrig-Croath,* Rock of the Sun. General Vallencey traces some appellations for the sun to the Chaldaic and Sanscrit. The Celts of Brittany borrowed their *Sul,* for sun, from the Roman *Sol. Caer Sedi* was an Irish cycle.

Bel is also the sun in Irish, as in eastern lands. Beli was their god of fire. *Bel-ain* were wells sacred to the sun. The Irish vernal equinox was *Aiche Baal tinne,* the night of Baal's fire. The sun's circuit was *Bel-ain,* or Bel's ring. A cycle of the sun, or an anniversary, was Aonach (pro. Enoch); and it is singular that we are told that the days of Enoch were 365 years.

Easter, as is well known, is connected with sun-worship. The Irish Dancing Easter Sunday is thus alluded to in an old poem :—

> "But, Dick, she dances in such a way,
> No sun upon an Easter day
> Is half so fine a sight."

People used to be out early on Easter Sunday to see the sun dance in honour of the Resurrection.

The sun and moon, according to the *Chronicles of St. Columba*, were to be seen on an altar of glass in the temple of the Tuath-de-Danaan, in Tyrconnal. For centuries, an Irish oath was accompanied with the hand on forehead, and the eyes turned to the sun. The round mounds, or Raths, enclosing the round dwelling, related to early sun-worship; the same may be said of the tradition that the battle of Ventry, between the Fenians and their foes, lasted 366 days.

Hecateus mentions the Hyperboreans of an island north of Gaul worshipping the sun. Diodorus speaks of the island's idolatry, saying, "The citizens are given up to music, harping, and chanting in honour of the sun." In Walker's *Bards*, we read of the Feast of Samhuin, or the moon, in the temple of Tiachta. "The moon," says Monier Williams, the great Vedas authority, "is but a form of the sun."

The circular dance in honour of the sun was derived from the East. Lucian says "it consisted of a dance imitating this god" (the .sun). The priests of Baal indulged in it. A Druid song has this account—"Ruddy was the sea beach while the circular revolution was performed by the attendants, and the white bands in graceful extravagance."

An ancient sculpture at Glendalough represents the long-haired Apollo, or Sun, attended by his doves. These were sun-images in Erin. In 2 Chron. xiv. 5, we read of Asa putting "away out of all cities of Judah the high places and the images"; or *sun-images* of the Revised Version.

At the *Lucaid-lamh-fada*, or festival of love, from Aug. 1 to Aug. 16, games were held in honour of the sun and moon.   Fosbroke alludes to the revolving, with the sun, as a superstition.   "At Inismore, or Church Island, in Sligo, in a rock near the door of the church, is a cavity, called *Our Lady's Bed*, into which pregnant women going, and turning thrice round, with the repetition of certain prayers, fancy that they would then not die in child-birth."

A Scotch writer observes—"The hearty Celts of Ireland say, 'The top of the morning to you.'   Are these expressions to be regarded as remnants of Dawn-worship? It may be so, for many similar traces of the worship of the sun and moon, as givers of good fortune, are still to be found."

An Ode to the Sun in the *Leabhar breac* has been thus rendered by an Erse authority :—

"Anticipate, my lays, O Sun! thou mighty Lord of the seven heavens—mighty governor of the heaven—sole and general God of man—thou gracious, just, and supreme King —whose bright image constantly forces itself on my attention.   To whom heroes pray in perils of war—all the world praise and adore thee.   For thou art the only glorious and sovereign object of universal love, praise, and adoration."

Similarly sang Orpheus of old—"O Sun! thou art the genial parent of Nature, splendent with various hues, shedding streams of golden light."   The *Rig Veda*, however, in one place calls the sun, "the most beautiful work of God"; while another of the Hindoo sacred books has this—"Let us adore the supremacy of the Divine Sun, the godhead."   Well might Capella exclaim in his Hymn to the Sun, "The whole world adores thee under a great number of different names."

Ossian sang—"When wilt thou rise in thy beauty, first of Erin's maids?   Thy sleep is long in the tomb.   The sun shall not come to thy bed, and sing, 'Awake Darthula!   Awake, thou first of women!   The voice of spring is abroad. The flowers shake their heads on the green hills. The woods wave their growing leaves.' Retire, O Sun! The daughter of Colla is asleep. She will not come forth in her beauty. She will not move in the steps of her loveliness."

Crowe, who observes, "The sun was a chief deity with us as well as the Greeks,"—adds, "I have long thought that the great moat of Granard was the site of a temple to the sun." The Rev. F. Leman, in 1811, spoke of an inscription upon a quartzose stone, at Tory Hill, Kilkenny, in old Irish characters, which he read *Sleigh-Grian*, hill of the sun. "Within view of this hill," said he, "towards the west, on the borders of Tipperary, rises the more elevated mountain of Sleigh-na-man, which, from its name, was probably consecrated to the moon."

When Martin was in the Hebrides, he came across observances reminding him of solar worship. "In the Island of Rona," said he, "off Ness, one of the natives needs express his high esteem for my person, by making a turn round about me, sun-ways, and at the same time blessing me, and wishing me all happiness." Again—"When they get into the Island (Flannan) all of them uncover their heads, and make a turn sun-ways round, thanking God for their safety." The Rev. Mac Queen mentions that every village in Skye had a rude stone, called *Grugach*, or fair-haired, which represented the sun; and he declares that milk libations were poured into Gruaich stones.

Travellers have written of Hebridean boats, going out to sea, having their heads rowed sun-ways at first for fear of ill-luck on the voyage. Quite recently one observed the same thing done by Aberdeen fishermen, who objected to turn their boat against the sun.

In all myths, sun-gods are very successful in their warlike enterprises during the summer, but frequently lose a battle in winter. In Egyptian paintings, the winter · sun is represented with only a single hair on the head ; this reminds one of Samson,—a word derived from *Shemesh*, the sun—losing strength in the loss of hair.

The shaving of the head, so as to leave a circular, bare spot, is a very ancient practice, and was done in honour of the sun, by certain priests of Jupiter and other deities. Mahomet forbade that idolatrous habit of his Arab disciples. Rhys calls the tonsure in Britain and Ireland, " merely a druidical survival."

While the image of the sun was, down to the great Revolution, carried in the priestly processions of Brittany, while Christians now, as the Peruvians used to do formerly, stand the plate-image of the sun upon the altar, and while we, though æsthetically, honour the sun-flower, we cannot too rudely condemn the ancient Irish for their reverent bowing to the material author of all earthly life.

FIRE-WORSHIP.

FROM the earliest time, the sun has been the object of human adoration. But the common flame itself, being destructive, yet beneficial, while ever mounting upward as if disdaining earth contact, became with most races of mankind a religious emblem, if not a Deity.

Pyrolatreia, or fire-worship, was once nearly universal. The Moloch of the Canaanites, Phœnicians, and Carthaginians, was the divinity of various nations under different names. Moloch was not the only deity tormenting simple maids and tender babes with fire. The blazing or fiery cross, in use among Khonds of India, was well known in both Ireland and Scotland. The Egyptians, with more modern Africans, have reverenced flame.

The Irish assuredly were not behind the most cultured peoples in this respect. The sanctity of their places for fire was notorious. The ancient lighting of fires was attended with solemn ceremonies. Even now, the trampling upon cinders in a household is regarded, in some way, as an indignity to the head of the establishment.

According to the old records of the *Four Masters* of Ireland, a curious spectacle was witnessed one St. George's day, having reference to this curious superstition. At Ross Dela, now Ross-dalla, of Westmeath, a tower of fire blazed up from a belfry for hours, while a great black bird, accompanied by a flock of smaller birds, kept flying in and out of the fire, the smaller taking shelter under the wings of the leader. When the great bird had finished its fiery purifications, it took up an oak tree by the roots, and flew off with it.

Persia was once the high seat of fire-worship. The Parsees of India were refugees from Persia at the time of the Mahometan conquest of that country, and these still retain the old fire religion. The natural flames that issued from the earth, and were regarded as divine, have pointed out to the practical moderns the mineral oil deposits of Baku. At the *Sheb-Seze*, or Fire-feast of Persia, says Richardson, birds and beasts were let loose with inflammable material about them.

American Indians, in some cases, retain this custom of their ancestors. Squier notes the supreme, holy, Spirit of Fire, *Loak Ishte-hoola-aba*, and the ignition of new fires at the solar festival. The priests got fire by friction. The Pawnees had a sacrifice of human beings in the fire at the vernal equinox. The Aztecs had a god of fire in Xiuhteuctli. The image of Hercules, the sun-god, was solemnly burnt once a year at Tarsus.

The Scriptures have many references to this worship.

A story is told in Maccabees of a priest who took sacred fire from the altar, and hid it in a cave. Upon Nehemiah sending for it, water only was found ; yet, when the liquid was poured over an altar of wood, the whole burst into flame. Phené remarks—"The British spire now fills the place, in the plains, of the once aspiring flame which ascended from the hill-altars."

The *Perpetual Lamps* of the ancients sanctioned the same idea. No less than one hundred and seventy Roman, Arab, and Mediæval writers record the finding of such lamps. In 1540 a lamp was reported still burning in the tomb of Cicero's daughter. Lights were buried in urns. Herodotus speaks of lamps in the tombs of Egypt. Augustine wrote of lights inextinguishable by either rain or wind. Asbestos wicks of lamps were known in Greek temples. Madame Blavatski says that Buddhist priests made use of asbestos wicks. Dr. Westcott, who records instances of Perpetual Lamps, adds, "There formerly existed an art that has been lost."

Ireland was not without her perpetual fire. St. Bridget and her nuns, in maintaining a constant flame in Kildare, were but continuing a very ancient heathen custom. Tradition says that Druidesses did the same, also, in sacred Kildare. As there was an Irish goddess Bridgit, Higgins remarked that the deity had become a saint, when the disciple of St. Patrick founded her nunnery at Kildare. The Welsh ecclesiastic, who wrote of the Norman Conquest of Ireland, says of this fire, that though ever recruited with fuel, "yet the ashes have never increased." It was fed with the wood of the hawthorn. The place of the fire is described as being twenty feet square, with a stone roof.

The virgin Daughters of the Fire were *Inghean au*

dagha; but, as fire-keepers, were *Breochwidh.* The Brudins, a place of magical cauldron and perpetual fires, disappeared with Christianity. Those flames were devoted by the Celts, &c. to Hestia, who stood in the place of Vesta. Being in *the Brudins* now means in *the fairies.* The Greek *Pyrtaneium* was, like the Brudins, a public feeding-house, where the fire never went out. The baptism of fire was an Indian institution. The Mexicans, Virginian Indians, and Peruvians, had their perpetual fire of a religious character. A curious sect arose once in Spain, that burnt a cross on the forehead of the child in baptism.

Lucius Florus said of Numa Pompilius, " He appointed a fire to be kept up by the Vestal Virgins, that a flame in imitation of the stars might perpetually watch as Guardian of the Empire."

The Archbishop of Dublin, in 1220, shocked at this revival of fire-worship, under the mask of Christianity, ordered the Kildare fire to be extinguished. It was, however, relighted, and duly maintained, until the suppression of the nunnery in the reign of Henry VIII. As an old poet sang :—

> " The bright lamp that shone in Kildare's holy fane,
> And burned through long ages of darkness and stain."

The Parsees of India have such a fire that has burned for twelve hundred years. This is at Oodwada, near Bulsar, which is much frequented by Parsee pilgrims during certain periods of the year. The writer once questioned a Parsee in Bombay on this matter. The gentleman repudiated the idea of Fire or Sun-worship, declaring that he saw the Deity better by that symbol than by any other.

As the Egyptian priests were said to acknowledge the same, it is possible that the Irish priests recognized in sun and flame but symbols of the invisible God.

Mrs. Bryant, however, asserts that "there is more trace of sun and fire-worship in the peasantry lingering among us to-day, than in the Bardic literature of the remote Irish past." Dr. Waddell, in *Ossian and the Clyde*, has no doubt of fire-worship being extant in Ossian's days. Dr. O'Brennan thinks that the Gadelians or Gaels everywhere they went established fire-worship. The *Gabha-Bheil* was an ordeal by fire.

Two sects were said to be in the island—the Baalites, or fire adorers, and the Lirites, or devotees of water. O'Kearney tells us—"It is probable that very violent contentions were once carried on in Ireland by the partizans of the rival religions, who were accustomed to meet and decide their quarrels at the place set apart for battle." The *Samhaisgs* were devoted to fire-worship, and the *Swans* to Lir worship.

May-day in Ireland was very strictly observed, as it had been in Babylon ages before. "Even now," says Mrs. Bryant, "in remote places, if the fire goes out in a peasant's house before the morning of the first of May, a lighted sod from the priest's house to kindle it is highly esteemed." On that day they once burnt hares, from a fancy that they stole the butter.

The eve of May-day was a trying time, as fairies were then extra frolicsome in stealing the milk. For preventative, the cows were driven through fires, as in distant pagan days. According to Hone (1825), in Dublin, folks would cast horses' heads into the bonfire ; horses were sun animals. May-eve rejoicings were known by the name of *Nech-na-Bealtaine*. According to the *Book of Rights*, Ultonian kings were not to bathe on May-day. O'Conor remarks that the May fire ceremonies were transferred by St. Patrick to the 24th of June, John Baptist's day. Leaping through fire symbolized human sacrifice.

Beltaine, or Baaltinne, was the Roman *Compitalia*, or glad times, for their beginning of the year. The *Tailtean* games of the Irish were said to have originated from Tailte, wife of Mac Erc, the last Firbolg king, killed in the Battle of Moy-tuir. May-eve was, with some, *Neen na Bealtina*, Baal's fire eve.

Keating, writing on the *Fair at Uisneach*, of Meath, says, "This fair, or assembly, was held on the first day of the month of May ; and they were wont to exchange or barter their cattle and other property there. They were also accustomed to make offerings to the chief god which they worshipped, named Bel ; and it was a custom with them to make two fires in honour of this Bel in every cantred of Ireland, and to drive a couple of every kind of cattle in the cantred between the two fires as a preservative."

Easter-time was duly celebrated in pagan as it is now in Christian times. The joyful season of awakening summer was being celebrated on Tara hill, at the very moment when St. Patrick was lighting his Easter fire on Slane hill, within sight of the King and his Court.

The *Book of Rights* informs us that "Patrick goes afterwards to Fearta Fear Feic. A fire is kindled by him at that place on Easter Eve. Laegaire is enraged as he sees the fire, for that was the *geis* of Teamhair among the Gaedhil." The King had, according to custom, ordered all fires out, as no fresh blaze could be kindled but directly or indirectly from his own fire.

This incident in the life of the Saint is the most interesting of his career, but can only be briefly referred to here. It was when standing on the site of the royal palace at Tara hill, and looking across the beautiful country to the distant hill of Slane, that we seemed to realize the legend. Druids had forewarned the King of the coming of strangers, but were as much astonished as he was at the sight of a blaze afar, when no light could be raised but by the Sovereign's command.

Orders were issued for the arrest of the bold intruders. St. Patrick and his shaven companions were brought into the presence of the Master of Fire.   Then he told his tale and lighted a flame in Erin never to be quenched.   The story, as given us there by a bent old woman of seventy years, will not be soon forgotten.   Leaning on her stick with one hand, and pointing over the almost deserted region to the hill of the Saint's fire with the other, heaving a sigh over the departed glories of Tara, she might have been taken for a Druidess herself.

That Paschal fire was the victor over pagan fires, with their abominable Moloch associations.

Midsummer fires served as sun charms to keep up the heat.   Midsummer Eve, however, afterwards nominated as John the Baptist's Eve, was a great fire-day far and wide.   Von Buch, the traveller, speaks of seeing the custom observed within the Arctic Circle.

An old writer about Ireland remarked—" A stranger would imagine the whole country was on fire."   Brand writes of the Vigil of St. John—" They make bonfires, and run along the streets and fields with wisps of straw blazing on long poles, to purify the air which they think infectious, by believing all the devils, spirits, ghosts, and hobgoblins fly abroad this night to hurt mankind."   One, writing in 1867, said—" The old pagan fire-worship still survives in Ireland, though nominally in honour of St. John.   On Sunday night bonfires were observed throughout nearly every county in the province of Leinster."

As Easter Day was of old devoted to Astarte, the Eastern goddess, so was St. John's Day to Baal.   But the eve of the first of November was the Hallow Eve or *Samhain,* when the fires were a thanksgiving to the sun at the end of harvest. Keating, who notes the sacred fire lighted by the Archdruid on Usnagh Hill, Kildare, tells of the fires on the hill of Ward, Meath County, on the last day of October. Some old writers identify this period, rather than Easter, as that of the meeting of St. Patrick and the King. The *Samhain* feast received a Christian baptism as the feast of the Annunciation of the Virgin Mary.

The festival known as the *Lucaid-lamh-fada*, or festival of Love, had no connection with the fires. It was held from the first to the sixteenth of August, in honour of the sun and moon, when games, more or less accompanied by greetings of the two sexes, were duly celebrated.

Baal or Bel is associated with the fires. *Beltane* was the Lucky Fire through which cattle were passed for purification. Spenser declared that in his day the Irish never put out a fire without a prayer. The *Gabha-Bheil*, or trial by Beil, subjected the person with bare feet to pass three times through a fire. A festival is mentioned, when birds and other creatures, previously caught, were set free with lights attached to them. There was an old Irish prayer, *Bealaine*, corrupted to *Bliadhain*. Then we have *Bealtinne*, or Baal's fire ; the cromlech, near Cork, of *Bealach magdadhair* ; *aiche Beltinne*, the night of Baal's fire ; *Baaltinglas* ; *Beilaine*, circle of Baal, &c.

Mrs. Anna Wilkes, in *Ireland, the Ur of the Chaldees*, sees in the Irish and Hebrew word *ur*, the sacred fire. A fire-priest was *Ur-bad*, or *Hyr-bad*. The perpetual fire in the monastery of Seighir, says the Tripartite Life, was at the place where St. Patrick first met St. Kieran. The *Rinceadh-fada* was a sacred dance of the Irish at Beil-tinne, like dances recorded of Phœnicia and Assyria. At Uisneach, the *Navel of Ireland*, where the Druids lighted the first fire of the season, courts were regularly held till long after Christian times.

The Venerable Bede records that even in his lifetime many of the Irish were given to fire-worship. Fraser assures his readers that " in the south of Ireland, the wayside beggar, whose appeals for charity have met with a liberal response, can think of no benediction so comprehensive as ' May the blessing of Bel rest upon you ! " '

Culdees, the recognized successors of the Druids in Ireland and Scotland, are said to owe their name—*cal*, *gal*, or *ceill*—to the word meaning *preserver of fire.* " It is still lucky," writes one, " for the young people to jump over the flames, or for cattle to pass between two fires." Another says, " Our forefathers sent their sons and daughters through the fire to Moloch." In Toland's day firebrands were cast about the fields of corn at Midsummer Eve, the survival of prayers to the fire-god to give heat for the harvest perfection. He calls the November fire, *Tine-tlached-gha,* or fire-ground. And yet, Arthur Clive considered fire-worship opposed alike to Druidism and the faith preceding it.

In the *Book of Rights,* so ably reproduced by J. O'Donovan, there are four seasons described—Earrach, Samhradh, Foghmhar, and Geimeridh, which he finds to be " undoubtedly Irish words not derived from the Latin through Christianity." Fires were lighted at Bealtaine in the beginning of Samhradh. The summer-end fires, Samhain, were known by the name of *Tlachtgha.* The new fire was produced by the wheel and spindle, with tow. The wheel, a solar symbol, must be turned by the spokes in the direction of the sun's daily course.

As Scotland, especially the western part, was largely peopled from Ireland, it would not be surprising to recognize Baal or fire-worship there.

All Hallow Eve ceremonies are well known, and especially

the passing through the fire, although the Council of Constantinople, 680, expressly prohibited the heathen practice of leaping through the fire. The Rev. Alan Stewart, referring to such fires in his parish of Kirkmichael, famous for its Druidical circle, said, " The practice of lighting bonfires prevails in this and the neighbouring Highland parishes." These were the *Tinegin* or *Needfires*.

Regular Baal-fires continued in Ayrshire till 1780, and milkmaids still like to drive their cows through the flames with a rowan stick. The proper way to light the fire is by friction. S. Laing writes of " the Bel-fires which, when I was young, were lighted on Midsummer night on the hills of Orkney and Shetland. As a boy, I have rushed, with my playmates, through the smoke of these bonfires, without a suspicion that we were repeating the homage paid to Baal in the Valley of Hinnom."

One cannot help remembering the passage in Isa. l. 11—" All ye that kindle a fire, that compass yourselves about with sparks, walk in the light of your fire, and in the sparks that ye have kindled." Virgil records a prayer to Apollo at Soracte :—

> " Whom first we serve, whole woods of unctuous pine
> Burn on thy Heap, and to thy glory shine ;
> By thee protected, with our naked soles,
> Thro' flame unsinged we pass, and tread the kindled coals."

The poet did not add that such devotees first applied a special ointment to their feet.

The Scotch Beltane, till lately, was observed in the Hebrides with something more heathen than the fire. The people lighted the fire by the old fashion of friction with two pieces of wood, and then ate the consecrated cake indulged in by pagan Syrians. The Scotch had the mixture of eggs, milk, and oatcake. This was broken up, and distributed among the assembly. Whoever got the black bit, hidden in the cake, was considered worthy of sacrifice to Baal, as the *cailteach bealtine*. He was pushed into the fire, though soon rescued, and afterwards had to leap three times through the flames. The term *Beltane carline* was ever a name of reproach.

In other places, at the Bealtine, a trench was cut round the fire, the young men assembled in the circle, and cast lots who should be the threefold leaper. Before eating the consecrated oatcake, a libation, in heathen style, was poured upon the ground. The Scotch generally are not now so given to sacramentarianism. Dr. Donald Clark conceives that the Beltane is not derived from Baal.

The Isle of Man, coming more under the influence of Ireland than any neighbouring land, has survivals of the old worship. Waldron asserts, " Not a family in the old Island, of natives, but keeps a fire constantly burning—or the most terrible devastations and mischief would immediately ensue." Train, in his account of the people, writes— " Almost down to the present time, no native of the Isle of Man will lend anything on either of the great Druidical festivals."

The *Deas-iul* dance, anciently in honour of the sun, is still practised there, going, like the sun, from east to south in its course, not *ear-tuia-iul*, or going round by east to north. Fires were kept up on the first of November, as at Hallowe'en.

Plowden, another historian of the place, remarks that— " The Scotch, Irish, and Manx call the first day of May, *Beiltein*, or the day of Baal's fire." A newspaper of 1837 has this paragraph—" On May-day the people of the Isle of Man have, from time immemorial, burned all the whin bushes in the Island, conceiving that they thereby burn all the witches and fairies, which they believe take refuge there."

In like manner, in the Isle of Lewis, they had the custom of *Dessil* (right hand), or *Dess*, from carrying fire in the right hand about houses and the stock. When a murrain occurred among the cattle there, all fires were formerly put out, and a fresh flame obtained by the rubbing of two planks together.

The Gaelic Councils tried in vain to arrest this fire devotion. James I. of Scotland has left a poèm on the custom—

"At Beltane, quhen ilk bodie bownis
To Peblis to the play—"

that is, at Beltane all went to the play or games at Peebles.

In Cornwall, another part under Irish influence, Midsummer Eve was kept up with fire rejoicings. At Penzance, until a few years ago, on that eve men carried two barrels on poles. Others had torches and rockets, and girls held flowers. All at once all joined hands, and ran through the streets, crying out, "An eye! an eye!"—when an eye was opened by a pair, and all passed through. The old country dance was one in the same style.

No one needs reminding how far Wales, long under Irish rule, had similar fire customs. At Newton Nottage, till very recently, people leaped through the Midsummer fires. Of this custom, Theodoret, in condemnation of it, admitted that it was held as an expiation of sin. Great fires were kept up formerly on the noonside rock of Brimham, a Yorkshire Druidical locality.

France, especially in Brittany, has survivals of fireworship. Such fires were useful to bless the apple-trees, and forward the harvest. A Breton priest was once called *Belec*, which means a servant of Baal. Outside Paris, Baal fires were lighted on St. John's Eve. Flammarion, in 1867, wrote—" In the evening the bonfires in honour of the feast of St. John were lighted all around Angoulême, and men and women were dancing before them, and jumping over them almost all night."

Russia and India have their leaping through the flames. In the first, a straw figure of Kupalo, a sort of representative of vegetation, was thrown in the fire. Germans had a straw image of the god Thor. In Mexico, babes on their fourth day were passed through fire.

Sonnerat had this account of the *Darma*, a Feast of Fire in India :—" It lasts eighteen days, during which time those who make a vow to keep it must fast, abstain from women, lie on the bare ground, and walk on a brisk fire. On the eighteenth day, they assemble on the sound of instruments, their heads covered with flowers, the body daubed with saffron, and follow in cadence the figures of Darma Rajah and Dobrede his wife, who are carried there in procession. When they come to the fire, they stir it to animate its activity, and take a little of the ashes, with which they rub their foreheads ; and when the gods have been three times round it, they walk, either fast or slow, according to their zeal, over a very hot fire, extended to about forty feet in length."

Fire-worship may be the purest form of idolatry ; as flame, so nearly immaterial, ever moving, always aspiring, is a type of the spiritual,—is useful, although dangerous. But no form of idolatry could be more cruel than the fiery adoration of the grim Moloch. Symbols are agreeable to fancy, and often helpful; but they may, and repeatedly do, lead men to crass idolatry.

STONE-WORSHIP.

IN many lands shapeless stones have been adored. Among several ancient nations the idea of Divinity was symbolized by a rough stone. That aërolites should be revered is not surprising, since they, as the idol stone of Ephesus, came down from heaven. A single pillar stone might well, in rude times, typify generative force. Jupiter, Apollo, Venus, Mercury, and Diana Patroa were adored as stone columns. A circle of upright stones has been reverenced from the Pacific, across the Old World, to the Atlantic.

Ireland was no exception to this lithic faith.

It has been customary to call circles, cromlechs, Logan stones, pillar stones, serpentine and allignment stones, by the appellation of *Druidical.* As these, however, are found in Japan, China, India, Persia, Arabia, Palestine, Barbary, every country of Europe, North and South America, as well as in the Pacific Isles, it would imply certainly a very wide range of Druids. No one could deny that in some parts, as Brittany and the British Isles, so-called Druids probably *used* such stones, as being already objects of reverence, without crediting them either as their builders, or as the originators of Stone-Worship.

Because of the superstition attached to such megalithic objects, Mahometan and Christian priests have alike sought their destruction. But Ireland and the islands adjacent exhibit many remains of so-called Druidical monuments. Some of these may be mentioned.

SINGLE STONES. Finn's finger-stone, *Clonduff* of Down, thrown by Finn McCoul; *Deer-stone*, of Glendalough; *Kiltulten* of Kildare; *Clogh-griane*, or Sun-stone; *Killeena*

of Antrim ; *Ardfert* of Kerry ; and several on Innis Murray.
Some old crosses have been rudely carved out of Bethels.

CIRCLES have suffered more destruction in Ireland than
in Great Britain.　One at Ballynahatna, near Dundalk, has
quite a Stonehenge character.　In 1810 the Rostrevor circle
was 120 ft. in diameter.　That at Mount Druid, Dalkey,
was 150 ft.　Killballyowen of Limerick has three circles.
Carrowmore of Sligo is half a mile across, and one near
Belfast must have been once nearly as large.　Brefin of
Cavan was a celebrated one two centuries back.　Then
there are circles at Deuman of Neath, Templebrian of
Cork, Ballrichan of Louth, Innisoen of Donegal, Rath
Hugh, Carrick-a-Dhirra of Waterford, and several in Louth.
Cobhail was a stone enclosure ; as were the Duns and
Casiols, that were often converted into oratories.　Ossian
repeatedly mentions the *Circle of Loda.*

LOGAN STONES are the *Rocking* ones, and were held as
Divining stones.　At Magee, south of Antrim, the weight of
one is twelve tons.　This is thought to be Ossian's Rocking
stone of Cromla.　His *Stone of Power* heard his hero's
voice.　In the Pass of Dunloe, Kerry, is one 24 ft. round.
That of Carrig-a-Choppian is near Macroon, and Sligo has
one at Ballina.

The DOLMEN or CROMLECH is known in Ireland generally as the burying-place of a giant or hero, if not the bed
of a Saint.　Whether *earth-fast* or not, it had a leaning or
cap-stone, resting on two or more upright stones, which
sometimes formed a sort of passage.　The House of flag-
stones was known as the *Fos-leac.*　As *Leaba-na-b-fian*, it
was the grave of heroes ; as *Leaba-na-Fearmore*, the grave of
giants.　An enormous one exists at Calry, Sligo Co.　One
bed, at Mayo, is 15 ft. long ; another is called Edward and
Grace's bed ; a third is named after the hero Diarmuid,
who ran off with the fair Graine.　A *Leaba-Diarmuid*

remains near Cleggan Bay, Galway. A Grannie's bed is at Glanworth of Cork. A *warrior's rest* lies at Hyde, Cork Co.

The capstones of some were as large as 24 ft. in length. One near Mount Brown weighed 110 tons. There are Cromlechs at Finvoy of Antrim, Dundonald of Down, Ballymascandlan of Dundalk, Rathkenny of Meath, Mount Venus of Dublin Co., Castlederg of Tyrone, Fairy Mount and others of Louth, Kinvyle of Galway, Leaba-na-bhfian, or Kissing-stone of Sligo, Loughrey of Tyrone, Sleigh-Grian of Kilkenny, Kilternan of Dublin Co., Castle-hyde of Cork Co., Ballintoy of Antrim, Sliabbcroabb and Drumgoolan of Down, Garry Duff of Kilkenny, Sugarloaf of Waterford, Burran and others of Clare, with those of Innishshark, Killeena, Fintona, Mullimast, Kilternail, Lennan, Knockeen, Dunmore, Lough Gur Isle, Headfort, Ballylowra, Gaulstown, Ballynageeragh, Killala, Castle Wellan, Mount Vernes, Brown, Rathkelly, Moytara, Carlow, Carrig-na-Crioth at Drumgoolan, &c.

While the cromlech of Howth, Dublin Bay, said to be the tomb of Oscar, son of Ossian, is the more romantic object, that of New Grange, by Drogheda, is the more wonderful. Formerly covered with earth, its interior was first made known in 1699. Standing on two acres of land, it rises 67 ft. At the base the diameter is 319 ft. ; at the top, 118 ft. There is a gallery of stones 62 ft. in length, with a number of chambers, one of which is 20 ft. in height.

Inscribed stones are not so common as in Wales and Scotland. But the symbols of discs, double discs, circles, concentric circles, bow and sceptre, volutes, wheels, spirals, zigzags, ogham writing, pentagons, triangles, spectacle-ornament, sceptres, serpents, horseshoes, mirrors and combs, fishes, boars, elephants, horses, bulls, camels, crosses, grooves, cups, &c., are not unknown in Erin. There are figures with kilts, and others with crowns. Some slabs, as at Lough Crew, are seen covered with various inscriptions. New Grange has a number of them ; like as in Scotland, France, India, the north of England, &c.

What meaning has been given to these monuments ?

In this scientific age, circles, &c., are simply called "the external adjuncts of Bronze-age burials." In the East they have been treated as *Bactyles*, or *Bethels*, to be duly anointed with oil or milk, and adored ; they are sometimes smeared over with the blood of sacrifices.

The Cabir doctrine came conveniently for others in explanation. The Cabirs were assuredly worshipped in caves. Some Welsh writers early claimed this theory to account for their Druids. These latter were said to be of Cabiric association. As Samothrace was the head-quarters of the Cabiri, which may have been of Phœnician origin, and as the Phœnicians visited the British Isles, it was concluded that Druidism was the same religion, especially as associated with fire and stones.

Anyhow, the stones were a puzzle. John Aubrey, just two centuries ago, introduced the Druidical theory, which was at once seized upon by Welsh, Scotch, English, and Irish scholars, as an easy solution. Still, as Professor P. Smith reminds us well, they were about as mysterious to the Greeks and Romans as to ourselves. And De Courson asked — "But were these grand sanctuaries of stone specially affected to the Druidic worship? Temples, altars, perfectly similar, exist, in fact, in all parts of the earth."

"If they are Druidical," says Picard, "the Romans would not have omitted to explain to us the nature of the place appointed for worship, for the Druids were their contemporaries." On the other hand, Morien, the modern Druid, declares these "temples were their Holy of Holies."

Morien's Master, the late Archdruid Myfyr, speaking of the greatest of British temples, remarked—" Its antiquity is so great as to reach behind the age of the circular temples themselves, inasmuch as it was in order to correspond with the different Bardic points that the stones were so arranged in those ancient temples."

Madame Blavatski gave the Theosophist's notion in these terms—" The Druidical circles, the Dolmens, the temples of India, Egypt, and Greece, the Towers, and the one hundred and twenty-seven towns of Europe which were found Cyclopean in origin by the French Institute, are all the work of initiated priest-architects, the descendants of those primarily taught by the ' Sons of God,' justly called ' The Builders.' "   Naturally, she sought a source anterior to the age of Druids.   She ascended to the ancient Aryan *Masters* in Thibet.   But Colonel Forbes Leslie advances further, saying—" It will not be disputed that the primitive Cyclopean monuments of the Dekhan were created prior to the arrival of the present dominant race—the Hindoos." Professor Benfey, too, called them pre-Aryan ; therefore over four thousand years in age, at least.

A letter of 1692, subsequently sent to the Society of Antiquaries, had these words—" Albeit from the general tradition that these monuments were places of pagan worship, and from the historical knowledge we have that the superstition of the Druids did take place in Britain, we may rationally conclude that these monuments have been temples of the Druids, yet I have found *nothing* hitherto, either in the names of these monuments, or the tradition that goes about them, which doth particularly relate to the Druids, or points them out."

This led Dr. Joseph Anderson, in his *Scotland in Pagan Times*, to observe—" It is clear from this lucid statement that, in the end of the seventeenth century, there was no tradition among the people connecting these monuments with the Druids. They were simply regarded as places of pagan worship."

Most persons may agree with Rivett-Carnac—" It seems hardly improbable that the ruins in Europe are the remains of that primitive form of worship which is known to have extended at one time over a great portion of the globe."

Not a few have detected in these monuments remnants of the old Phallic worship,—some illustrating the male principle, and others symbolizing the female. Dudley's *Symbolism* detects the worship of the former in the circle, and the female in the quadrangular. Others would see the feminine in the circular, and the masculine in the standing stone.

Astronomy, some think, furnishes a solution. The circle of 12 stones, or any multiple of 12, might represent the constellations, as 19 would suit a lunar period. Dr. Kenealy, a proficient in mystic studies, wrote—" The Druidical temples called *Ana-mor* were composed of 48 stones, denoting the numbers of the old constellations, with a Kebla of 9 stones near the circumference, on the inside, to represent the sun in its progress through the Signs."

We may accept the dictum of Dr. Clark, that the stone circles were the temples of the British Isles; that down to the Reformation the general name in Gaelic for a church was *Teampull*, and is still applied to the old Culdee churches of the Outer Hebrides. Forlong says, " In such monuments as these you see the very earliest idea of the temple." The columns took the place of tree-stems; and, later on, became circular or solar forms.

St. Martin of Tours mentions " a turreted fabric of highly-polished stones, out of which rose a lofty *Cone.*" This had relation to Phallic superstition. The worship of stones was expressly forbidden by the Council of Nantes

in the seventh century, and as late as 1672, by an ecclesiastical ordinance, ordering the destruction of circles.
Welshmen were shown the impotence of these objects,
by the power of St. David splitting the capstone of Maen
Ketti, in Gower.

The Irish, like their neighbours, venerated their lithic
temples. They not only anointed them, as may be still
seen done to the sacred cone in India, but, down to a late
period, they poured water on their sacred surface that the
draught might cure their diseases. Molly Grime, a rude
stone figure, kept in Glentham church, was annually
washed with water from Newell well ; so was the wooden
image of St. Fumac washed in water from a holy well
near Keith. Babies were sprinkled at cairns in Western
or South Scotland down to the seventeenth century. Some
stones were kissed by the faithful, like the Druid's Stone
in front of Chartres Cathedral, once carefully kept in the
crypt.

The *Cloch-Lobhrais*, of Waterford, had a great reputation
for deciding difficult cases. But this virtue was lost under
circumstances thus narrated—"But the Good Stone, which
appears to have been a remnant of the golden age, was
finally so horrified at the ingenuity of a wicked woman
in defending her character, that it trembled with horror and
split in twain." It seems to have been as sensible and
sensitive as were those Pillar-stones near Cork, which, as
devoutly attested, being carried off to serve some vulgar
building purposes, took the opportunity of nightly shades
to retreat to their old quarters. At last, in vexation, the
builder shot them into the water. After waiting the
departure of their sacrilegious captors, they mysteriously
glided back to their former standing-place.

These were not the only Holy stones endowed with sense
and motion. At the command of a Saint, they have safely

borne over bays and streams one standing upon them. The stone at the grave of St. Declan was seen to float over the sea with his bell, his vestments, and his candle. St. Senan, sitting on a stone, was carefully lifted with it by angels to the top of a hill.

St. Patrick is connected with the cromlech of Fintona, the so-called *Giant's Grave.* To rebuke one sceptical as to the Resurrection, he is said to have struck the grave with his *Staff of Jesus*, when the giant rose from the dead, thankful for a temporary respite from the pains of hell. After learning he had been swineherd to King Laogaire, the Saint recommended him to be baptized. To this rite he submitted. He then lay down in his grave in peace, secure against further torment.

Stories of giants were common of old. Jocelin speaks of Fionn Mac Con as one of them, and Ossian's heroes were often gigantic. Boetius records Fionn as being fifteen cubits high. But St. Patrick's giant was represented by one bard as one hundred and twenty feet in length. The twelve stones of Usnech were said to have been cursed by the Saint, so that they could not be built into any structure.

In the cromlech on the Walsh Hills, Fin-mac-coil was said to have kept his celebrated hounds. A cromlech was a Bethel, or house of God. St. Declan's Stone, Waterford, had a hole through which people crawled for the cure of maladies. The Pillar Stone of Fir Breige had the gift of prophecy, and was duly consulted by those who had lost their cattle. One Pillar Stone, much frequented in pagan times, split with a great crash after a discourse on the better faith, when out leaped a cat—doubtless a black one.

The Rock of Cashel—for ages a consecrated place—was once known as St. Patrick's Stone. Cashel was said to have been the place where angels were waiting for the Saint's arrival in Erin. The tooth of the Saint was a venerated piece of sandstone, which somewhat resembled a tooth in shape ; possibly as much as Guatama's footstep on Adam's Peak in Ceylon.

St. Columba, likewise, among the Hebrides, had a reputation for stones. There is his Red Stone, his Blue Egg Stone in Skye, his Blue Stone of Glen Columkillo, his stony beds of penitence, his Lingam Stones, which worked miracles. He was born on a stone, he was sustained in famine by sucking meal from the Holy Stone of *Moel-blatha.*

There are Pillar Stones, indicating Phallic origin. That on Tara Hill was popularly known as *Bod Thearghais*, with especial reference to generative force. Several of them bore names connecting them with the Tuatha ; as the *Cairtedhe Catha Thuatha de Danann*, their pillar stone of battle. The Ship Temple of Mayo was *Leabha na Fathac*, the *Giant's Bed*.

The *Clochoer*, or gold stone, at Oriel, Monaghan County, spoke like an oracle. So did the *Lia Fail*, the Ophite Stones of old, the anointed *Betyles* of Sanchoniathon. It is even reported of Eusebius, that he carried such in his bosom to get fresh oracles from them. Mousseaux calls some *mad stones.* Pliny notices moving stones. The old Irish had their *rumbling stones.* The Celtic *Clacha-brath*, *or judgment stones*, must have been gifted with sounding power. Yet La Vega has a simple way of accounting for these reverential objects, as—"the demons worked on them." One may credit priests with hypnotic power, or we may think, with a writer, that without magic there could have been no speaking stones.

Some holy stones had curious histories. The hallowed pillow-stone of St. Bute had been flung into the brain of

Conchobar mac Nesse, where it stayed seven years, but fell out one Good Friday. Another stone was mentioned, in the *Book of Leinster*, as causing the death of an old woman, 150 years old, who, having been brought into a great plain, was so charmed with the sight, that she would never go back to her mountains, preferring death there by knocking her old head upon the stone.

Elf-shots—the stone arrow-heads of their ancestors—were long regarded with reverence. As with Western Islanders, they served as charms for the Irish—being sometimes set in silver, and worn as amulets about the neck, protecting the wearer against the spiritual discharges of elf-shots from malignant enemies. They were the arrows of fairies. They ought not to be brought into a house. In 1713 Llwyd found this superstition existing in the west.

Martin speaks of finding at Inniskea a rude-looking stone kept wrapped up in flannel, and only in the charge of an old woman, as formerly with a pagan priestess. On a stormy day it might be brought out, with certain magical observances, in the confident expectation of bringing a ship on shore, for the benefit of the wreck-loving Islanders. The *Neevougi*, as the stone was called, did service in calming the sea when the men went out fishing. It was equally efficacious in sickness, when certain charms were muttered over the stone. We have been privately shown, by an Australian aborigine, a similar sacred stone, a quartz crystal in that case, wrapped up in a dirty rag, protected from the eyes of women. Pococke, in 1760, saw pieces of a stone on Icolmkill used to cure a prevalent flux.

Walhouse regarded such superstitions as belonging " to the Turanian races, and as antagonistic to the Aryan genius and feeling." Gomme esteems " stone-worship as opposed to the general basis of Aryan culture." The unshapely stones worshipped in India belong to non-Aryan tribes.

Authors, then, contend that this Irish form of belief came not from the Celts, though accepted by them. Rhind amusingly talks of a "non-Aryan native of Ireland, who paid unwelcome visits to this country as a Scot ; that Scot by and by learned a Celtic language, and insisted on being treated as a Celt, as a Goidel." As it was the non-Aryan, or Tartar race, that introduced magic and devils into Assyria, so may the same have been here the originators of Stone-worship, and other superstitions, long before the Celts reached these Islands.

As with other peoples, the Pluto and his attendants were believed to have been no less connected with celebrated stones than were the giants themselves.

The story told by a Welsh visitor into Ireland, seven hundred years ago, preserves an Irish tradition of stones—

"There was in Ireland, in ancient times, a pile of stones, worthy of admiration, called the *Giants' Dance*, because giants from the remotest parts of Africa brought them into Ireland ; and on the plains of Kildare, not far from the Castle of the Vaase, as well by force of art as strength, miraculously set them up. Those stones, according to the British story, Aurelius Ambrosius, King of the Britons, procured Merlin, by supernatural means, to bring from Ireland into Britain."

This origin of Stonehenge was long accepted as history. If not holy stones, they were, at least, indebted for their rambling to the exercise of demoniacal or occult powers. They came not from heaven, as did those of Phrygia, Mount Ida, &c.

Various authors have contended that our ancestors in the British Isles were never so lost to common sense as to worship or reverence stones, though other peoples may have done so. O'Curry considers cromlechs "never were intended and never used as altars, or places of sacrifice of any kind; that they were not in any sense of the word Druidical." In this opinion he is opposed to Welsh, English, and Irish writers. But Arthur Clive declared— "Our Irish ancestors of Aryan race worshipped the air, *stone*, and fire."

Forbes Leslie conceives that many figures represented on stones "are disconnected from any Christian symbol." Certainly the *Comb* shape, so common upon inscribed stones, may be viewed on Indo-Scythian coins. The *zigzag* was a Gnostic sign. The double disc and sceptre symbol may refer to solar worship, as that of the crescent and sceptre to lunar worship.

A Buddhist origin is attributed to inscriptions by Dr. G. Moore. Dr. Longmuir considers them "the earliest existing records of the ideas" cherished in these Islands. Leslie looks at them as associated with old Oriental divin-ation. Tate esteems them "to express some religious sentiments, or to aid in the performance of some religious rites." Not a few regard them as emblems of religious worship.

The meaning of the *Cup* symbol—observed on stones at Fermanagh, and in the west of Kerry—has puzzled the learned. In India it is frequently found both with and without grooves. The common observance upon kistvaens, and on mortuary urns, would seem to bear a religious significance. Professor T. J. Simpson imagines the emblem "connected in some way with the religious thought and doctrines of those who carved them." He saw no reason to doubt the origin of cup and ring being still earlier than even the age of the earliest Celts.

Vallencey, commenting upon the spiral marks at New Grange, fancifully says, "The three symbols (3 *spirals*) represent the Supreme Being or First Cause."

The most wonderful and deeply reverenced Irish stone

was the *Fál*, by some strangely enough identified with the Coronation Stone brought by King Edward from Scotland to Westminster Abbey. Arbois de Jubainville gives this account of it:—

Conn Cetchathach, chief King of Ireland. in the second century, accidentally put his foot on a magical stone called *Fál*, which had been brought to Ireland by the Tuatha de Danann. It cried out, so that all in Tara heard it. Three Druids present were asked what the cry meant, where the stone came from, whither it would go, and who had brought it to Tara? They asked a delay of fifty-three days, when they answered all but the first question. They could only say that the stone had prophesied. The number of its cries was the number of the kings of the royal race, but the Druids could not tell their names. Lug then appears to them, takes Conn to his palace, and prophesies to him the length of his reign, and the names of his successors. A number of idle legends are attached to the *Fál* stone.

As late as 1649, Commissioners were appointed by the Scottish General Assembly to dispel the popular superstitions respecting sacred stones. In Ireland the superstitious observances had a longer possession of people's minds.

As circles are known in Icelandic as *domh-ringr*, or doom rings of Judgment, it has been suggested that Stonehenge itself may have been a chief Seat of Judgment with the foreign colony, whose capital on Salisbury Plain may have been Sorbiodunum, afterwards Sarum.

Clemens Alexandrinus spoke of stones as images of God. Aurelius Antoninus brought to Rome a black stone, and paid homage to it. The Laplanders, until lately, sacrificed the reindeer to a stone. Lactantius records the worship of *Terminus* in the form of a stone. Damascius mentions consecrated stones in Syria. Black stones are still honoured at Mecca, Benares, and elsewhere. Herodian names one worshipped by the Phœnicians, since it fell from heaven. In a letter to Sir Joseph Banks, by our Neapolitan Minister, the antiquary Sir William Hamilton, there is an allusion to a standing stone at Isurnia, that was duly dedicated to Saints Cosmo and Domiano. Astle, F.R.S., in 1798, remarked—"The ancient practice of consecrating pagan antiquities to religious purposes has been continued to modern times."

ANIMAL WORSHIP.

THAT religion was early associated with animals admits of no question. The Apis worship of Egypt prevailed several thousand years before Christ. Animals have served as *Totems* to the tribes of America and other parts, but have been certainly regarded as religious symbols in most lands. The four Evangelists are to this day symbolized by such creatures. How far this reverence, from association with an idea, degenerated into absolute worship of the living thing, is a well-recognized fact of history.

Every one knows that the twelve signs of the Zodiac, to distinguish periods of time, were named after animals, and are so to this day. The Chinese cycle is called after the rat, ox, tiger, hare, dragon, serpent, horse, goat, monkey, cock, dog, and pig. Abel Remusat notes "the cycle of twelve animals, imagined by the Kirghis, and now in use through nearly all eastern Asia."

Irish literature is full of tales respecting animals, particularly in connection with sorcery. Cats, dogs, bulls, cows, horses, and boars, figure largely therein. St. Kiaran frustrated the mischief intended by a cat, in the discharge of a red-hot bar from a blacksmith's forge. Because so many Irish stories are about the magical feats of lower animals, and such a number of places in Ireland are named after them, it has been supposed, said Patrick Kennedy, that the early Irish paid them the same divine honours as the Egyptians had done.

Birds share in the veneration. The Dove, which was held sacred at Hierapolis, and the symbol of Mithras, was honoured in West Scotland and in Ireland ; for Bollandus records that "a snow-white dove, with a golden bill, was wont to sit on the head of St. Kentigarn while occupied in sacred rites." The name of St. Columba also suggests the dove.

The Wren is not yet forgotten in Ireland. It was thought to be the king of birds. It was hunted as the Cutty wren, and is still hunted on St. Stephen's Day, the 26th of December, the winter solstice. There, and in Western Scotland, it has been known as the Lady of Heaven's hen, with this refrain :—

> " The wren ! the wren ! the king of all birds,
> St. Stephen's Day was caught in the furze ;
> Although he is little, his family's great,
> I pray you, good landlady, give us a *tratè*."

The French hunt and kill it, devotionally, on Twelfth Day. Contributions should then be collected in a stocking. After the bird has been solemnly buried in the churchyard, a feast and a dance terminate the ceremony.

The wren in some way symbolized the sun, and was once sacrificed to Pluto. It perhaps represented the weak sun. Morien tells his readers—" The Druids, instead of a dove, employed a wren to symbolize the sun's divinity escaping into an Arkite shrine, to save himself from his murderous pursuers." " The worshipful animal," says J. G. Frazer, " is killed with special solemnity once a year ; and before or immediately after death he is promenaded

from door to door, that each of his worshippers may receive
a portion of the divine virtues that are supposed to emanate
from the dead or dying god."

The Hare, in like manner, was hunted once a year, but
that was on May-day. The modern Irishman fancied it
robbed his milch cows of the sweet draught that belonged
by right to himself. On the other hand, hares have been
styled St. Monacella's Lambs—being placed under her
special protection.

The hare, however, was certainly reverenced in Egypt,
and at Dendera was to be seen the hare-headed deity.
Cæsar mentions that the Celts would not eat of the animal,
any more than did the Pythagoreans. In Irish tales witch-
hares are declared to be only caught by a black greyhound.
Elsewhere it is stated, that in the Cashel cathedral an
ornament figures a couple of hares complacently feeding
upon some trilobed foliage, as the shamrock.

Only a few months since a traveller gave an illustration
of the persistence of some meaning being attached to the
hare, even among the educated and Christian fishermen
of Aberdeen. When out at sea, and in some danger from
bad weather, it is thought unfortunate, and even calamitous,
for any one in the boat to mention the name of this
creature.

That animal reverence, to say the least of it, continued
not in Ireland alone, but even in Scotland, among
those of the same race, to quite modern times, is manifest
from the fierce denunciation of certain practices relating
thereto. The Presbytery of Dingwall, Ross, on September
5, 1656, made special reference to the heathenish customs,
then prevalent in the North, of pouring out libations of
milk upon hills, of adoring stones and wells, and above
all, of sacrificing bulls !

The *Ossianic Transactions* contain some references to

the Irish Holy Bulls and Cows. The bull has been called the Deity of the Ark. In Owen Connelan's translation of *Proceedings of the Great Bardic Institution*, is an account of a magical cow which supplied milk to nine score nuns of Tuam-daghnalan. This is very like the tale of the Tuath smith's *Glas Gaibhne*, or Grey Cow, which nourished a large family and its numerous dependants. Though stolen by the General of the roving Fomorians, she contrived to live on, and practise her benevolence until the fifth century. Her camping places, numerous as they were, are localities recognized by Irish country folk to this day. There is also the story of Diarmuid Mac Cearbhall, half Druid, half Christian, who killed his son, because he had caused the death of a Sacred Cow.

As to the nine score *nuns* of Tuam, it must be noticed that the word *caillach* served alike for nun and druidess. This led W. Hackett, in the *Transactions*, to observe— " the probability is that they were pagan Druidesses, and that the cows were living idols like *Apis*, or in some sense considered sacred animals."

The PIG must be placed among the sacred animals of Ireland, as it was of various nations of antiquity. Was not the place known of old as *Mucinis*, or Hog Island ? Did not Giraldus Cambrensis say in the twelfth century that he had never seen so many swine as in Ireland ? And who would dispute the honour given still to " the gentleman who pays the rent " ?

The Boar was sacred to Diana, who sent forth the destroying Calydonian boar to ravage the country, but which was slain by Theseus. The Hindoo divine mother Varahi was the *Earth Sow*. The third Avatar of Vishnu, Varaha, had a boar's head. A Cyprus gem bears the image of a flying boar, believed to represent Adonis, who was killed by a boar. Sacrifices of black pigs were made to Mars Sylvanus. The sow was sacred to Isis, and sacrificed to Osiris. It was sacred to Demeter or Ceres, as representing the corn spirit. In Egypt, during later periods, the boar personated Typhon. In the picture of the Last Judgment, to be seen on the famous sarcophagus at the Sloane Museum of Lincoln's Inn Fields, the condemned soul is observed transformed into a pig. One of the Phœnician gods is beheld holding one by the tail.

The Jews were not to keep, ·eat, or even touch the creature, which was held sacred, as devoted to evil. Certain passages, as Isa. lxv. 3 and 4, and lxvi. 3 and 17, are curious in relation to it. " Although swine and their herdsmen," says Gladstone, " were deemed unclean, there was a very particular and solemn injunction for the sacrifice of two swine to Osiris, and to the moon, by every Egyptian. The poor, who could not supply the animals, offered the figures of swine made of dough." The Phœnician priests, like those of Druidism, were called *swine*. A sow figure has þeen found in the ruins of the Mashonaland Zimbabwe, both on pottery and carved in soapstone. Mahomet was satisfied that so unclean an animal did not exist before the Ark days. The pig was once slain for divination purposes.

The Prophet of old condemned those who sacrificed in gardens, and who ate swine's flesh. Was it because the neighbouring Syrians were accustomed, in fear, to do homage to the destroyer of Adonis ? Or, did the Jews abstain from eating it, from the fear of offending an adverse power ? The Norsemen offered the pig to their sun-god, killed at the winter solstice. The animal appears on Gaulish coins, under or over a horse and the *fleur-de-lis*. It was the national symbol of Gaul, as seen in their standards.

The sow and its young are oddly associated with a search after a sacred spot. Æneas, when in Italy, was said to have built his town where he met a sow with thirty sucklings. On the front of Croyland Abbey may still be seen the sculptured sow and pigs, under a tree, that led the founder of this monastery to fix his abode on the island of the fens.

A Breton poem, *Ar Rannock*—(the Numbers) mentions a wild sow, with her five young ones, that called the children under an apple-tree, when the wild boar came to give them a lesson. A Welsh poem begins with—"Give ear, little pigs"—meaning disciples. One of the Triads speaks of three powerful swineherds. The priest of Ceridwen or Hwch was Turch, the boar. The animal is prominent on the Cross of Drosten, Forfarshire. Glastonbury is said to be derived from Glasteing, who, after a cow with eight legs, found her with her young ones under an apple-tree; upon which he was content to die on that spot. Both St. Germanus and St. Patrick are associated with the animal. Down to the Middle Ages, says an author, some supernatural power is ascribed to it, as we read of a sow being tried for witchcraft, pronounced guilty, and duly executed. It may be presumed that no one, however much admiring pork, partook of her flesh.

The Irish Brehon law had these two references to it— "The pig has a tripartite division : one-third for her body, one-third for her expectation, and one-third for her farrow." The "trespass of swine" is described as "the crimes of the pigs." All such creatures were ordered to be kept in the stye at night.

The story of the boar of Beann Gulbain, which caused the death of Diarmuid, the captor of the beautiful Graine, after he had killed it, through his heel being pierced by its bristles, is very like the classical one of the death of Adonis.

Heroes were accustomed to fight against wild boars and enchanters.

Druids were rather fond of pigs, since these had a liking for acorns, the produce of the saintly oak. Yet they, as priests, were the *Swine of Mon,* and *Swine of the Sacred Cord.* Like the Cabiri, they were *Young Swine.* The Druids were much given to transforming persons into what were known as Druidic pigs. When the Milesians sought for Ireland in their voyage, the Tuatha, by magic, caused a fog to rise so as to make the land assume the appearance of a large pig; whence it got the appellation of *Inis na Muice,* or Isle of Pig ; or *Muc Inis,* Hog Island.

A wonderful tale is told of a fabulous pig kept by a King of Leinster, Mesgegra mac Datho, who fed it daily from the milk of sixty cows. Welsh stories are told of fighting swine. At the end of a Welsh bonfire, the people used to shout out, " The cropped black sow seize the hindermost ! " when all would run in haste away. The pig—in Irish, *muc, orc,* and *torc*—when a possessed animal, was a decided danger as well as nuisance. The hero Fionn had several notable adventures in pursuit of such, as the torc of Glen Torein, and the boar of Slieve Muck.

According to an Ogham inscription at Ballyquin, the pig was sacred to the goddess Anar Aine. It is said, " A sacrifice of swine is the sovereign right of Ana." There are still sacred pigs in some Buddhist temples. Tacitus speaks of the Aestii (of North Germany) worshipping the goddess Friga, after whom our *Friday* is called, in the form of a pig. As the Rev. J. Rice-Byrne translates the passage— " They worship the Mother of the gods. As the emblem of their superstition, they are used to bear the figures of boars " : *i. e.* in sacred processions to Friga.

In the *Proceedings of the Great Bardic Institution* (Irish), there is a paper by W. Hackett, who writes—" In pagan

times, the pig was held as sacred in Ireland as it is held at
the present day in the religious systems of India and China."
It was his expressed opinion that "all the legends of
porcine animals, which abound in Ireland, Wales, and
Scotland, had reference to the suppression of a form of
idolatry, analogous to, if not identical with, the existing
worship of the Hindoo deity, Vishnu, in his Avatar as a
Boar."

Certainly, the Irish, like the Germans, are still admirers
of the pig. Witches and pigs are mixed up in stories ; but,
then, Gomme's *Ethnology in Folklore* tells us—"The connection between witches and the lower animals is a very
close one." It has been affirmed that the footmarks of St.
Manchan's cow can yet be distinguished upon the stones
it walked over in Ireland.

Animals were known to be offered by Irish and Scotch
down to the last century, and it is recorded that a calf
was publicly burnt in 1800 by Cornishmen to stop a
murrain. A sheep was sometimes offered for the like
purpose in some parts of England. In 1678 four men were
tried "for sacrificing a bull in a heathenish manner in the
Island of St. Ruffus—for the recovery of health of Cirstane
Mackenzie." Animals were also killed in honour of St.
Martin's day.

A remarkable story is quoted by the President of the
Folklore Society, from an old writer, of sheep being offered
to a wooden image in times of sickness. The skin of the
sheep was put round the sick person, and the neighbours
devoutly ate the carcase. This occurred at Ballyvourney,
County Cork. The story is related in the *Folly of
Pilgrimages.*

THE SHAMROCK, AND OTHER SACRED PLANTS.

THE Shamrock is even more typical of Ireland than the Oak is of Britain, and was the greater object of reverence and regard.

> " Chosen leaf
>   Of Bard and Chief,
> Old Erin's native Shamrock !
>   Says Valour, ' See
>   They spring for me,
> Those leafy gems of morning ! '
>   Says Love, ' No, no,
>   For me they grow,
> My fragrant path adorning ! '
>   But Wit perceives
>   The triple leaves,
> And cries,—' O do not sever
>   A type that blends
>   Three godlike friends,
> Love, Valour, Wit, for ever ! '
> O ! the Shamrock, the green, immortal Shamrock ! "

But Moore might have added the claims of Religion. Is it not a sacred emblem of the Trinity? Does not the legend remind us of St. Patrick convincing his doubting hearers of the truth of the *Three in One* doctrine, by holding up a piece of Shamrock? It is true that the *Philosophical Magazine*, June 1830, throws some doubt on the story, since the three-leaved white clover, now accepted as the symbol, was hardly expanded so early in the year as St. Patrick's Day ; and Irishmen to this day do not agree which is the real Shamrock.

The trefoil that was sour was certainly eaten by the primitive Irish, while the white clover, not being sour, was not eaten. It may, therefore, have been the Wood Sorrel, a trefoil out in early spring. Spenser says—" If they found a plot of watercresses or shamrocks, there they flocked as to a feast." Wyther wrote—" And feed on shamrooks as the

Irish doe." The word *Shamrock*, or *Shamrog*, is applied
to various trefoils, however, by Erse and Gaelic writers,
though ancient herbalists knew only the sour variety by
that appellation. The Gaelic *seamarog* is the little *seamar*
trefoil. Dr. Moore of Glasnevin declares the *black nonsuch*
(Medicago lupulina) to be the true shamrock, though the
white clover is often sold for it.

The pious Angelico introduced the white clover in his
sacred pictures, like the Crucifixion, and as Ruskin thinks,
"With a view to its chemical property." Its antiquity is
vouched for. Dr. Madden sings—

> " 'Tis the sunshine of Erin that glimmer'd of old
> On the banners of *Green* we have loved to behold,
> On the Shamrock of Erin and the Emerald Isle."

Ancient bards declare that it was an object of worship
with the remote race of Tuath-de-Danaans. It was the
emblem of the Vernal Equinox with the Druids. Greek
emblems of the Equinox were triform. As the *Seamrag*,
it was long used as an anodyne, being seen gathered
for that purpose by Scotch wives as late as 1794; it
must, however, be gathered by the left hand in silence,
to preserve its virtues. The four-leaved shamrock is
called Mary's Shamrock. According to an engraving in
Ledwich's *Antiquities of Ireland*, the shamrock appears on
the oldest Irish coin. It is the badge of the Order of St.
Patrick, founded in 1783, but the national badge since
1801. Pale or Cambridge blue, not green, is the true
national colour of Ireland. But Ireland cannot claim sole
possession of it as a sacred symbol. It was the three-
leaved wand of Hermes, the triple oracle of the ancients.
It was the three-leaved sceptre of *Triphyllian Jove*. It
was seen on the head of Isis, of Osiris, and of a god of
Mexico. It was recognized both on Persian and Irish
crowns. We perceive upon a monument from Nineveh a

couple of sacred hares engaged in devouring it. The Berlin Museum has a representation of some rude satyrs jestingly offering it to a woman. Artists, in the Middle Ages, have shamelessly made it the plant presented by the Angel to the Virgin Mary. The Bismarcks use the shamrock with the motto " In trinitate robur." The sacred Palasa of India has triple leaves. The French, like the Irish, retained it as a national symbol. To this hour the *three-leaved*, or Fleur-de-lis plant is preserved as a sacred symbol in architecture, on altar-cloths, &c., the emblem being now seen in Nonconformist churches as well as in the Episcopalian.

It was the three-in-one mystery. "Adorning the head of Osiris, it fell off at the moment of his death. As the trefoil symbolized generative force in man, the loss of the garland was the deprivation of vigour in the god; or, as some think, the suspension of animal strength in winter."

In the Dublin Museum is a beautiful copper vessel, or plate, with the trefoil, from Japan. In the Mellor church of Derbyshire is a very ancient font, with rude figures of horses, and men with Norman helmets. The tails of the horses, after passing round the body, end in a rude form of trefoil, which another horse, with open mouth, is prepared to eat, while its own long tail is similarly presented to the open mouth of its equine neighbour. The shamrock was mysteriously engraved on the neck of the oriental crucified figure in the relic collection at Glendalough.

The OAK was also venerated by the early Irish. We read of *Kil-dair*, the Druids' cell or church of the oak; *Maig-adhair* or *Dearmhagh*, the field of oaks ; the *Daire-calgaich*, now Londonderry, the wood of Calgac ; *Dairbhre* (now Valentine, Isle of Kerry), the place producing oaks. Derrynane was *Doire-Fhionain*, the oak grove of the Finian ; *Doire-maelain*, now Derryvullan, the grove of

Maelain ; *Derrada-Doire-fhada*, the long oak grove ; *Derrybeg*, little oak ; *Derry Duff*, black-oak wood. Derry is from *Doire* or *Dair*, oak. Kildare was *Cill-dara*, the church of the oak. St. Bridgid of Kildare built her cell, it is said, under a very high oak. Hanmer wrote— " Bridget builded a cell for her abode under a goodly faire oke, which afterwards grew to be a monasterie of virgins called *Cylldara*, in Latin *Cella quercus.*"

Druids were so named from *Dair, Doire*, or *Duir*—the oak. The Druids were *Dairaoi*, or dwellers in oaks. There was the Gaulish *Drus* or *Drys*, the Gaelic *Daru*, the Saxon *Dre* or *Dry*, the Breton *Derw*, the Persian *Duracht*, the Sanscrit *Druh.*

The oak was thought sacred from its acorns being food for man in his savage state. It was dedicated to Mars and Jupiter. Etrurian inscriptions appear about the oak. The temple of the oracular Dodona was in an oak forest. We read that 456 B.C., a Roman Consul took an oak solemnly to witness as a god. That tree was the symbol of the Gaulish deity Hesus, as it was of the German Thor. The Dryades were priests of the oak. It was associated with the *tau* or cross. " So far as I know," says Forlong, " the cutting of a live oak into a *tau*, or deity, is unique on the part of the Druids." The stones in Sichem were placed under an oak. The oak or terebinth of Mamre was worshipped as late as the fourth century. The oak was sacred, as the acorn and its cup represented the male and female principles.

The MISTLETOE had an early reputation as a guide to the other world. Armed with that *golden branch*, one could pass to Pluto's realm :—

> " Charon opposed—they showed the Branch.
> They show'd the bough that lay beneath the vest ;
> At once his rising wrath was hush'd to rest."

Its connection with health, as the *All-heal*, is noted by the poet Callimachus, under the appellation of panakea, sacred to Apollo :—

    "Where'er the genial panakea falls,
      Health crowns the State, and safety guards the walls."

As the seat of the life of the Oak, as then believed, it had special virtues as a healer. The Coel-Creni, or omen sticks, were made of it, and also divining-rods. It had the merit of revealing treasure, and repelling the unwelcome visits of evil spirits. When cut upon St. John's Eve, its power for good was greatest. "While the shamrock is emblematic of the equinox, the mistletoe is associated with the solstice," says St. Clair.

The ancient Persians knew it as the healer. It told of the sun's return to earth. Farmers in Britain used to give a sprig of mistletoe to the first cow calving in the year. Forlong points out the recovery of old heathen ideas ; saying, "Christian priests forbade the mistletoe to enter their churches; but yet it not only got in, but found a place over the altars, and was held to betoken good-will to all mankind." It was mysteriously associated with the dove. The Irish called it the *uil-iceach :* the Welsh, *uchelwydd.* The *County Magazine* for 1792 remarked— "A custom of kissing the women under the mistletoe-bush still prevails in many places, and without doubt the surest way to prove prolific." Pliny considered it good for sterility. It was the only thing that could slay the gentle Baldur. In England there are some twenty trees on which the mistletoe may grow.

Certain plants have at different times been objects of special consideration, and worshipped as having divine qualities, or being possessed by a soul. Some were thought to manifest sympathetic feeling with the nation by which they were cherished. The fetish tree of Coomassie fell when Wolseley's ultimatum reached the King of Ashantee. The ruthless cutting of trees was deemed cruel. Even if they had no living spirit of their own, the souls of the dead might be there confined ; but perhaps Mr. Gladstone, the tree-feller, is no believer in that spiritual doctrine.

In Germany one may still witness the marrying of trees on Christmas Eve with straw-ropes, that they may yield well. Their forefathers' regard for the *World-tree*, the ash Yggdrasill, may incline Germans to spare trees, and raise them, as Bismarck loves to do. Women there, and elsewhere, found consolation from moving round a sacred tree on the approach of nature's trial. The oldest altars stood under trees, as by sacred fountains or wells. But some had to be shunned as demoniac trees.

The Irish respected the *Cairthaim*, quicken-tree, quickbeam, rowan, or mountain ash, which had magical qualities. In the story of the *Fairy Palace of the Quicken-tree*, we read of Finn the Finian leader being held in that tree by enchantment, as was Merlin by the fairy lady. MacCuill, son of the hazel, one of the last Tuath kings, was so-called because he worshipped the hazel. Fairies danced beneath the hawthorn. Ogham tablets were of yew. Lady Wilde styled the elder a sacred tree ; and the blackthorn, to which the Irishman is said to be still devoted, was a sacred tree.

Trees of Knowledge have been recognized east and west. That of India was the *Kalpa*. The Celtic Tree of Life was not unlike that of Carthage. The Persians, Assyrians, and American Indians had their Trees of Life. One Egyptian holy tree had seven branches on each side. From the Sycamore, the goddess Nou provided the liquor of life ; from the Persea, the goddess Hathor gave fruits of immortality. The Date-palm was sacred to Osiris six thousand years ago. The Tree of Life was sometimes depicted on coffins with human arms. The Lotus, essentially phallic, self-produced, was an emblem of self-created deity, being worshipped as such at least 3000 B.C. Homa was the Life-tree of Zoroaster. The bean was thrown on tombs as a sign of immortality. The banyan and the onion denote a new incarnation.

The Indian and Cingalese Bo or Asvattha, *Ficus religiosa*, sheltered Gautama when he gained what is known as Entire Sanctification, or Perfection. The sacred *Peepul* is the male fig, the female being *Ficus Indica*. The fig. entwines itself round the palm. The Toolsi, *Ocymum Sanctum*, and the *Amrita* are also worshipped in India; so are the *Lien-wha*, or Nelumbium, in China; the cypress in Mexico, and the aspen in Kirghizland.

Trees and plants were devoted to gods: as the oak, palm, and ash to Jupiter; the rose, myrtle, and poppy to Venus; the pomegranate to Proserpine; the pine-apple to Cybele; the orange to Diana; the white violet to Vesta; the daisy to Alcestis; the wild thyme to the Muses; the laurel to Apollo; the poplar to Hercules; the alder to Pan; the olive to Minerva; the fig and vine to Bacchus; the lotus to Hermes. The leek of Wales, like the shamrock of Ireland, was an object of worship in the East, and was associated with Virgo. The *Hortus Kewensis* states that it first came to Britain in 1562. The mandrake or Love-apple was also sacred. Brinton gives a list of seven such sacred plants among the Creek Indians. The Vervain, sacred to Druids, was gathered in Egypt at the rise of Sirius the Dogstar.

WELL-WORSHIP.

THAT so wet a country as Ireland should have so great a reverence for wells, is an evidence how early the primitive and composite races there came under the moral influence of oriental visitors and rulers, who had known in their native lands the want of rain, the value of wells. So deep was this respect, that by some the Irish were known as the *People of Wells.*

In remote ages and realms, worship has been celebrated at fountains or wells. They were dedicated to *Soim* in India. Sopar-soma was the fountain of knowledge. Oracles were delivered there. But there were Cursing as well as Blessing wells.

Wells were feminine, and the feminine principle was the object of adoration there, though the specific form thereof changed with the times and the faith. In Christian lands they were dedicated, naturally enough, to the Virgin Mary. It is, however, odd to find a change adopted in some instances after the Reformation. Thus, according to a clerical writer in the *Graphic,* 1875, a noted Derbyshire well had its annual festival on Ascension Day, when the place was adorned with crosses, *poles,* and arches. All was religiously done in honour of the Trinity, the vicar presiding. Catholic localities still prefer to decorate holy wells on our Lady's Assumption Day.

It was in vain that the Early Church, the Mediæval Church, and even the Protestant Church, sought to put down well-worship, the inheritance of extreme antiquity. Strenuous efforts were made by Councils. That of Rouen in the seventh century declared that offerings made there in the form of flowers, branches, rags, &c., were sacrifices to the devil. Charlemagne issued in 789 his decree against it—as did our Edgar and Canute.

As Scotland caught the infection by contact with Ireland, it was needful for the Presbyterian Church to restrain the folly. This was done by the Presbytery of Dingwall in 1656, though even worse practices were then condemned ;

as, the adoration of stones, the pouring of milk on hills, and the sacrifice of bulls. In 1628 the Assembly, prohibiting visits to Christ's well at Falkirk on May mornings, got a law passed sentencing offenders to a fine of twenty pounds Scot, and the exhibition in sackcloth for three Sundays in church. Another act put the offenders in prison for a week on bread and water.

Mahomet even could not hinder the sanctity attached to the well Zamzam at Mecca. More ancient still was holy Beersheba, the *seven wells.*

Wales, especially North Wales, so long and intimately associated with Ireland, had many holy wells; as St. Thecla's at Llandegla, and St. Winifrede's of Flintshire Holywell. St. Madron's well was useful in testing the loyalty of lovers. St. Breward's well cured bad eyes, and received offerings in cash and pins. St. Cleer's was good for nervous ailments, and benefited the insane. The Druid magician Tregeagle is said still to haunt Dozmare Pool. Henwen is the Old Lady Well. The Hindoo Vedas proclaim that "all healing power is in the waters."

Hydromancy, or divination by the appearance of water in a well, is cherished to the present time. One Christian prayer runs thus:—

> "Water, water, tell me truly,
> Is the man that I love duly,
> On the earth, or under the sod,
> Sick or well—in the name of God."

Irish wells have been re-baptized, and therefore retain their sanctity. A stout resistance to their claims seems to have been made awhile by the early missionaries, since St. Columba exorcised a demon from a well possessed by it. They all, however, liked to resort to wells for their preaching stations. In one of the Lives of St. Patrick, it is related that "he preached at a fountain (well) which the Druids worshipped as a God."

Milligan assures us, "The Celtic tribes, starting from hot countries, where wells were always of the utmost value, still continued that reverence for them which had been handed down in their traditions." This opinion may be controverted by ethnologists. But Croker correctly declares that even now in Ireland, "near these wells little altars or shrines are frequently constructed, often in the rudest manner, and kneeling before them, the Irish peasant is seen offering up his prayers."

It is not a little singular that these unconfined Irish churches should be in contiguity with Holy Oaks or Holy Stones. Prof. Harttung, in his Paper before the Historical Society, remarked of the Irish—"They have from time immemorial been inclined to superstition." He even believed in their ancient practice of human sacrifices.

Pilgrimages to wells are frequent to this day. The times are fixed for them; as the first of February, in honour of Tober Brigid, or St. Bridget's well, of Sligo. The bushes are draped with offerings, and the procession must move round as the sun moves, like the heathen did at the same spot so long ago. At Tober Choneill, or St. Connell's well, the correct thing is to kneel, then wish for a favour, drink the water in silence, and quietly retire, never telling the wish, if desiring its fulfilment.

Unfortunately, these pilgrimages—often to wild localities—are attended with characteristic devotion to whisky and free fights. At the Holy Well, Tibber, or Tober, Quan, the water is first soberly drunk on the knees. But when the whisky, in due course, follows, the talking, singing, laughing, and love-making may be succeeded by a liberal use of the blackthorn.

In the story of the *Well of Kilmore* is an allusion to

mystical fishes. An old writer says, " They do call the said fishes *Easa Seant*, that is to say, holie fishes." In the charming poem of *Diarmuid*, there is an account of the Knight of the Fountain, and the sacred silver cup from which the pilgrim drank.

Giraldus, the Welsh Seer, beheld a man washing part of his head in the pool at the top of Slieve Gullion, in Ireland, when the part immediately turned grey, the hair having been black before. The opposite effect would be a virtue.

Prof. Robertson Smith, while admitting Well-worship as occurring with the most primitive of peoples, finds it connected with agriculture, when the aborigines had no better knowledge of a God. The source of a spring, said he, " is honoured as a Divine Being, I had almost said a divine animal." " Such springs," remarks Rhys, " have in later times been treated as Holy Wells."

River-worship, as is well known, has been nearly universal among rude peoples, and human sacrifices not uncommonly followed. The river god of Esthonia sometimes appeared to the villagers as a little man with blue-and-white stockings. Streams, like wells, are under the care of local deities. Even our river Severn was adored in the time of the Roman occupation, as we know by Latin inscriptions.

Wells varied in curative powers. St. Tegla's was good for epilepsy. Rickety children benefit from a thrice dipping. Some, by the motion of the waters when something is thrown in, will indicate the coming direction of wind. Some will cure blindness, like that at Rathlogan, while others will cause it, except to some favoured mortals.

Offerings must be made to the spirit in charge of the well, and to the priestess acting as guardian. If in any way connected with the person, so much the better. A piece of a garment, money touched by the hand, or even a pin from clothes, is sufficient. Pins should be dropped on a Saint's day, if good luck be sought. As Henderson's *Folklore* remarks, "The country girls imagine that the well is in charge of a fairy, or spirit, who must be propitiated by some offering." Some well-spirits, as Peg O'Nell of the Ribble, can be more than mischievous. Besides the dropping of metal, or the slaughter of fowls, a cure requires perambulation, sunwise, three times round the well. On Saints' day wells are often dressed with flowers.

Otway has asserted that "no religious place in Ireland can be without a holy well." But Irish wells are not the only ones favoured with presents of pins and rags, for Scotland, as well as Cornwall and other parts of England, retain the custom. Mason names some rag-wells :—Ard-clines of Antrim, Erregall-Keroge of Tyrone, Dungiven, St. Bartholomew of Waterford, St. Brigid of Sligo.

The spirits of the wells may appear as frogs or fish. Gomme, who has written so well on this subject, refers to a couple of trout, from time immemorial, in the Tober or well Kieran, Meath. Of two enchanted trout in the Galway Pigeon Hole, one was captured. As it immediately got free from the magic, turning into a beautiful young lady, the fisher, in fright, pitched it back into the well. Other trout-protected wells are recorded. Salmon and eels look after Tober Monachan, the Kerry well of Bally-morereigh. Two black fish take care of Kilmore well. That at Kirkmichael of Banff has only a fly in charge.

"The point of the legend is," writes Robertson Smith, "that the sacred source is either inhabited by a demoniac being, or imbued with demoniac life." It is useful, in the event of a storm near the coast, to let off the water from a well into the sea. This draining off was the practice of the Islanders of Innis Murray. The Arran Islanders derive much comfort from casting into wells flint-heads used by their forefathers in war. Innis Rea has a holy well near the Atlantic.

What was the age of Well-worship? The President of the Folklore Society, who deems the original worshippers Non-Aryan, *i. e.* before Celts came to Ireland, identifies the custom with the erection of stone circles. The scientific anthropologist, General Pitt-Rivers, tells us, " It is impossible to believe that so singular a custom as this, invariably associated with cairns, megalithic monuments, holy wells, or some such early Pagan institutions, could have arisen independently in all these countries."

Enough has been said to show, as Wood-Martin observes, that "Water-worship, recommended by Seneca, tolerated by the Church in times of yore, is a cult not yet gone out." But one has written, " The printer's blanket somehow smothers miracles, and small pica plays the very mischief with sanctified wells."

HOLY BELLS.

HE who has visited Burmah or Russia will have no doubt about the reverence for bells, and special reverence being paid to special bells. There are fixed bells, and portable bells ; the last being held in the highest estimation.

Their special virtue lay in dominion over the powers of darkness. Duly baptized bells, down to latter days, have been endowed with ability to disperse demons. When the Swedes under Charles XII. defeated the Russians at Narva, the courage of the Muscovites was revived by incessant ringing of bells, throughout Holy Russia, to drive devils from the sacred soil. That superstition still prevails with the followers of Siva in India.

Baptized bells possess other powers. St. Teilo brought

a celebrated one from Jerusalem, that had such inherent sanctity, as to make known, in some way, its detestation of particular crimes.

Bells could even work miracles by their enchantments. The children of Lir were said by ancient Irish bards to have been changed by a Druidic wand, more powerful than that of a harlequin, into four swans. They had a dreary time of it for a few centuries. At first they dwelt in Loch Derg for three hundred years. Then they flew to the Sea of Moyle, between Erin and Alba. But the poor creatures still inhabited the bodies of swans. Their release, according to bardic tales, was thus effected :—" The bell that rang in the first Mass celebrated on Inis na Gluaise (Isle of Glory) restored them to their human shapes ; but they were now emaciated and decrepid, and only waited for baptism to flee away to rest eternal."

Holy bells of Ireland are of distinct Buddhist shape, being of an irregular cylindrical form, as in India, &c., and not round as in Christian lands. Irish bells were often ornamented with crosses, the fleur-de-lis, and the pomegranate. St. Finnian's bell resembles that seen in Jain temples of India.

A number of so-called St. Patrick's bells are still preserved, as in the instructive and interesting Dublin Museum. They are of various sizes, the largest being a foot in height. He is said to have had fifty. The sweetest sounding one is known by the name of *Finn Faidheach*. Most of his bells were of bronze, often beautifully adorned after an oriental fashion. The *Betechan* is half iron. The *Clogdubh* or black bell of the Saint, an alloy of different metals, is about twelve inches high, and five by four otherwise.

The *Tripartite* Life of the Saint records his flinging a little bell under a dense bush, and in time a birch grew through its handle, revealing it to the eyes of Dieuill.

When he drove the demons into the sea at Croagh Patrick, Mayo, he flung after them his bell. It is not certain whether this was the *Bearnan Brighde* or the *Dubh-duaib-seach*. O'Donovan explains the occasion—" According to all the Lives of the Irish apostle, he remained for forty days and forty nights on this lofty mountain, which was then infested by malignant demons, who opposed his progress in preaching the gospel in this dreary region; but whom he drove thence headlong into the sea." This was effectually done by means of his bell.

Another account is that a bell was brought down for St. Patrick by angels from heaven, when a spring gushed forth at the place. He scared the demons away by it, aided by blows, and not by the mere ringing.

The shrines of these cherished bells have always drawn forth much admiration. Miss Stokes, in her beautiful work on *Early Christian Art in Ireland*, said, " Such covers or shrines for bells seem to be unknown to any other branch of the Christian Church."

Among other Irish bells may be mentioned one with a very handsome border. This was twelve inches high, nine broad, and nine and a half deep. There were the *Clog Beannaighthe*, the *Clogdubh*, the *Cumaseach* MacAntils of the Archbishop of Armagh, the *Doumragh* of Fenagh, the gapped bell of St. Culann, the golden bell of St. Sevan, the bronze one given by St. Patrick to the Bishop of Cloghir, the magnificent bronzed one with gold filagree of exquisite workmanship, and the bells of St. Ruadhan, St. Mura, St. Mogue, or Maidoc, &c., &c.

The Dublin Museum has bells of St. Columba, which had the same virtue as those of St. Patrick in the expulsion of demons, and as the heathen Burmese still relate of their own holy bells. Bells were brought from Rome by St. Patrick, St. Columba, and St. Mungo or Kentigern, of

Glasgow fame. It is singular that in the ruins of Zim-
bahwe, of Mashona Land, travellers have found some
double iron bells. No bell has any charming power until
duly consecrated by the priest of some faith.

IRISH CROSSES.

WHO could write the history of the Cross? It is the
most ancient, and the most deeply reverenced of all religious
symbols. To the men dwelling beside the Nile or the
Euphrates, to the inhabitants of India to the East and of
Mexico to the West, to those sojourners in Egypt before
the Great Pyramid was built, not less than to modern
Christians, the *Cross,* whatever may have been the meaning
attached to it, in the ever-changing systems of faith, has
been a source of wonder, of mystery, and of comfort.

When the Christians assaulted the Osirian temple at
Alexandria, and with destructive force entered its sacred
precincts, they saw a huge cross occupying the marble
pavement. Great, too, was the surprise of the Spaniards
to find the same emblem in the temples of aboriginal
America. The *Tau* or Cross meets one's view in the
ornamental relics of many lands.

Ancient Ireland was no exception in the display of
cruciform objects.

The *Edinburgh Review* of 1870 truly said, " It appears
to have been the possession of every people in antiquity ;
the elastic girdle, so to speak, which embraced the most
widely-separated heathen communities ; the most signifi-
cant token of a universal brotherhood." It can, it adds,
be traced " to the remotest antiquity, and is still recognized
as a military and national badge of distinction."

The Rev. A. Hislop, in his *Two Babylons*, boldly asserts

that "the cross was known to Adam." It is strange that
the chosen people should have preserved no tradition of it,
and that the only mention of it in the Old Testament (Ezek.
ix.) should be a mark or *tau* on the forehead of idolaters,
as may be seen to this day in the bazaars of India.
Baring-Gould thinks " it is more than a coincidence that
Osiris, by the Cross, should give life eternal to the spirits
of the just." Is he not here confounding the archetypical
emblem with the antitypical ?

Oliver, the authority on Freemasonry, ventures this connection between Pagan and Christian crosses—" The system
of salvation through the atonement of a crucified Mediator
was the main pillar of Freemasonry ever since the Fall." (!)
Were this true, Popes need not have excommunicated
the Brotherhood.

The Spaniards saw the Indians bowing to the cross in
worship. It has been found on the breasts of statuettes
from the Indian cemetery of Jingalpa, Nicaragua, of
unknown antiquity. Tablets of gypsum, in Mexico, bore
it in the form of that cross adopted by the Knights in
Malta. The Peruvians and Babylonians had the Maltese
cross. The Druids were said to have made their cross of
the stem and two branches of the oak.

The Buddhist *tau* or *Swastika* is a cross—having sometimes a Calvary, with buds and leaves. The Tree of
Immortality in the palace of Assyrian Khorsabad forms
a cross. Etruria and Pompeii exhibit the same symbol.
The *Reviewer* of 1870 says, " Our commonplace book
contains nearly two hundred distinct representations of
the Pre-Christian Cross."

Only in recent days have British Protestants cared to
use the cross. Now it may be seen on and in Methodist
and Nonconformist chapels. It was once thought distinctly
Papal in origin. But Tertullian, Jerome, and Origen, notify

its use in their day. Processions in its honour were known
in the fifth century. Cyprian records its use on the brow
in baptism. The first Protestant Prayer-book (Edward
VI.) ordered its mark on the infant's breast and forehead.
The whole Christian world has either bowed to it, or raised
but a feeble voice against its use.

Ireland has been, and is, the very land of crosses. Long
before St. Patrick came to its shores, wise men from the
East had brought it in Mediterranean galleys.

What did the Irish think of the Cross ? What elevating
ideas did it convey to them ? Was the Pre-Christian
emblem anything to the mass of the natives, or pertaining
only to the foreign settlers encamped upon their coast ?
Did Irish Druids, mixing more with the people, adore the
Cross, as was the custom with British Druids ?

To the Christianized Irish, whether Culdees or not, it
was the symbol of the once suffering but now exalted
One. In bowing to it they beheld the image of their
Saviour, and indulged the hope of a happier Home Beyond.
If the heathen cross came to them from the East, it was
from the East it afterwards approached them with a higher
and nobler faith.

The pagan crosses being just the same in appearance as
those subsequently introduced by Christian missionaries,
we may reasonably be puzzled to distinguish one class from
the other. Dr. Graves, Bishop of Limerick, compared
Irish and Coptic crosses. " These," said he, " were brought
into both Egypt and Ireland from Palestine, Syria, Asia
Minor, Byzantium." He found oriental crosses with or
without circles on Ogham Irish monuments.

Wakeman, in his *Irish Inscribed Crosses,* believes they
" were used by the people of Erin as a symbol of some
significance, at a period long antecedent to the mission of
St. Patrick." Rubbings from the stones on the Island of

Inismurray, of Sligo, overlooking the Atlantic, led him to say—" We have the elements of all, or nearly all, spirals, chevrons, lozenges, cups and dots, crosslets, foliage, cable, wavy and other mouldings, upon cinerary urns, golden or bronze ornaments and implements, and most notably upon megalithic structures, associated with the practice of cremation, all of which are beyond the range of Western history."

Pre-Christian crosses he identifies at Dowth and New Grange upon the Boyne, Knockmany of Tyrone, Deer Park of Fermanagh, Cloverhill of Sligo, Slieve-ha-Calliagh near Lough Crew of Meath. These are like the heathen inscriptions in Scotia Minor or Lesser Ireland, which we know now as Scotland.

Tuath-de-Danaan crosses are associated with Snakes, and are not likely to be Christian ones. The Tuath ones resemble those of Buddhist countries. That at Killcullen, county Kildare, bears the figures of nine Buddhist priests in oriental garb, and even with a sort of Egyptian beard. Keane, of Round Tower story, writes—" Gobban-Saer means the sacred past, or the Freemason sage, one of the Guabhres or Cabiri, such as you have seen him represented on the Tuatha-de-Danaan Cross of Clonmacnoise." The latter was adorned with birds and other animals.

Clonmacnoise was a sacred spot before Christianity came. It is ten miles from Athlone, in King's Co. The North Cross, thirteen feet high, bears carvings of priests or Brehons. The South Cross, twelve feet, has some splendid figures of birds, deer, &c. There are staves, with bunches of leaves. A dog appears among the animals. That would have no meaning with a Christian cross, but the sacredness of that friend of man in Zend books classes that cross among those of oriental origin.

The human figure has an eastern look, fully clothed

and crowned. It holds two sceptres crossed in the arms, with crosses at the top. That Clonmacnoise was a sacred spot is evidenced by the two remaining Round Towers there. Its sanctity was continued, though in a Christian channel. Besides the cathedral, there are remains of nine churches. The author of the *Round Towers of Ireland* is led to exclaim, " Within the narrow limits of two Irish acres, we have condensed more religious ruins of antiquarian value, than are to be found, perhaps, in a similar space in any other quarter of the habitable world."

That writer is disposed to see proofs of some connection between the ancient Irish faith and that of the Zendavesta of Cyrus. Referring to the dog on those crosses, he says— " The personation of a dog—their invariable accompaniment, as it is also found among the sculptures of Persepolis, and in other places in the East—would in itself be sufficient to fix the heathen appropriation of these crosses, as that animal can have no possible relation to Christianity; whereas, by the Tuath de Danaans it was accounted sacred, and its maintenance enjoined by the ordinances of the State."

Buddhist crosses are well known throughout the East. The Rev. Ernest Eitel, of Hongkong, describing one on Amitabha Buddha, writes, " It is exactly the same diagram which you may have seen engraved on ancient church bells in England, and which learned antiquarians invariably declare to be the hammer of Thor (the Scandinavian god of Thunder). Perhaps, also, you remember to have heard that among the German peasantry, and in Ireland, this same figure is used as a magical charm to dispel thunder. Well, you turn to your friend (*Chinese*). 'What is the meaning of this?' He informs you that it is the mystic shibboleth of the believers in the Western Paradise, an accumulation of lucky signs." Anyhow it had a different significance to that we now recognize in the cross.

One need not be alarmed at the discovery, that not only the Cross, but the Crucifixion, was a sacred symbol many hundreds of years before the birth of Jesus. Yet, in Christianity, a different and more moral and elevated idea became associated with the figure of a crucifix. Mithras, as the Sun, is represented as crucified at the winter solstice. Vishnu, Buddha, and Indra were, also, said to have been crucified on the cross. The Scandinavians had a crucifixion of the sun ceremony on the shortest day.

Ireland, like other lands, had Pre-Christian crucifixions. The most remarkable one seen by us was that at Glendalough. The Persian head-dress, and the ancient kilt, were observed with the oriental crown. That character was afterwards imitated in Christian times, as some suppose, down to the twelfth century.

Clonmacnoise has the figure fully clothed and crowned. The figures of Knockmoy, Galway, and Cashel wear the kilt of the East. As has been remarked, " The Hindoo Puranas corroborate to an iota this our Knockmoy crucifixion." That of India refers to the death of Sulioahana upon the tree. The Knockmoy figure has the same sort of philibeg, or kilt, as that worn by the arms-extended Deity in Nubia.

Another peculiarity noticed in some of the Irish Pre-Christian illustrations of the Crucifixion is the absence of nails ; the legs being bound with cords at the ankles. Cords, also, pass round the chest, and under the arms. The arms are not fully outstretched, but rather hang downward. At Monasterboice the figure is bound by cords. As Keane observed—" Such a mode of representing the crucifixion never could have occurred to the early Irish Christian missionaries and bishops, who are universally allowed to have made the Scriptures their chief study." The crown resembles that worn by the goddess Diana. Keane is pleased to say of the whole—"It represents the Cuthite crucifixions of primeval tradition."

The Irish shrine of St. Manchin led that same writer to add—"The crucified figure in the sculptures from a Persian Rock Temple may assist in explaining the mummy-like figures on the Irish shrine. The similarity of the design would seem to confirm the idea that the figures were intended to signify the inmates of the Ark, undergoing the process of mysterious death, which was supposed to be exhibited in Arkite ceremonies."

O'Brien's *Round Towers*, which, with the exception of some extravagances, has been largely approved by the learned, alludes to a bronze crucifix, with arms extended, and with an oriental crown and kilt, in these words— "could not have been intended for our Saviour, wanting besides the INRI, and wearing the Iranian royal crown, instead of the Jewish crown of thorns. Therefore we are justified in ascribing it to its owner Buddha, whom again we find imprinted in the same crucified form." The supposed Virgin and John figures on one of the Round Towers, he declares to be Rama and Buddha's mother.

It is singular that the dress of one crucified figure, as worn about the loins, corresponds with that of the fabled crucified Christna. That Christian artists, who, as seen in the beautiful works of ancient Irish art, borrowed so much from the East, should imitate oriental Pre-Christian crucifixions, ought not to surprise us. Christian symbolism is generally borrowed, with new adaptation, from heathen mythology.

Myfyr, the late Welsh Archdruid, has this explanation of the mystery, viz.—"Hu, of light, died on the cross at the equinox, descending to the southern hemisphere, and was re-born at Christmas, when rising toward the northern summer lands."

Scotland, peopled by the same race, on its western side, as Ireland, had the like veneration for stone crosses. Donald Clark, a Gaelic scholar, derives Inverary from the river *Aray* and *Aoradh* (worshipped). "This place," says he, "is still called *Crois-an-Sleuchdte* (kneeling cross), because the pilgrims on arriving there were wont to kneel in prayer. Before, however, they arrived here, they had to ford the river Aray at a point where the cross came in sight, and in sight of the cross they *aoradh* (worshipped), and the stream was from this association called *uisge aoradh* (water of worship), not simply *aoradh* (worship)."

One cross of Kintyre is made of four round bosses, with a fifth in the centre. At Keills, of Kintyre, the cross is highly sculptured. A winged figure appears in the top compartment, and the centre is circular, with three bosses inside, surrounded by four dogs. Captain White finds "the conical or pyramidal weather-cope on so many of the Irish crosses is conspicuously absent in the Scottish examples." He observed, however, that "the primitive kind of four-holed cross, met with in Knapdale (Kintyre) is common to Wales, Cornwall, Cumberland, and other western districts."

His remarks on serpent crosses are as follows—"The representations of serpents, so prevalent in the one set of sculptures (*Irish*), are almost unknown to the other, though on the eastern pillar-shafts they so frequently appear. I cannot recall a single instance of a serpent delineated on a West Highland ecclesiastical carving in the mainland districts I have traversed ; it appears, however, on a cross in Islay, and on one in Iona." The open wheel, so prevalent in Ireland, occurs, according to Captain White, but thrice in Scotland.

Eugene Hucher, in *L'Art Gaulois*, has some remarkable illustrations of the cross among a kindred people to the Irish across the Channel. It is there associated with the pig, lion, serpent, eagle, winged horse, bird, chariot, pig under a horse, fleur-de-lis, &c. The Gaulish coins have the cross frequently impressed on them.

Some Irish crosses are distinguished by the Buddhist symbol in all sorts of positions. The *Triple Tau* of India is equally manifest. The Thor's-hammer cross is very common among other Pre-Christian crosses. Fosbroke affirms that there are twenty-two instances of the cross on Ogham stones, but none on the fifty-three inscribed stones in Rath chambers. It is his opinion that "stone crosses owe their origin to marking Druid stones with crosses, in order to change the worship without breaking the prejudice."

The Irish cross within a circle has been seen not only in the far East, but in the Indian Mounds of Ohio. The Druid's Cross is fully acknowledged in the *Two Babylons* of the Rev. A. Hislop. The form of the Philistine Dagon is detected in the sculptured mermaid on Meath's cross, and at Clontarf cathedral; where the fish-woman has a forked tail. The *Tau*, mentioned in Ezek. ix. 4, is declared by St. Jerome to have been a cross.

The base of the cross at Kells, Co. Meath, has the figure of a centaur with the trident, another centaur behind armed with a bow and arrows, birds, fishes, and a sacred hare. The sandstone cross of Arboe, by Lough Neagh, 20 feet high, is covered with men and horses, trees and serpents. That of Monasterboice, 23 feet in height, has figures on the panels. Brash has interesting records of the sculptured crosses of Ireland. He describes those of Kilkenny and Clonmel, of sandstone, having in the centre of one, coiled around the boss, four serpents. On the panel of the left arm is a hunting scene ; on the right are chariots, horsemen, and dogs. A human head had a forked, oriental-looking beard.

Lucan mentions that the Druids wrote over the cross, *Pan Daran, Lord of Thunder*, bearing *Hesus* or *Hu* on the right arm, and *Beli* on the left.

Mrs. Wilkes, in her *Ireland the Ur of the Chaldees*, has thus declared her views—" The cross as a symbol is traceable to the crossed rods of the Chaldæan Shepherd Kings, —as ancient as the fish and the serpent signs, and as the ring and cup cuttings to be seen on the stones of Scotland and Ireland." Again, " The inhabitants of Erin, previous to the arrival of St. Patrick, were well acquainted with the cross as a symbol." Further she writes, " As we find the Christian emblem was general among the Druids, no one need fear assigning to many of the crosses of Ireland and Scotland a period far anterior to the introduction of Christianity."

The *crann tau-ré*, or *crois-tau-ré*, the Fiery Cross, which was carried through the Highlands thirty miles in three hours, in the year 1745, at the Stuart Rebellion, was known in very remote times among the western Celts, as it still is in India. When dipped in the blood of goats, and bearing a flame, it was the message of alarm among the wild tribes. A serpentine figure was often twisted round the cross in heathen times.

It is curious to find that the pagan crosses of Central India resemble many still existing in Cornwall and Ireland. A St. Andrew's cross marked the ancient Holy Cakes of Egypt. A Buddhist god bore the cross and trident in his hand. The Emperor Decius had the cross on coins. Some of the early Fathers were led to call the old heathen cross an invention of the devil.

The cross of Finglas has a romantic history. It was

exhumed in 1816, after having been buried for ages. Its cross was represented in a sun figure, as in Egypt. There were the marks of the snake about it, though much defaced.

The so-called Druidical temple of New Grange, one of the most wonderful monuments of old Ireland, is in the form of a Latin cross. There are four angled crosses or *fylfots* within a circle. The emblem, seen also on cromlechs, may be a reminiscence of Baal, or of the Scandinavian Thor, both being associated with crosses. The pyramidal cross, observed at New Grange, was known in countries as far apart as India and the Tonga Isles. Every one knows that the several deities of ancient Egypt are recognized by the cross they hold in their hands.

They who would study the subject further may consult O'Neal's *Irish Crosses*, and Rolt Brash's *Sculptured Crosses of Ireland*. By comparing the information therein with accounts of Egyptian, Persian, Phœnician, Babylonian, Hindoo, and other ancient crosses, the conviction will be strengthened that, from whatever sources derived, Ireland was acquainted with the Cross, as a religious emblem of some sort, long before the Christian era.

THE SACRED TARA HILL.

TARA, Temor, Temhuir, or Temoria, is intimately connected with the early religion of Ireland, and has been associated with singular theories. As *Tea-mur*, it was the mount or home of Queen Tea, wife of the Milesian King Heremon. The centre of Druidical song and power, the seat of ancient royalty, Tara was a favourite subject of glorification by ancient annalists, and has been immortalized in the poem of Moore. But, while bards record a great assembly being held there 921 B.C., Dr. Petrie, the eminent antiquary, is disposed to regard the place as existing only between 200 and 300 years after Christ.

The high civilization at Tara has been a favourite subject for Bards. The old lady guide at Tara told us that only gold and silver vessels were used at the banquets. Dr. Ledwich laughs at the yarns about its twenty-seven kitchens, and its amazing bill of daily fare. He assures us that the story of Tara rests only upon the fragment of a fragment in the Seabright collection, that had neither the name of its author nor a date. The earliest Romish ecclesiastics, and mediæval writers, knew nothing of early Irish culture or wealth.

We must refer to the works of Dr. Petrie for a description of the several halls, mounds, raths, cairns, and tombs still to be traced, with distinguished appellations connected with heroes and prophets of old. The *Feis*, or Irish Parliaments, were wont to meet in the so-styled Banqueting Hall. An ancient Celtic bard had this account of the grave of the Queen that came from Spain—

> " Tephi was her name ! She excelled all virgins !
> Wretched for him who had to entomb her.
> Sixty feet of correct measurement
> Were marked as a sepulchre to enshrine her."

The Tara stone, or the *Dallan*, Stone of Destiny, referred to by writers of the tenth century, is declared by Dr. Petrie to be the cylindrical obelisk still seen six feet out of the ground, with other so-called Druidical monuments. The tourist is shown the spot where Lucad the Druid was burned in the house, from which Benen, St. Patrick's disciple, had escaped. The story, as told in Latin by Maccuthenius, contains one of the traditions connected with the reputed life of Ireland's apostle, and illustrates the contest at Tara between the Saint and the Druids—

"All these things being done in the sight of the King between the magicians and Patrick, the King says to them, 'Cast your books into the water, and him whose books shall escape uninjured we will adore.' Patrick answered, ' I will do so.' And the magician said, ' I am unwilling to come to the trial by water with that man, because he has water as his god' (alluding to baptism). The contest was to be settled, therefore, by fire. A house was constructed of boughs, half green and half dry. The magician went into the green part, and Benin into the dry. The fire came and consumed the green, with the Druid, but the Christian was not hurt."

Other stories connected with the preacher at Tara are narrated elsewhere in the present work, and relate to a period subsequent to the institution of the Ollamh Fodhla college at Tara. But the modern school of Anglo-Israel attach other ideas to that ancient seat of sanctity. Heber of the bards is to them Hebrew. Tara is named from Terah. Jeremiah fled thither after the siege of Jerusalem, carrying away the treasures of the temple ; as, the ark, the sceptre of David, the Urim and Thummim, and others. Some persons at this day affect to believe that in the Hill of Tara might yet be found these memorials of Judaism, and hope to recover thence David's harp, carried to Ireland by Jeremiah and the Princess Scota, daughter of Pharaoh.

The Rev. F. R. A. Glover, M.A., has no doubt about its possession of the sacred stone; saying, "The Foundation Pillar which the Jews regarded for six hundred years with veneration, as Jacob's Pillow, in their temple on Araunah's threshing-floor, and which, being lost in the destruction of their sanctuary, B.C. 588, has appeared in Ireland as the precious *Liag Phail*, brought thither by Hebrew men in a ship of Dan, *cir.* 584."

The same authority elsewhere advances the following—

" In Ireland, in the royal precincts of Tara, *cir.* B.C. 582-3, there was a Hebrew system and transplanted Jerusalem, set up in a sort of abeyance in sanctuary ; actual, operative, but unknown ; real, but for some wise purpose kept out of sight ; a throne set up by a Hebrew prophet (Jeremiah) reset in sanctuary." Some pious friends of the Anglo-Israel movement have desired a digging search over Tara, now a wilderness region, to discover the missing treasures from Solomon's temple.

The romance connected with Tara we thus perceive still blossoming at the end of the nineteenth century. It began with heathens, was discoursed on by Catholics, is reverenced by Protestants. We still dream and sing of " The harp that once through Tara's halls."

The Rath on the slope, between the hill of Tara and the river Boyne on the west, was the site of the burial of the heroes of the Battle of Gavra. The grave of Oscar is still shown.

> " We buried Oscar of the red arms
> On the north side of the great Gavra."

The palace of Teamair, or Tara, was held by the Tuatha. The chief college of the Druids was at Tara. There was held the national convention of the Teamorian Fes. It was associated with the marriage sports of the Tailtean. The foundation is attributed to the wise Ollam Fodhla.

O'Hartigan, of the tenth century, the author of the *Book of Ballymote*, spoke of it—

> " Fair was its many-sided tower,
> Where assembled heroes famed in story ;
> Many were the tribes to which it was inheritance,
> Though decay lent a green grassy land."

He sang its praises under Cormac O'Cusinn, when it was a fortress ; when, at banquets, three hundred cup-bearers handed round three times fifty goblets, "which cups were of gold or of silver all."

" In Meath," said Hollinshed, "is a hill called the Hill of Taragh, wherein is a plaine twelve score long, which was named the Kempe his Hall; where the countrie had their meetings and folkmotes at a place that was accounted the high palace of the monarch.—The Irish hammer manie fables in this forge, of Fin Mac Coile and his chieftains. But doubtless the place seemeth to beare a show of an ancient and famous monument."

When Widow Feelin, the guide,—wrinkled, freckled, wasted, wizen, bent at an angle of 45 degrees,—hurried over the ground with the weight of 75 years to show us the wonders of Tara, she pointed out the "plaine twelve score long," as the site of the far-famed Banqueting Hall. She told us of the vessels of gold and silver, served by three hundred butlers. She could show no stone remains, for sure, the palace was of polished oak. She gloated over the graves of fifty croppies (soldiers); and, seating herself on the turf, sang a long ballad of past glory, in which O'Connell was duly remembered, and the Repeal meeting on Tara Hill, at which she had been present. Looking round upon nine counties, she mourned the loss of Erin's pride, as an aged Fenian Druidess might have done. She said that some persons wanted to search the grave-mounds over Tara's departed heroes, but that she had roused the villagers, who drove off the sacrilegious party. To her patriotic ardour, the sanctity of Tara and its departed Druids and Princes may be safely confided.

Mrs. Wilkes reads in the antiquity of Temora as the Teman of Edom, of Midian as the old name for Meath, of Padan Aram, of Laban, of Levi now Lewes, of Danaans from Dan, of Jacob's pillow Lia Fail, of the Irish genealogy in the first of Chronicles, of the tablets of Druids being the *peeled rods* of Jacob, &c., &c., testifying to the glory of Tara. The old Patriarchal religion of Chaldæa was one with the ancient faith of Erin.

Lastly, and not to be forgotten, the association of the Holy Stone with Tara signifies the place above all in some persons' estimation. Dr. Petrie discourses eloquently upon the *Bod Thearghais*, which bears, however, a surprising phallic signification. " It is," says he, " an interesting fact that a large obeliscal pillar stone, in a prostrate position, occupied, until a recent period, the very situation on the Hill of Tara, pointed out as the place of the Lia Fail by the Irish writers of the tenth, eleventh, and twelfth centuries; and that this was a monument of pagan antiquity, an Idol Stone, as the Irish writers call it, will seem evident from its form and character."

Tara, therefore, occupies no mean position in the history of religion in Ireland.

———

HOWTH HILL, overlooking Dubhlinn or Dublin Bay, not far from *Eblana*, Dublin, and rising 578 feet above the water, was a hallowed spot long before St. Patrick was at Tara. It was the *Ben Edir* or *Edair* of the Fenians, and so called from its oaks. The Danes destroyed its Halls in 819. The *Book of Howth* chronicles events from 432 to 1370. The Danish word *Howeth* is from *Hoved*, a head. Ptolemy's *Edras* became *Edar*. A Fenian poem runs thus :—

> " How sweet from proud Ben Edir's height
>   To see the ocean roll in sight;
>   And fleets, swift bounding on the gale,
>   With warriors clothed in shining mail.
>   Most beauteous hill, around whose head
>   Ten thousand sea-birds' pinions spread ;
>   May joy thy lord's true bosom thrill,
>   Chief of the Fenians' happy hill."

Ireland' Eye, a little isle north of Howth harbour, is also associated with early religious history. It was the *Inis Nessan,* from St. Mac Nessan, of the Royal family of Leinster, who, in the sixth century, had his oratory at *Inis Erean,* as then it was called. The word *Eye* is from the Danish *Ey,* Island. There it was that the holy man was assailed, as the story goes, by the formidable chief of hell, who sought to terrify him by his gigantic and terrible form. The Saint, excited, threw his book at the fiend, driving him against a rock which, splitting open, received him within itself.

The Abbey of Howth was erected in 1235. Fin Mac Coul's *Quoit,* a stone of many tons weight, is now seen covering a cromlech, upon which these verses were written by ·S. Ferguson, Q.C., recording the burial of the fair Fenian, Aideen—

> " They hewed the stone ; they heaped the cairn :
> Said Ossian, ' In a queenly grave
> We leave her 'mong her fields of fern,
> Between the cliff and wave.'
> The cliff behind stands clear and bare,
> And bare above, the heathery steep
> Scales the blue heaven's expanse to where
> The Danaan Druids sleep.
>
> And here hard by her natal bower,
> On lone Ben Adair's side we strive
> With lifted rock, and signs of power,
> To keep her name alive.
> That while from circling year to year,
> The ogham letter'd stone is seen,
> The Gael shall say, ' Our Fenians here
> Entombed their loved Aideen.' "

ROUND TOWER CREED.

WITHOUT entering upon a description of these ancient and graceful architectural objects, it may properly be

asked, " Do they throw any light upon the question of
religion in Ireland ? "

The first inquiry will be as to their age. If, as some
authorities declare, they date from Christian times, they
may be regarded as silent, so far as prior heathenism is
concerned. If, however, as others contend, their structure
and arrangements indicate a period of greater antiquity,
they may tell a tale of pagan symbolism.

As writers of the twelfth century assure us that there
were then no stone churches in Ireland, these buildings
must, if Christian, have been raised since the Norman
conquest of that Island. And yet, as Marcus Keane informs us—" more than eighty of the supposed sites of
towers are associated with the names of fifth and sixth
century Saints, or of heathen divinities."

One has affirmed that a celebrated tower was built by
the devil in one night. To this, Latocnaye says, " If the
devil built it, he is a good mason." Others may still ask,
" Who erected the rest ? " While over a hundred are
known to us now, their number must have been much
greater formerly, if, as that ancient chronicle, the *Ulster
Annals*, declares, 75 fell in the great Irish earthquake
of 448.

We have been told that they were fire-towers, belfries,
watch-towers, granaries, sepulchres, forts, hermit dwellings,
purgatorial pillars, phallic objects of worship, astronomical
marks, depositories of Buddhist relics, Baal fire-places,
observatories, sanctuaries of the sacred fire, Freemason
lodges, &c., &c. They were Pagan and Christian, built
long before Christ, or a thousand years after.

As showing the diversity of opinion, we place before the
reader some of the views,—especially where they bear upon
the subject of Irish religion.

Most Christian writers of the Island, jealous alike for

their faith and the honour of the country, pronounce them Christian edifices. The most eminent, perhaps Dr. Petrie, asserts that they "are of Christian ecclesiastical origin, and were erected at various periods between the fifth and thirteenth centuries;" that is, mostly raised by the Norman conquerors of Ireland as belfries. O'Curry regards Petrie as unassailable. Miss Stokes is deservedly a high authority for her *Early Christian Architecture in Ireland;* but she would place them as pre-Norman.

Petrie and others point to the fact of skeletons being found in some, and these lying east and west, as a proof of Christian origin. Yet, as is replied, all this existed under paganism. Christian emblems, found only in three out of sixty-three, have been regarded as modern alterations. The silence about the Towers in Irish hagiography, as the *Acta sanctorum*, &c., would seem to indicate a non-Christian origin, as early monkish authors forbore reference to paganism.

It is further asked, Where is the Christian prototype? If an Irish style of Christian building, why did it not appear in countries known to have been under Irish missionary influence,—as in Cornwall, Isle of Man, Scotland, France, Germany, &c.? Why did not Culdees leave such memorials in the Hebrides, in Lindisfarne, and other localities?

"There are weighty authorities on both sides," writes Gradwell, "but there are sufficiently high names who maintain they were already in existence when the Saint was brought to Ireland. If they belong to a later period, when Ireland was Christian, it seems strange that the architects of those times should have displayed such surpassing skill in the construction of these Towers, for which it is difficult to assign any adequate purpose; and not, on the other hand, have left us no monuments whatever of a more useful kind."

It is obvious enough, as has been pointed out, that " St. Patrick and his followers almost invariably selected the sacred sites of paganism, and built their wooden churches under the shadow of the Round Towers, *then* as mysterious and inscrutable as they are to-day."

Mrs. S. C. Hall, noting the carvings on the Devenish Tower, writes, " Some of the advocates of the Christian theory, on looking at these carvings, and at those of Cormac's Chapel in Cashel, and on the corbel stones in the interior of the Ardmore Tower, would argue a Christian period of erection. We confess we cannot see them in the same light."

The anchorite theory was mentioned by the Rev. Thomas Harmer, in 1789. He saw a parallel in the hermitage of St. Sabba ; saying, " The height of the door of the Tower belonging to St. Sabba is a circumstance in which it appears to agree with the Scotch and Irish Towers." A bell on the top served as a warning of the approach of foes to the hermits. Some saw them as serving to sustain such self-martyrs as Simon Stylites.

Wright, the antiquary, observed, " Some will have them to have been watch-towers or beacons ; but their low situation seems rather to argue against it. Others are of opinion that they are purgatorial pillars, by which the penitent was elevated, according to his crime, by a ladder, to fast and pray, and so purge away his sins." " They are certainly not belfries," says Higgins ; " and the fire-tower scheme being gone, I have not heard anything suggested having the slightest degree of probability." To Bede they were an enigma.

H. O'Brien, on the *Round Towers*, held that they were built by the Tuath de Danaans, and " were specifically constructed for a twofold purpose of worshipping the Sun and Moon, as the authors of generation and vegetable heat.

Again—" I do deny that the Round Towers of Ireland were fire receptacles,"—(but) " in honour of that sanctifying principle of nature, emanating, as was supposed, from the Sun, under the denomination of Sol, Phœbus, Apollo, Abad or Budh, &c. ; and from the Moòn, under the epithets of Luna, Diana, Juno, Astarte, Venus, Babia or Batsee, &c."

Miss Stokes thought it was absurd to say, as the early Welsh historian did, that Ireland had no stone buildings before the eleventh century, and she maintained that the towers were of the tenth century, being half strongholds, half belfries. Her opinion is that Irish art is not from Greece, but of purely native growth. Many Irish traditions point to their Danish origin. St. Bernard wrote that the Archbishop of Armagh first built a stone house, and was blamed for it by his Irish flock.

That they had great antiquity might be conjectured from the fact, that the great battle between Tuaths and Firbolgs was known as the *Field of the Towers*. Petrie found the tradition of their structure by Goban Saer, the poet, or mason, a myth of very olden date.

Dudley's *Symbolism* dilates on their geometric form and phallic characteristics. A MS. says that "the use to which our antient Irish put these towers was to imprison penitents." Forlong deemed them phallic ; and Bishop Rothe, 1647, memorials of conquest. Kenrick's thought of their Phœnician origin is combated on the ground of there being none like them in Palestine.

In 1605, a work appeared with this title, *De antiquitate Turrum Belanorum Pagana Kerriensi, et de architectura non campanilis Ecclesiastica*," and containing many engravings of Round Towers. An author of Louvain, 1610, esteemed them, says Hargrave Jennings, the Rosicrucian, "heathen Lithoi or obelisks, in the sense of all those referred to in other parts of the world (*phalli*). They were raised in the early religions, as the objects of a universal worship."

The popular idea in Ireland, that they were erected by the Danes, is met with the difficulty that there are none such in Denmark, or in England.

Sir Thomas Molyneux declared them belfries. One Smith, 1750, supposed their date between 900 and 1000. An Irish MS. called them *Inclusoria*, for the imprisonment of criminals. Governor Pownall gave them an Arkite origin ; another, a Pictish ; a third, as the work of Scythian Sabæans. Brereton, of the Society of Antiquaries, said, in 1763—" I think them rather ancient Irish than either Pictish or Danish."

The Towers must not be confounded with the Brochs or Pictish houses of Caithness, &c., which were forts with the residence between two circular walls ; nor with the so-called vitrified forts, known in Scotland, and of great antiquity. But they may be likened to the *Nurhaghs* or Giants' Towers of Sardinia, Gozo Island, Balearic Isles, &c., though these towers are much more complicated in structure, and rather conical. Like our Towers, they are splendid specimens of masonry.

The Nurhaghs are numerous—even thousands remaining. As round towers, they slope inward about ten degrees. They are seen from 20 to 140 feet in diameter, having a spiral staircase. At Gozo, one, with a diameter of 100 feet, has one chamber 80 feet by 50. Fergusson, architectural scholar, declares them pre-Roman in age. He thinks they did not grow out of Dolmen, nor Dolmen out of them. The word *Nur* means *fire ;* but, if fire-temples, why so many of them ? As few bodies are ever found in them, they could not have been tombs. Oliver considered the Nurhaghs were granaries in time of peace, but fortresses in war.

There is great uncertainty as to the object or origin of Towers. Being roofed in, they resemble the domed tumuli at Mykenna of the Pelasgians, or like Buddhist Dagobas. Captain Oliver, describing the Maltese Towers, calls attention to " the use of the numerous recesses, more like small cupboards, cut in the stone slabs," and which resemble the recesses in the Round Towers. " It may be conjectured," said he, " that these loculi may have been intended to hold the small idols, whose trunks (headless), made of stone or clay, are not dissimilar to the conventional female figures of Hindoo representations, on the numerous large and small rudely shaped *conical stones* (possibly sacred symbols, analogous to the larger stone cones, on which female *mammæ* are found engraved in the ruined nuragghi of Sardinia) which are found in those ruins. Somewhat similar small pyramidal cones, which by some have been supposed to represent the sun's rays, are to be seen in the hands of priests kneeling before the sacred serpent god in Egyptian paintings."

All this reference to phallicism in the Nurhaghs, maintained by Arnim, De la Marmora, and other Italians, apparently tends to support phallic theories on the Round Towers. Other authorities, as Manno, Peyron, &c., see in them only sepulchres ; while Angius, Arri, and Münter take the fire-worship view. The word *Nuraggh* is Turanian according to the Rev. J. Taylor ; but, to Dr. Charnock, it is Phœnician.

Round Towers have been also compared to the Towers of Silence by Fergusson, though those are but Parsee burial-places. Some see resemblance to the pagodas of the Polygars of the Circars. One near Benares is 50 feet high ; that at Bahar has the door reached by a ladder. They have been compared with the Dhila iron shaft, 48 feet high, erected in the fifth century.

The *Chouchas* of North Africa are in groups, from 7 feet to 40 feet diameter, of regular masonry. The towers of Etruria, like those of Ireland, had several stories. Lucian wrote of a priapus near Hieropolis three hundred cubits high.

A likeness to the Topes of Bhilsa, or the lofty Buddhist Stupas, had many advocates. Yet Fergusson asserts that no stone building of India was existing 250 B.C.; and Cunningham dates the Topes no earlier. Masson assures us that tumuli invariably accompany Topes. Chinese towers have nine stories. In Persia, Pulwar valley, is a stone tower 40 feet high, with a door 15 feet high, considered by Morier a fire-temple. Under one stupa were found two stone vessels containing bones, pearls, and gold-leaf; under another, a sacred box. A Sarnath stupa is recorded by Hwen Thsang to have been 300 feet in height. King Asoka's pillar, 70 feet, was erected three hundred years before Christ.

Marcus Keane wrote nearly thirty years ago his *Towers and Temples of Ancient Ireland.* He held that the oriental Cuthites raised them, as giants built the Tower of Babel, and that long before the Celts came to Erin; that the Irish were then a cultured people, as St. Patrick is said to have burnt 180 volumes of their literature; that the Saints identified with old churches were heathenish; that St. Diul or St. Deuil, was Dia Baal, the god Baal; that stone crosses existed there before Christianity; that St. Kevin's bed had a mystic and pagan meaning; that the Gobban Saer, said by Irish tradition to be the Tower-builder, was none other than the grand-master of the Cuthite masons, &c.

But his great contention was that the Round Towers were designed to exhibit the male productive principle, and, indirectly, the productive power of the sun. He fancied that the dispute which led to the dispersion at the Tower of Babel was none other than the rivalry between the believers in the *Father Principle* and those adopting the *Mother Principle.* He declared that the Cuthites or Scotis were upholders of the first, and that, being defeated by the other party, they emigrated to Ireland, and raised the towers as monuments of their faith.

The Magian or Fire theory, associated also with sun-worship, had advocates in Weld, O'Conor, Bethan, Webb, Moore, Lanigan, &c.

Dr. Lanigan found buildings in India with an interior like that of Irish Towers. "Those temples," says he, "were usually round, and some of them were raised to a great height. The lower part of an Irish Round Tower might have answered very well for a temple ; that is, a place in which was an altar, on which the sacred fire was preserved, while the middle floors could have served as habitations for the persons employed in watching it. The highest part of the tower was an observatory, intended for celestial observations, as I think evidently appears from the four windows being placed opposite to the four cardinal points." Finding most doors facing the west, he is the more confirmed in the fire-worship theory, as Magians always advanced from the west side to worship the fire.

We are reminded of the words of Diodorus Siculus, that an Isle opposite Gaul, and nearly as large as Sicily, had temples of a *round form*, dedicated to the sun, in which priests with harps sang praises to their god. The *Psalter of Cashel* distinctly speaks of the preservation of their sacred fire.

Dr. O'Brennan, who thought they were raised by the Tuaths, recognized the fire-worship of the Gadelians in Ireland, and the use of the towers for that purpose. Though known of old as *Bell-houses*, he observes—" That these towers might have been, in after times, used as bell-houses, is another question." Miss Beaufort says—" The object for which the towers were built is distinctly mentioned in the ancient history, called the *Psalter of Cashel*, and that of *Tara*, to be for the preservation of the sacred fires of Baal, the Baal-Theine." Elsewhere, she writes—" The Druidic temples of Vesta, in which were kept the sacred or eternal fire, were called *Tlachgs*, or temples of Cybele, being of the same construction with the *Pyrathea* of the ancient Persians."

Windele thus expresses his views—" Their Irish names, *Tur-aghan* or *adhan*, *Feidh-neimhedh* and *Cileagh*, are of themselves conclusive as to their pagan origin, and announce at once a fane devoted to that form of religion, compounded of Sabæism or star-worship and Buddhism, of which the sun, represented by fire, was the principal deity."

Buddhism is here a sort of sun-worship, and not after the teaching of the Founder. However pure the sentiments originally taught, and now professed in Esoteric Buddhism and Theosophy, all travellers admit that ancient pagan ideas have come through to the surface of Buddhism, and largely represent idolatrous action. Yet, they who recognize in the Irish Towers the former presence of Buddhist missionaries, fancy the buildings might have contained the relics of Budh. H. O'Brien regards the Sacred Tree of Budh to have been primarily a lingam, and secondarily a tree. He reads in the Irish *Budh-gaya* an allusion to generativeness. Forlong looks upon the tower as a deposit for lingam articles in secret recesses.

Anna Wilkes in *Ireland, Ur of the Chaldees*, writes— " There can be no doubt the Towers in the interior of Hindostan bear more than a striking likeness to those remaining in Ireland. These resemblances are to be found in such great quantities in the latter place, that it is impossible but to believe that Ireland was the centre from which a great deal of the religion of Budh developed. This will not appear strange when we consider, in connection with the point, that many of the Saints bear Aryan and Semitic names."

The bells, asserted by tradition to have belonged to the Towers, furnish an argument for the advocate of Buddhism, so closely associated with bells.

Glendalough, in its sculptures, appears also to favour this idea. No one can visit St. Kevin's Kitchen there without being struck with such resemblances. Ledwich has pointed out some of these. As among the most ancient structures in Ireland, and singularly allied to the Tower near, St. Kevin's Kitchen peculiarly aroused the attention of the writer. It was not only the position occupied by the serpent, the bulbuls or doves, the tree of life, or Irish *Aithair Faodha*, or *tree of Budh*, but the stone roof and the peculiar cement of the walls bore witness to its antiquity.

The Buddhist form of the Crucifixion, so different from anything in early Christian art, is another singular feature. In the Tower of Donoughmore, Meath county, is one of these sculptures; as Brash describes—"very diminutive rude figure with extended arms, and legs crossed."

In Irish we read of the Danaan King, *Budh* the red; of the Hill of Budh, *Cnox Buidhbh*, in Tyrone; of other Budh hills in Mayo and Roscommon; and, in the *Book of Ballymote*, of *Fergus of the Fire of Budh*. Buddhism was a great power in remote ages; and, as Allanson Picton points out, "not so much in its philosophical conclusions, as the feeling out of the soul towards an unlimited loyalty to the infinite." Still, if Round Towers owe anything to Buddhism, why are they only in Ireland?

While Larrigan thought them pagan, Lynch, O'Halloran, Ledwich, O'Curry, and Petrie held them Christian. A phallic origin is given by H. O'Brien and Sir W. Betham ; a cemetery memorial, by Westropp ; a baptistery by Canon Smiddy ; a hermitage, by Dean Richardson and E. King ; and a penitentiary, by Sir R. Colt Hoare. Who can decide when such authorities disagree ?

OSSIAN THE BARD.

A WILD storm of controversy once raged, when Macpherson put forth a work purporting to be a collection of old Gaelic songs, under the name of the "Poems of Ossian," who was the last of the Fenian Chiefs, and who, as reported, on his return to Ireland after his enchantment, failed to yield his paganism to St. Patrick's appeals.

While generally condemned as the inventor of the lays, the charms of which enthralled even Byron and Goethe, he must surely have been a poet of great merit, if they were of his own composition. But if they were remains of ancient traditions, carried down by word of mouth, Macpherson might at least be credited with weaving them into more or less connected narratives.

There has been much debate as to the possibility of such rude people, as in Erin and on the opposite shore of North Britain, having so retentive a memory, with the ability to transmit ideas at once beautiful and refined, in language of imagination and taste. But, as with the Edda, and the folklore of other semi-barbarous nations, facts prove the reality of extraordinary memory. It is not generally known that many Jews could repeat faithfully the whole of their sacred scriptures.

The history of the poems is interesting. The Rev. John Home, the author of *Douglas* and other publications, found a Tutor with transcripts taken down from old northern people, which were sent on to Professor Hugh Blair. Macpherson was requested to translate some of them, and these were published by Blair in 1760. Search was then made for similar traditions by Macpherson himself, who found in Lord Bute a patron for the publishing of *Fingal* in 1762. Dr. Johnson, the hater of all that was Scotch, furiously attacked the book.

In 1849, Dr. Lounrost published 22,793 verses rescued from memory. The 1862 edition of the Dean of Lismore's book gives, in the appendix, a long poem taken down from the mouth of an old woman as late as 1856. Sir Walter Scott collected many Scotch ballads in the same way. The story of Grainne and Diarmuid has been long known in the cabins of Ireland. Fenian poems have been circulating for ages among the peasantry of Ireland and Scotland. In 1785, Ford Hill published an ancient Erse poem, collected among the Scottish Highlands, to illustrate Macpherson's *Ossian.*

In Gillies's *History of Greece*, we are told that "the scattered fragments of Grecian History were preserved during thirteen centuries by oral tradition." Bards did the same service for Roman history till the second century before Christ. "The *Dschungariade* of the Calmucks," the learned Heeren writes, "is said to surpass the poems o Homer in length, as much as it stands beneath them in merit ; and yet it exists only in the memory of a people which is not unacquainted with writing. But the songs of a nation are probably the last things which are committed to writing, for the very reason that they are remembered."

Dr. Garnett, in his *Tour in Scotland*, 1798, says, "It seems to me wonderful that any person who has travelled in the Highlands should doubt the authenticity of the Celtic poetry, which has been given to the English reader by Macpherson." He speaks of the Macnab being "in possession of a MS. containing several of the poems of Ossian and other Celtic bards, in their native tongue, which were collected by one of his *ancestors*." At Mull, he continues, "Here are some persons who can repeat several of the Celtic poems of Ossian and other bards. The schoolmaster told me he could repeat a very long one on the death of Oscar, which was taught him by his grandfather."

The Royal Irish Academy had, in 1787, a notice of "ancient Gaelic poems respecting the race of the Fians (Fenians) collected in the Highlands of Scotland in the year 1784, by the Rev. M. Young, D.D., Fellow of Trinity College, Dublin."

Upon this, the *Hibernian Magazine* for 1788, remarks— "Dr. Young gives very copious extracts from Ossian, with a literal, or at least a close, translation; and proves decidedly that the poems of that bard are Irish, not Scotch compositions, and that Mr. McPherson has egregiously mutilated, altered, added to, and detracted from them, according as it suited his hypothesis. He appears particularly to have suppressed every line of the author, from which it might be deduced they were of Irish origin."

There seems ground for the latter statement. There was the prejudice in favour of the Scotch origin of the poems, although the narratives clearly deal more with Irish history and manners. Dalriada was, however, inclusive of south-west Scotland and north-east Ireland.

Croker declares that "many Irish odes are ascribed to Oisin." The *Inverness Gaelic Society* quotes G. J. Campbell—"The spirit is felt to be ancient and Celtic. There can be no doubt regarding the existence of Ossianic poems and ballads for ages before McPherson." Donald

Ross, Inspector of Schools, wrote in 1877—" A careful analysis of the thought of the *West Highland Tales* (by T. E. Campbell) points to an antiquity beyond the introduction of Christianity into Scotland."

The Rev. Dr. Waddell, in his *Ossian and the Clyde*, had no difficulty, in spite of some apparent geological changes, in identifying some of the localities mentioned in the poems. "In Ireland," says he, "the joint tombs of Lamderg, Ullin, and Gelchosa, with the adjoining tomb of Orla and Ryno, might be identified on the northern slope of the Carrickfergus ranges, between the upper and lower Carncals (Ossian's Cormul), and Lake Mourne." Yet, as he adds, "The topography of Ossian was a mystery to Johnson, to Pinkerton, to Laing, and a wilderness of error to Macpherson himself."

The Homeric dispute as to authenticity is recalled by the Ossianic one. Thoreau thought Ossian "of the same stamp with the *Iliad* itself." Homer appears to us in connection with blind reciters, as does Ossian.

The subject of Homer has had exhaustive treatment under the genius and research of a Gladstone. Yet not a few learned men detect a different author in the *Odyssey* to that of the *Iliad*. The two poems depict different conditions of civilization, the *Iliad* being the older, with different ideas as to the Future Life. If, then, there be such difficulty in deciding upon Homer, obscurity may be imagined in relation to Ossian. In both cases, probably, there was need of a compiler of the scattered bardic lays, the Macpherson of the period.

Dr. Shaw's *Gaelic Dictionary* asserts that—" Fion is not known in the Highlands by the name of Fingal. He is universally supposed to be an Irishman." King James, in 1613, in a speech, said—" The ancient Kings of Scotland were descended from the Kings of Ireland." Of the several migrations northward from Ireland, that led by Carbry Riada, King Cormac's relative, founded Dalriada of Argyle. The Irish certainly carried their own name of *Scots* into the northern country.

It may be said of Ossian, as Girardet said of Homer— "We know nothing of his birth, life, or death." But tradition calls him the son of Fion, stolen by a magician, and ultimately becoming the chief bard of the *Fianna* or Fenians. When these people were crushed at the battle of Gavra, he was spirited away by a fair lady, and lived with her in a palace below the ocean for a hundred and fifty years. Allowed to return to Erin, the story goes that he met with St. Patrick, to whom he related the events of the past, but refused to be a convert to the new faith. Another tale declares that, when staying with the Saint, he objected to the larder.

The *Harp*, a periodical of 1859, remarks, that other bards got hold of the poems of Oisin or Ossian, "and linked them together by the addition of a suppositious dialogue between the old bard and the Saint." The *Harp* fancies Ossian had met with "some of the missionaries of the Faith who preceded St. Patrick into Erinn."

Miss Brook, a distinguished Irish authority, thinks some of the so-called Ossianic poems arose as late as the eighth, ninth, and tenth centuries. Anyhow, those coming down to our day betray a remarkably heathenish character, and preserve the manners and opinions of a semi-barbarous people, who were endowed with strong imagination, high courage, childlike tenderness, and gentle chivalry for women.

Goethe makes Werther exclaim—"Ossian has, in my heart, supplanted Homer." Windisch, no mean critic, has these observations—"The Ossian epoch is later than that of Conchobat and Cuchulinn, but yet preceded the in-

troduction of Christianity into Ireland." Skene, justly
esteemed one of the first of Scottish historians, sees that
Windisch "regards the figures of Finn and Ossian as a
property common to the Gaels of Scotland and Ireland."
He thus expresses his own opinion—" The Scotch legend
attaches itself evidently to the Irish legend ; the Irish
legends and poetry have passed from Ireland to Scotland."
He says elsewhere—" The old blind poet Ossian is a poetic
invention, which has taken birth, and which found itself at
first created in Ireland."

In the chapter on Irish superstitions, reference is made
to some traditional ideas of the olden times. It is sufficient
here to observe that, whatever the views which may be
entertained as to the authenticity of Ossian, those poems do
throw some light upon the religious belief of the ancient
Irish race. Their tales accord with those of other semi-
barbarous people, and need interpreting after a similar
manner. The legendary heroes are not all of flesh and
blood.

THE CULDEES OF DRUIDICAL DAYS.

So many questions have been raised concerning the
mysterious community, called *Culdees,* and such various
opinions have been expressed concerning them, that one
may be excused inquiring whether in their midst we can
trace reminiscences of old Irish faiths. The notion has
been long prevalent that the Culdees were only Scotch,
having nothing to do with Ireland ; whereas, they were
originally from that country.

Their most bitter enemy in early Christian days was the
Venerable Bede, who denied their claims to orthodoxy.
But, since he was a Saxon, and a priest under Roman rule,

his charges have been slightly heeded. Their maintenance of an hereditary priesthood was not merely Jewish, as he supposed, but of Druidical sympathy.

Prof. Rhys judiciously remarks—"Irish Druidism absorbed a certain amount of Christianity, and it would be a problem of considerable difficulty to fix on the period where it ceased to be Druidism, and from which onwards it could be said of Christianity in any restricted sense of that term."

As both St. Patrick and St. Columba have been regarded by some modern writers as simply Culdees, and not following orthodox views and methods, might not the many stories told of their conflicts with Druids have been brought forth by ancient chroniclers, in refutation of the slanders abroad concerning their heretical, Druidical tendency? The same supposition may be equally directed against the early Welsh missionaries, though these were almost all from Ireland. Certainly their assumed miraculous powers inclined to the old traditions of Druidical performances. They had all of them a control over the powers of nature, and had even raised the dead; at least, their biographers claimed it for them.

Dr. Carpenter speaks thus :—" The incidents in St. Columba's life have been originally recorded in the contemporary *fasti* of his religious foundation, and transmitted in unbroken succession to Abbot Adamnan, who first compiled a complete *Vita* of his great predecessor, of which there exists a MS. copy, whose authenticity there is no reason to doubt, which dates back to the early part of the eighth century, not much more than one hundred years after St. Columba's death. Now, Adamnan's *Vita* credits its subject with the possession of every kind of miraculous power. He cured hundreds of people afflicted with inveterate diseases, accorded safety to storm-tossed vessels, himself walked across the sea to his island home, drove demons out of milk-pails, outwitted sorcerers, and gave supernatural powers to domestic implements."

All this reminds one strongly of the powers attributed by tradition to the Druids of the period, and points suspiciously to some outgrowth from Druidism in his case.

Columba was an Irishman of Donegal, and died, as it is said, in 597. Adamnan declares that his staff (without which a Druid could do but little), when once left behind at Iona, went of itself over the sea to its master in Ireland. He founded a monastery at Durmagh, King's Co. At Iona the ruins are those of the Cluniac monks ; for, says Boulbee, " not a trace can well remain of the primitive settlement of Columba." But Iona was certainly a Druidical college at first.

Like the Druids before them, the Culdees formed communities. Richey tells us—" The Church consisted of isolated monasteries, which were practically independent of each other ; the clergy exercised no judicial power over the laity." On the other hand, Wood-Martin of Sligo supposes, " Christianity must have been first introduced into Ireland by missionaries of the Greek Church." He notes the fact that Bishops were to be found in almost every village. It is also pointed out that Columba never sought Papal sanction for the conversion of the Picts.

The Iona tonsure, like that of St. Patrick's time, was the shaving of all the hair in front of a line drawn over the top of the head from ear to ear. The Roman, as all know, was a circle at top, and appears to have been first adopted at Iona early in the eighth century. The first, or crescent, shape was Druidical.

It was about that date, also, that the Roman way of keeping Easter succeeded the so-called Irish mode. At the Council of Whitby, Colman of Iona was outvoted, though protesting the antiquity of his own practice. McFirbis's MS. speaks thus of the year 896—" In this year the men of Erin consented to receive jurisdiction and one rule from Adamnan respecting the celebration of Easter on Sunday on the 14th of the moon of April, and the coronal tonsure of Peter was performed upon the clerics of Erin." Again, it says, " The clergy of Erin held many Synods, and they used to come to those Synods with weapons, so that pitched battles used to be fought between them, and many used to be slain." After this authority, one need not wonder at the assertion that Irish Druids formerly led contending parties.

Iona had certainly a Druidical college till the community was expelled by Columba for his own community, and the Highlanders still recognize it as the *Druid's Isle.* An old statistical work says, " The Druids undoubtedly possessed Iona before the introduction of Christianity." It must be admitted that the Culdees wore a white dress, as did the Druids, and that they occupied places which had a Druidical reputation. They used the Asiatic cross, now called that of St. Andrew's. Dr. J. Moore is pleased to say, " The Culdees seem to have adopted nearly all the Pagan symbols of the neighbourhood."

As to the origin of the word, Reeves might well remark in his notes on Columba's Life, " Culdee is the most abused term in Scotic church history." As the *Ceile De,* the *Four Masters* mentions them in 806. Todd writes of them thus—" The earliest Christian missionaries found the native religion extinct, and themselves took the name of Culdees from inhabiting the Druids' empty cells." Jamieson styles them *Culdees* or *Keldees, Kyldees, Kylledei.* O'Brien has them the Irish *Ceile De,* servant of God. Another calls them *Clann Dia,* Children of God. Barber considered them Mithraists.

Higgins, in *Celtic Druids,* will have Culdees only changed Druids, and regarded the Irish hereditary Abbots of Iona, the *Coarbs* or *Curbs,* as simply Corybantes. Latin writers knew them as *Colidei* or God-worshippers. Bishop Nicholson thought them *Cool Dubh,* from their black hoods. As *C* and *G* are commutable letters in Irish, we have *Giolla De,* Servant of God. The word Culdee was used by Boece in 1526. Dr. Reeves, in the Irish Academy, calls the *Servus Dei* by the Celtic *Celi-Dé,* and notes the name *Ceile-n-De* applied to the Sligo Friars in the *Four Masters,* 1595. Monks were reputed *Keledei* in the thirteenth century. Brockham's Lexicon finds regulars and seculars called so in the ninth century.

The *Four Masters* record that "Maenach, a *Celæ-Dé,* came across the sea westward to establish laws in Ireland." In the poem of *Moelruein,* it is the Rule of the *Cele-n-dé.* The *Keledei* of Scotland, according to Dr. Reeves, had the same discipline as the Irish *Colidei.* One *Collideus* of the Armagh church died in 1574. One *Celi-dé* of Clonmacnois, dying in 1059, left several sons, who became Abbots after him.

The canons of York were Culdees in Athelstan's time. Ceadda, Wilfrid's predecessor, was a Culdee. They were also called, from their mode of celebrating Easter, *Quartadecimans.* The last known in Scotland were in 1352. As Bede says, the Irish, being Culdees, would as soon communicate with pagans as with Saxons; the later following Latin or Romish Christianity.

Ireland, as reported by Giraldus, had a chapel of the *Colidei* on an island of Tipperary, as he declared some were on islands of Wales. They were in Armagh in 920. Ussher, Archbishop of Armagh, asserts that the Northern Irish, "continued still their old tradition," in spite of the declaration of Pope Honorius. In Tirechan's *Life of St. Patrick, Cele-de* came from Briton to Ireland in 919; but in 811 some were said to have been miraculously conveyed across the sea. Bede, who opposed them, whether from Ireland or Scotland, was shocked at their holding his religion " in no account at all," nor communicating with his faithful " in anything more than with pagans." He banished those who came to his quarter.

He found these Irish, Welsh, and Scotch Christians to have, in addition to many heresies, the Jewish and Druidical system of hereditary priesthood. Property of the Church even descended from father to son ; and, says Dr. Reeves, " was practically entailed to members of certain families." He adds that they were understood in the 12th century as " a religious order of clerks who lived in Societies, under a Superior, within a common enclosure, but in detached cells, associated in a sort of collegiate rather than cœnobical brotherhood."

Giraldus, as well as Bede, complained of their hereditary priesthood. The same principle prevailed in the Druidical region of Brittany, and only yielded to the force of the Council of Tours in 1127.

Although St. Columba had no exalted idea of the other sex, saying, " Where there is a cow there will be a woman, and where there is a woman there will be mischief"—yet his followers practised marriage. But while, says Mylin, they " after the usage of the Eastern Church, had wives, they abstained from them, when it came to their turn to minister." The " Woman's Island" of Loch Lomond was one of the female sanctuaries on such an occasion. Their opposition to celibacy brought them much discredit with other priests.

Archbishop Lanfranc was shocked at their not praying to Saints, not dedicating churches to the Virgin or Saints, not using the Roman Service, and because, wrote he, " Infants are baptized by immersion, without the consecrated chrism."

St. Bernard was distressed at what he heard of these Irish Culdees, who had no Confession, never paid tithes, and lived like wild beasts, as they disdained marriage by the clergy. In his righteous anger, he stigmatized them as " beasts, absolute barbarians, a stubborn, stiffnecked, and *ungovernable* generation, and abominable ; Christian in name, but in reality pagans." This harsh language is not worse than that employed by the Pope, when he entreated our Henry II. to take over Ireland, so as to bring the Irish into the Christian Church, compel them to pay tithes, and so civilize them.

One would fancy, with Algernon Herbert, that the Culdees performed secret rites, and indulged, like their Druidical fathers, in human sacrifice, from the legend of St. Oran being buried underneath the church erected by Columba, to propitiate the Powers, and secure good fortune. In that case, however, St. Oran offered to be the victim, so as to avert evil from bad spirits.

If St. Patrick, St. Columba, and other early Irish Saints had been true monks, why did St. Bernard, in his *Life of Malachy*, Archbishop of Armagh, 1130, say that up to that time there was not a monk in Ireland ? Columba certainly took Culdeeism to Scotland from Ireland. In the Bog of Monaincha are two islands. On one was a monastery for men, their wives occupying the neighbouring Woman's Isle. Giraldus Cambrensis, who wrote of the Community of Monaincha in the twelfth century, called it the church of the old religion, and politely designated as " Demons " all who belonged to that former church. The Abbey church, the ruins of which still remain, and which was 38 feet by 18 feet in size, was erected after the time of Giraldus.

Thus R. F. Gould, in his *Freemasonry*, had some grounds for saying—" The Druidism of our ancestors must have been powerfully influenced by the paganism of the Empire

at the period when Christianity dawned on Britain." He
deemed it probable that the early clerics of Christianity,
" the *cultores deorum*, the *worshippers of the gods*, gradually
merged into *cultores Dei*, worshippers of the true God."
So it might be that, as Higgins wrote, " The Culdees
were the last remains of the Druids."

THE FUTURE LIFE, OR LAND OF THE WEST.

No more touching or inspiring belief was there among
the ancient Irish, than in the hope of another life beyond
the grave.   Nature restored the dead forest of winter to
the wealth of foliage in spring ; why should not the breath-
less form of man once more find joy in life ?   But this
happy thought, with our Islanders, was associated with two
things—the sea-wave and the western sunset.

The soul of the Maori, it was said, took its flight to the
Reinga, the northernmost promontory of New Zealand, and,
from the branch of an overhanging tree, dropped into the
ocean in search of its subaqueous home.   The Irish, in like
manner, knew that his next tenement would be beneath
the flood.

The dying Egyptian beheld with the eye of faith his
spirit following the setting sun.   The Irish looked forward
to the West as the place to which his ethereal nature would
take its flight.   The roar of the Atlantic was music to his
ears, for it was but the echo of the voices of his forefathers,
and departed loved ones, in the western Land of the Blest.

Pindar sang—

> "Where mortals easiest pass the careless hour ;
> No lingering winter there, nor snow, nor shower ;
> But ocean ever, to refresh mankind,
> Breathes the cool spirit of the western wind."

Penelope's suitors, slain by her returning lord, were thus led by Mercury to the Shades—

> " So cowering fell the sable heap of ghosts,
> And such a scream filled all the dismal coasts.
> And now they reach'd the earth's remotest ends,
> And now the gates where evening Sol descends."

Chronos slept in his palace of glass in Ogygia, Isle of the West. The Hesperides and its apples lay in the happy West. The Teutones went to the glass Isles of the West, as did the Norsemen and Celtiberians. Arthur was rowed to Avalon in the West. The Sacred Isles of the Hindoos were to the West. Christian hymns still speak of crossing the waters to Heaven. How many of us have been delighted with Faber's beautiful hymn—" The Land across the sea ! " The Gaulish *Cocagne*, the Saxon *Cockaign*, the Lusitanian *Cocana*, or Happy Land, were beyond the sea-shore. Prof. Rafinesque might well say, " It is strange, but true, that, throughout the earth, the place of departed souls, the land of spirits, was supposed to be in the West."

> " To Rhadamanthys of the golden hair,
> Beyond the wide world's end ; Ah ! never there
> Come storm or snow ; all grief is left behind,—
> And men immortal, in enchanted air,
> Breathe the cool current of the Western Wind."

Procopius had a story of the West. Thither the souls are conveyed by ghostly fishermen to an island for rest ; and tales are told of ears detecting the calling over of names, as the boat touches the mystic strand, and wives and husbands being summoned to their arriving mates.

Erebos was the gloom that fell after sunset. The word in Assyrian was from *eribu*, to descend, as suns then dropped below. Odysseus turned to Erebos when offering his sacrifice to departed hero-gods. Ghosts were there wont to assemble, and might be seen flitting to and fro in the uncertain light. The main entrance of Greek temples was in the East, so that the worshippers might face the Happy West.

Homer's reputed poems are unlike in their records of the dead. The *Iliad* knows no apotheosis ; the *Odyssey* has it. Coleridge observes, " In the *Iliad*, Castor and Pollux are mentioned in the ordinary language denoting death and burial, and no more. In the *Odyssey*, we have the account of their ultimate resuscitation, which finally became the popular fable."

Alluding to the Homeric Hades—Aïdes and Erebos— W. E. Gladstone writes—" A particular portion of the unseen world, apparently special in its character, is stated to be situate as far below Aïdes as our earth is below heaven. It bears the name of Tartaros, and it appears to have been reserved for preter-human offenders." The condition of the departed generally was not very joyous ; Gladstone shows this as follows—" The Hellenic dead are wanderers in the *Shades*, without fixed doom or occupation." Again—" The Greek personages, recently dead, do not appear to have been either rewarded or punished ; and Achilles bitterly complains of the sheer want of interest in this life."

In Homer's *Nekromanteia*, we have the intercourse of Ulysses with the dead. He employs necromantic arts in his descent into Hades, which were strictly of a Babylonian character, and the whole description reminds us of the fabled descent of the Assyrian goddess to the Sheol. The ghosts gather round Ulysses at the smell of the blood of his offerings, and, inspired thereby, " expressed dark things to come." Tiresias then says—

> " Know to the spectres that thy beverage taste,
> The scenes of life recur, and actions past."

We are assured that when the hero sought to embrace a friend—

" Thrice in my arms I strove her shade to bind,
Thrice through my arms she slipp'd like empty wind."

Coleridge exclaims, " The whole of the *Nekromanteia* is remarkable for the dreary and even terrible revelations which it makes of the conditions of the future life. All is cold and dark ; hunger and thirst and discontent prevail." The ghost of Achilles was made to say—

" Rather I'd choose laboriously to bear
A weight of woes, and breathe the vital air,
A slave to some poor hind that toils for bread,
Than reign the sceptred monarch of the dead."

Ulysses, horrified at the sight of the *Underworld*, exclaims—

" No more my heart the dismal din sustains,
And my cold blood hangs shiv'ring in my veins."

Horace writes more cheerfully of the locality—the land of plenty and of peace

" No bear grins round the fold, no lambs he shakes ;
No field dwells there with pois'nous snakes,
No heat annoys ; the ruler of the gods
From plagues secures these blest abodes."

Renouf, in his translation of the *Book of the Dead,* has this Egyptian prayer—" Let me have my heart, that it may rest within me. I shall feed on the food of Osiris. Hail to you, O ye Lords of everlasting Time and Eternity ! Let not my heart be torn from me. I shall not surrender to thee this heart of the Living. Come forth to the bliss towards which we are bound."

Prof. Whitney thus speaks of the Hindoo faith—" There is no attempt made, in any Vedic hymn, to assign employments to the departed in their changed state, nor, for the most part, to describe their condition, excepting in general terms as one of happiness."

How far these old pagan views of the Future Life reached the shores of Erin may be seen in what follows in this chapter. A perusal of Ossianic songs, as elsewhere noted, will give the popular conception of the Unseen World just before the reception of Christianity. The *Purgatory of St. Patrick* might be, also, consulted for information upon the same subject. As to what opinions were cherished on the reception of Christian truths, we may perhaps discover some in the writings of Eastern Fathers, upon the supposition of some that the earliest teachers of Erin came from the Levantine regions.

The following passages from their writings may exhibit some notions about the *Hereafter* prevalent in the early Oriental Church.

Gregory of Nyssa tells us—" After due curative treatment, and when the fire shall have destroyed all foreign matter, then the nature even of these shall improve." St. Gregory writes—" It is not just that they should perish eternally who are sustained by His breath and Spirit. The fallen angel will begin to be that which he was created, and man, who had been expelled from Paradise, will be once more restored to the tilling of Paradise." St. Basil trusted that "everything of wickedness in man shall cease." Gregory of Nazianzus, 370 A.D. declares that "all will be loosed who groan under Tartarine chains." Origen affirms— "God will be all, seeing evil nowhere exists." Clement, 190 A.D., hopefully says, " He, by the Father, will direct the salvation of all." Only Tertullian, from unfriendliness to the theatre, exults in seeing "the tragedians more tuneful under their own sufferings."

The story of the Purgatory of St. Patrick declares another order of teaching, introduced later on into Erin, one more in consistency with the Babylonian "doctrine of devils," and which still survives with its lurid light. A recognition of *Our Father* is more elevating, helpful, and comforting.

The heathen Irish did certainly dwell upon a *Land*

Beyond. In Dr. Malden's *Ossian and the Clyde* we read, "When the warrior, who was also a hunter, reposed, his dog was laid beside him on the left, as if waiting his summons to attend his master on fields of air beyond the verge of earth—like Oscar's at Glenree, and like Cuthullin's by Lake Lego." And, yet, in the *Songs of Selma*, one mourns forth—"No more shall he hear thy voice, no more awake at thy call. When shall it be morn in the grave to bid the slumberer awake?" In the Chapter on "Superstitions" are references to the ghost belief of other days.

In the account of the *Land of Youth*, given by the heathen Fenian Oisin to St. Patrick—when the hero was carried off from the field of battle by the golden-haired fairy Niamh—the region was divided into states under sovereigns, as in the *Land of the Living*. It lay beneath the waves in the West, in a lovely climate.

How easy it was in so blessed a place to lose ideas of time! When Oisin obtained leave from his beautiful captor to revisit earth, he alluded to the rapidity of time passed in this retreat by his three months' imprisonment—

> "'Three months!' replied the Fair, 'three months alone;
> Know that three hundred years have roll'd away
> Since at my feet my lovely phœnix lay.'"

In Dodsley's fairy collection, one King Porsuma was carried off by a Zephyr—the princess taking him for a phœnix, and conveying him, as in the case of Oisin, to *Thierna-na-Oge*, the paradise of eternal youth.

Oisin had a fanciful description of his happy home—

> "You shall obtain the diadem of the King of the Land of Youth,
> Which he never gave to any person beneath the sun;
> It shall shield you both by night and day,
> In battle, conflict, and hard struggle.
> You shall get one hundred satin shirts,
> One hundred cows, one hundred calves;
> One hundred sheep with fleeces of gold,
> And one hundred precious stones not found in the world.

You shall have one hundred merry young maidens,
Bright and shining like the sun ;
Who excel in shape, form, and features,
And whose voices are sweeter than the melody of birds," &c.

Then there was *Flath-innis,* the *Island of the Good,* which word is still the Irish for *Heaven.* An old Gaelic poem had this description of it—

"The Isle spread large before him like a pleasing dream of the soul, where distance fades not on the sight, where nearness fatigues not the eye. It had its gently sloping hills of green, nor did they wholly want their clouds. But the clouds were bright and transparent, and each involved in its bosom the source of a stream ; a beauteous stream, which, wandering down the steep, was like the faint notes of the half-touched harp to the distant ears. The valleys were open and free to the ocean ; trees, laden with leaves, which scarcely waved to the slight breeze, were scattered on the green declivities and rising ground. The rude winds walked not on the mountains ; no storm took its course through the sky. All was calm and bright. The pure sun of autumn shone from his blue sky on the fields. He hastened not to the West for repose, nor was he seen to rise from the East. He sits in his middle height, and looks obliquely on the noble Isle. In each valley is its slow, moving stream. The pure waters swell over the banks, yet abstain from the fields. The showers disturb them not, nor are they lessened by the heats of the sun. On the rising hills are the halls of the departed—the high-roofed dwellings of the heroes of old."

In the tale of the *Voyage of Condle the Hunchback,* a wise woman sings thus to him, as translated from Irish by a French author—

"Tu éprouves, à cause de moi, du plaisir.
Sur les vagues, ton chagrin serait oublié,
Si, sur la barque de verre, nous arrivions ;
Si nous avions atteint la cité divine de victorieux."

Many Celtic legends relate to a voyage in a glass ship. As Sophocles tells us, Orithyia was carried off by Boreas to the ancient garden of Apollo.

A spirited translation of *The Battle of Gabhra*, by N. O'Kearney, affords English readers another picture of the Land of the Blessed.

> " Tiro na n-Og is the most beautiful country that can be found,
>   The most productive now beneath the sun ;
>   The trees are bending under fruit and bloom,
>   While foliage grows to the top of every bramble.
>   Wine and honey is abundant in it,
>   And everything the eye ever beheld ;
>   Consumption shall not waste you during life,
>   Neither shall you see death nor dissolution."

The distinguished historian, Lecky, has this allusion to another ancient fancy ; saying, " Among the many half pagan legends that were connected with Ireland, during the Middle Ages, one of the most beautiful is that of the Islands of Life and of Death. In a certain lake in Munster, it is said there were two islands ; into the first, Death could not enter, but age and sickness, and the weariness of life, and the paroxysms of fearful suffering were all known there, and they did their work, till the inhabitants, tired of their immortality, learned to look upon the opposite island as upon a haven of repose. They launched their barks upon the gloomy waters ; they touched its shore, and they were at rest."

In Joyce's translation of *Connla of the Golden Hair*, the hero is tempted by the fairy in these words—

" I have come from the *Land of the Living*,—a land where there is neither death nor old age, nor any breach of law. The inhabitants of earth call us *Aes-shee*, for we have our dwellings within large, pleasant green hills. We pass our time very pleasantly in feasting and harmless amusements, never growing old ; and we have no quarrels or contentions."

Beseeching Connla to go with her, his father, Conn of the Hundred Fights, called his Druid Coron to contend with her, and she was shouted off by him. But Connla leaped into her canoe, and was lost.

> "A land of youth, a land of rest,
>   A land from sorrow free ;
> It lies far off in the golden West,
>   On the verge of the azure sea.
> A swift canoe of crystal bright·
>   That never met mortal view—
> We shall reach the land ere fall of night,
>   In that strong and swift Canoe ;
> We shall reach the strand
>   Of that sunny land,
>   From druids and demons free ;
>   The land of rest,
>   In the Golden West,
> On the verge of the azure sea."

Tradition says that one Creidé, the god of goldsmiths, had a magic palace beneath the western sea, where he was drowned, while bringing gold to Ireland from Spain. Earl Desmond descended below Lough Gur, and has since been usually seen once in seven years. He is ultimately to escape as Oisin did. The Grey Sheep's cave, near Kilkenny, is the outlet. A piper, long confined there, has been heard to play on his pipes upon a May-day morning.

Ireland was associated with the west by the old Welsh, or, as Professor Rhys observed, with Wales. Taliesin, the great Welsh Druid, was stolen by an Irish pirate vessel of the period, but he escaped in a magic coracle before reaching Erin. The *Land beneath the Sea* was beyond Cardigan Bay, the Annwn of the old Sun. The Welsh Avalon, or Island of Apples, the everlasting source of the Elixir of Life, the home of Arthur and other mythological heroes, was in the Irish direction. As Morien writes, " The district of Hades beneath the earth, and beyond the river, was the fairy-land of our ancestors, the source of the passive principle of life."

So with Ireland itself; it was the western Arran-more Isle of the Bay of Galway, from which the quick-sighted, upon a fine day, could discern *Hy-Bræfailth*, or the Enchanted Isle. Moore alludes to the tradition—

"And as echo far off, thro' the vale my sad orison rolls,
I think, O my love, 'tis thy voice from the Kingdom of Souls."

The Spanish Bay of Souls lies west of Cape Finisterre. Ogygia was thought by Plutarch five days' sail west of Brittia. The ancient Egyptian ritual spoke of the Happy West. The home of Calypso was in the west. Bailly, writing to Voltaire, in 1778, said, "The giant Gyges (hundred-handed) inhabited the island of Atlantis, which is the same as Ogygia." The Bretons had their western *Ifern*, which was the *Flaitheas*, or Isle of Heroes, the Welsh *Gwynvyd*. Vinland the Good was westward, as were the Fortunate Isles. Spanish tales tells of seven cities below the western ocean, where still dwell Christians·who fled from the Moors and some of whom return after hundreds of years. America was probably visited by eastern voyagers long before Columbus knew it.

Lalla Rookh of Moore has similar references, as—

"I know where the Isles of Perfume are,
Many a fathom down in the sea,
To the south of sun-bright Araby."

Mythical allegory may give meaning to these stories.

In the Transactions of the Ossian Society is the following sketch of the *Land of Youth*, by Bryan O'Looney—

"This Elysium is supposed to be divided into different states and provinces, each governed by its own king or ruler. It is all peace, tranquillity, and happiness. The Land of Life is supposed to give perpetual life to the liberated spirits of the just. They are supposed to be located somewhere about the sun's setting point, and have means of approach, chiefly through the seas, lakes, and rivers of this world, also through raths, duns, and forts. The seas, lakes, and rivers act as cooling atmosphere, while the raths, duns, and forts serve as ingress and egress to and from them."

Speaking then of the fabled city in Liscannor Bay, he adds—

"The white breaking waves are said to be caused by the shallowness of the water over this enchanted little city, which is believed to be seen once in seven years, and of which, it is observed, that those who see it shall depart this world before the lapse of seven years to come ; but it is not supposed that these persons die, but change their abode, and transmigrate from this world of toil into the elysium of the just, where they shall, at once, become sportive, young and happy, and continue so for ever. It is also believed that those who see these enchanted spots, are slightly endowed with the gift of prophecy."

The life is not greatly different from that found here, since Oisin, in his reported dialogue with the Irish saint, admitted—

> "I had, by golden-headed Niamh,
> Of children, of surpassing beauty and bloom,
> Of best form, shape, and countenance,
> Two young sons and a gentle daughter."

In the story of Cûchulainn's adventures through this mysterious realm, is a full detail of its palaces and landscapes. The hero went thither in a bronze boat, which awaited his return thence. They who were admitted to a brief visit to the upper regions of earth were duly admonished, that if they once dismounted from their magic steeds, they would never again be able to return.

Bove Derg went to visit the Dagda deity at the Brugh of Mac-an-Og, where dwelt Augus Og, the god's son, and where Oscar and other Fenian heroes were entertained. Fiachna is recorded to have come to Connaught from *the agreeable plain*, in order to obtain help in a contest with other deities. He disappeared in a lake, and fifty warriors dived in after him. War was, with the Irish, as with other people of German or Norse descent, a most pleasant way of beguiling time in the world beyond. Even Cûchulainn was induced to undertake his perilous voyage, that he might gain a goddess for a wife, by promising to help her family in a fight.

There they heard noble and melodious music of the gods, travelled from realm to realm, drinking from crystal cups, and entertaining themselves with their beloved. No wonder that a hero returned thence declared to an Irish sovereign that not for his kingdom would he relinquish a single night with the gods.

In Irish so-called history, we read of the emigrations of Nemed, son of Agnomen, from *Mag more*, the great plain, or *Trag mâr*, the great coast, or *Mag meld*, agreeable plain. Nennius supposed this was Spain. It was, however, the country from which all came, and to which at death all must return. In the legend of *Tuân mac Cairill*, says M. Jubainville, Nemed's four thousand and thirty men, and four thousand and thirty women, voyaged from *The Great Plain*, and all died ; *i. e.* went there again.

The same French writer remarked how the relations which had existed here were continued there, even to the repayment of debts contracted on earth. " The life of the Dead," said he, " in the mysterious region beyond the sea is for each a second edition, so to speak—of the life led by the departed on this side of the ocean."

O'Beirne Crowe, treating of the *Book of Leinster*, and other MSS., says—" The point of departure from this world, as well as the entrance to the next, whether for pain, or bliss, or business, was always in the West, and the route west-wards. For the ancient Irish beliefs on this point we can appeal to the Vision of Adamnan, which gives the angels of the West the guardianship of the entrance to the regions of punishment, as well as to the cave of Loch Derg, which is most decidedly a pagan relic. This cave of Loch Derg is situated in the west of Ireland, as the corresponding cave Avernus is situated in the west of Italy."

Again, he remarks—" Somewhere, far away in the western ocean, there was supposed by the ancient Irish to be a spiritual country, called generally *The Lands of the Living*, and *Traig Mar* (great strand) and *Tir Tairngire* (Land of Promise) of Christian origin, as in the *Dind-senchus*, and *Tir Mar* (great land) as in another legend." Further— " The Land of the Living was the happy spirit's home of the Irish pagans until after the purification of all things by fire."

Parthalon was said in Irish legends to have come from Spain, not from the country of the Dead. Tethra, conquered in the battle of Mag Tured, became King of the Dead beyond the ocean. Chronos, also, reigned over the departed. The plain where these infernal deities dwelt was the Irish *Mag cetne*.

As the son of Manannân-mac-Lir returned to earth again, so did the Ossianic Find-mac-Cumaill, and Cailté ; evidencing the Celtic belief in the soul's immortality.

According to some traditions, the Better-land of the Druids floated in Neamhagas, as the Trimurti of the East were said to do in Akass or celestial ether. A bridge as fine as a hair, like Mahometans believe to this day, connects this world with that beyond, which they truly styled the *Greater Island.* The inhabitants were robed in white at *Murthemne*, the flowery plain.

Sepulchral rites were as essential to the comfort of the Irish in their Sheol as to the Greeks in theirs. As burial of the body was required in the latter case, so was the funeral song, feast, or cry over the corpse of the former—more or less performed to this hour by their Christian descendants. There would otherwise be dismal wanderings alone beside the Irish Styx, as with Homeric heroes.

The ghosts are variously described. The Ossianic ones appear indistinct and mystic in cloudland, floating with the wind. Such phantoms were of the worst sort, says O'Kearney; who adds—"Irish pagans never dreamed of spirits after death having assumed any such forms, either in Tir-na-n-Og, Flaith-innis, or any other happy abode of departed heroes. The spirits from Elysium always appear in their proper shape, and spoke and acted as if they were still in possession of mortal life."

There are many elements regarding ideas of the Dead which are common to both Greeks and Irish, though not direct borrowings. Entrances to the nether world were recognized in portions of the East; and Joyce tells us—"In my boyhood day, the peasantry believed that the great limestone cavern near Mitchelstown, in the county Cork, was one of the entrances to Tir-no-noge."

Dermat, in company with a wizard, or Knight of the Fountain, descended a well, and came into a country of delightful flowers and trees, palaces and castles. There a lady fair cured Dermat of the wounds he had received in battle, besides entertaining him with music. In the *Fate of the Children of Turem MS.*, we read of the Island of Fincara, which was sunk beneath the waves by a Druidic spell long ago. Then, one Brian, in quite modern times, provided with a magic water dress and crystal helmet, saw most charming-looking ladies. In the *Voyage of Maildun*, also, a privileged person was enabled to behold the *Mog-Mell* plains of pleasure, though these rather belonged to Fairydom.

In Plato, we have an account of banquets in Hades. In Irish MSS. are many references to the good things below.

There was a lesser god, Miders, married to Etain, one of the goddesses. The lady, tired of her situation, or company, came up, and obtained Eochaid-Airem, King of Ireland, for a husband. Miders followed the faithless one ; but she declined any further connection with one "who has no genealogy, and whose ancestors are unknown." The forsaken one engaged the king in a game of chess, in which the loser was to grant the request of the winner. The king, losing, was requested to give up his wife. This he refused to do. The disconsolate one then turned to win over the goddess. He sang to her of the *Pleasant Plain*, and invited her to return with him to a happier home than Ireland could give. He would give her there more tasteful pork, sweeter milk, and more intoxicating beer. There were rivers warm with hydromel, and even wine. Youth never aged, and love was not forbidden. All this, and more, may be read in the *Lealthair na hllidhre.*

It was to the mysterious realm of Tethra, beyond the sea, that the fabled Fomorian race of Irish retreated, when finally vanquished by the next comers. But the able Editor of the Irish *Battle of Gabhra*, has the following story of the ancient emigrants, or conquerors, of Erin—

"The Firbolg and Fomorian races, being more or less sea-faring men, placed their Elysium far out in the sea, and called it by various names, such as *Island of the Living, Island of Breasal, Island of Life*, &c. The Firbolgs are said to have lived under the waters of our lakes. The Tuath de Danans, being devoted to civil and literary pursuits, and their Druids having held their seminaries in caves and other secluded subterranean abodes, fancied their Elysium placed under the earth, while the Milesians steered, as it were, a middle course between both, and made their Elysium in a sort of indescribable locality to which a subterranean passage led. This they called *Tir-na-n' Og*, *i. e.* the country of perpetual youth. In this they supposed the virtuous and brave to roam among fields covered with sweet flowers, and groves laden with delicious fruits. Here some, as the taste inclined, promenaded in happy groups, some reclined in pleasant bowers, while others exercised themselves with hunting, wrestling, running races, martial feats, and other manly exercises. No person ever grew old in this happy abode, nor did the inhabitants feel tedious of enjoyment, or know how centuries passed away."

The early Christian preachers tried hard to dispel these images of the heathen paradise, and that by details of a terrible *Hell*—the *Avernus* of the pagan Orientals. When, however, St. Patrick told Oisin, as is recorded, that the hero Fingal was roasting in hell, the old Fenian cried out—" If the children of Morni, and the many tribes of the clan Ovi, were alive, we would force brave Fingal out of hell, or the habitation should be our own."

In the early ecclesiastical writings of Ireland, there is the same strange medley of old pagan superstitions and supposed scriptural ideas, to be found in other lands of the period. But this is also mixed up with the Babylonian horrors that found their way into the Talmud, making the Jewish idea of the Future so different from that of the Prophets in Scripture. We have but to read of the so-called Purgatory of St. Patrick for an apt illustration.

The entrance to this Purgatory was that known to the heathen Irish as leading to the Nether World. But the application came centuries after the usually recognized date of the Saint, and was unknown to such writers as Nennius and Probus. Irish tradition preserved the notion of descent into the lower regions, as with Oisin and others. Ecclesiastics, in like manner, record visits to St. Patrick's Purgatory, Lough Derg.

Henry of Saltrey, in the twelfth century, spoke of the Saint hearing there the cries of those in Purgatory. The Knight Owain, in King Stephen's time, went down, and saw the horrors. Some were fastened down by their hair, to be bitten by fiery snakes; others were in molten metal, rivers of pitch, or lakes of cold. A wall of glass afforded sufferers a view of the joys of Paradise.

One monk, writing in the thirteenth century, affirms that any doubts as to Purgatory would be at once dispelled by going to Lough Derg. Froissart knew one who had been there. William Staunton, 1409, saw "orrible bastes" tormenting men. Yet the Pope, in 1497, ordered the cave to be closed up, upon the report of a Dutch monk that there was no truth in the stories circulated concerning the locality.

Notwithstanding the papal authority, the superstition still exists, and vast numbers of pilgrims frequent the scene of St. Patrick's Purgatory. The descent into hell by Istar, Orpheus, Hercules, &c., yet lives in the stories of Irish visitants to the lower regions.

In the ancient *Book of Lismore* is the following narrative —"Howbeit the devil there revealed the gates of hell to Brenaina. And Brenaina beheld that rough, hot prison, full of stench, full of flame, full of filth, full of the camps of the prisoners' demons, full of wailing, and screaming, and hurt and sad cries, and great lamentations, and moaning and hand-smiting of the sinful folks; and a gloomy, sorrowful life in cores of pain, in prisons of fire, in streams or the rows of eternal fire, in the cup of eternal sorrow, and death without limit, without end."

The Irish traveller beheld there demons torturing men and women, "monsters yellow, white, great-mouthed; lions fierce, greedy; dragons red, black, brown, demoniac—a place wherein there are streams frozen, bitter, ever stinking, swift, of full fire," &c., &c. Altogether, a disagreeable contrast to the happy *Land beyond* of Irish pagans.

They might have had no clearer vision than Homer's Greeks of the fate of the Dead, though their lively fancy pictured a pleasant home. They had some glimmerings of light beyond the deepening shadows, while conceiving the ghosts of the departed as conscious of the past, and not unmindful of beloved ones left behind.

Some wild roamers on the rock-bound shores of Erin had a dim perception of a Better Land. The heart of the purer, the intelligence of the nobler, dreamed, however faintly, of a realm of peace beyond, of a scene of tranquil beauty, of a restful time in the fabled Isles of Happy Ones, where storms would be unknown, where never-withering flowers would greet the grateful eye, and where the Blessed West foretold repose.

We may fancy some white-haired sage of Erin, feeling the sands of life slowly but surely sinking, who would seat himself on the tempest-tossed cliffs beside the Atlantic, watching a sunset in those western waters, where the gradually lessening glow foreshadowed his own departure. There he might recall the friends of his youth, the deeds of manhood, and the lessons of age. There, too, he might weep at the recollection of loved ones gone before, and yet smile at the prospect of re-union in the country of Ever-lasting Youth. Such a man, at such a time, may well have imagination quickened to a perception of the *Onward and Upward* in the Inner Life of poor Humanity.

ANCIENT IRISH LITERATURE.

THERE are such contradictory views upon the originality, authenticity, and reliableness of Irish literature among Irish scholars and experts, that it is necessary to give various ideas of this question, as has been given upon other subjects treated of in this book.

Some Irish authorities, like not a few Welsh ones, are ready to accept without hesitation a narrative written by their countrymen, as if it were a point of patriotism to do so. Others, not so credulous, are desirous to explain away any seeming errors or incongruities, especially if regarded in the interest of a Church, or the exigency of a political party. Then, there are a few, influenced by the modern spirit of inquiry, or scepticism, prepared not only to reject what are palpable absurdities, but, sometimes, unreasonably to deny what is not immediately capable of proof.

Too much praise cannot be given to many, such as Sir Charles Gavan Duffy, who are trying to popularize ancient Irish literature.

It is harsh, indeed, to say, as Dr. Ledwich does in his *Antiquities of Ireland*, after quoting a list by Ware and Keating—"It savours, as all Irish MSS. do, of modern forgery." But no student of history can exempt the annals of Ireland from the charge of misrepresentation of facts, or absolute invention of falsehoods. Prof. Harttung, who considered the old Irish "a distinctly unhistorical and unsettled people," has this opinion of their ancient literature—"Imagination and the works of scholars, especially after the tenth century, supplied that which was painfully wanting in actuality."

No better illustration can be given than the remarkable series of books on the lives of St. Patrick and St. Columba. One's faith is tried thereby to the uttermost, leading not a few to deny the very existence of the two missionaries. That early Irish literature was afterwards much corrupted may be admitted, without throwing doubt upon all records because of interpolations and changes, through indiscreet zeal, or love of the marvellous.

Spenser, though an Englishman, did justice to Ireland when he wrote—" It is certain the Irish hath had the use of letters very anciently and long before England." Let us acknowledge with Faber, that " fictions of ancient poetry . . . will be found to comprehend some portion of historic truth." It is Bede, no real friend to the Irish, who tells us that " many both of the nobles and the low state left their country, and, either in search of sacred learning, or a stricter life, removed to Ireland." Camden quotes St. Sugenius, of the eighth century—

> " Exemplo patrum, commotus amore legendi,
>   Ivit ad Hibernos Sophiâ mirabile claros."

Skene, in *Celtic Scotland*, observes, " Others of these legends are undoubtedly purely artificial, and the entire legendary history of Ireland, prior to the establishment of Christianity in the fifth century, partakes largely of this character." Dr. Todd, however, warns us " that the pagan character of a passage fails to prove its antiquity,"—as " early Christianity itself was deeply tinged by pagan influences." In the same sense, Eugene O'Curry writes— " The tales relating to the pre-Christian period have in some form or other floated down the stream of tradition, preserving in the midst of a richly-developed Christian mythos much of their original pagan character."

The latter author draws a comparison between Irish and Welsh literature, not much to the advantage of the latter, saying, that there is in the first " a definite localization of all the personages and incidents of the tales " ; whereas the Welsh poems " bear incontestable evidence of having been recast in the twelfth or thirteenth century." He deplores the great destruction of Irish MSS. for several centuries before the Norman conquest of Ireland, much information being only preserved by tradition. The country must have been for ages in a fearful state of feud and anarchy before the twelfth century. Toland, in his *History of the Druids*, agrees with O'Curry in the statement that Irish MSS. are older and more numerous than Welsh. Many are scattered in the libraries of Europe, particularly in Paris, Spain, Copenhagen, and the Vatican.

Leland, time of Henry VIII., accounts for some destruction of MSS. As the Norman conquerors of Ireland built churches wherever they established themselves, Leland says that the native Irish made a practice of burning churches in their hatred to the new men. As the pious Normans were great patrons of monasteries, these buildings often shared a similar fate from the like cause, and vast collections of Irish MSS. so perished in the flames. The Danes, in the pillaging of Armagh, and other centres of ancient learning, were responsible for much of the Vandalism.

A curious story is told by Christopher Anderson. " In the reign of Elizabeth," says he, " the King of Denmark applied to England for proper persons who might translate the ancient Irish books in his possession ; and an Irishman in London, then in prison, being applied to on the subject, was ready to engage in the work. But, upon a council being called, a certain member, it is said, who may be nameless, opposed the scheme, lest it should be prejudicial to the English interest."

Of one thing there can be no doubt ; viz. that Irish scholars find great difficulties in reading and translating Irish MSS. They are so obscure and rude, have been so often interpolated at various periods, and are so liable to be misunderstood by the most conscientious and painstaking student, that outsiders are puzzled by the contradictory results of examination.

It is generally allowed that the Fenian poems are the most classical. Hardiman, in *Irish Minstrelsy*, is " fully convinced of the antiquity of these Fenian poems " ; but, he adds, " the language is so obsolete that it cannot be understood without a gloss ; and even the gloss itself is frequently so obscure as to be equally difficult with the text." The mixture of barbarous and abbreviated Latin increases the embarrassment. English readers of such translations have to take much upon faith. The Fenian poems are by far the finest extant. The *Pursuit of Diarmuid*, or Dermot, has been translated into many languages. The *Battle of Gabhra* and the *Lamentations of Oisin* relate to the final destruction of the Fenian warriors by the Milesians.

The Irish Academy and other literary institutions have done excellent service in translations. Walker's *Irish Bards* and Miss Brooke's *Reliques of Irish Poetry* may be consulted with advantage, as well as Hardiman's *Irish Minstrelsy*. The collection of Erin's ancient poets would not by any means approach in size that of the Finnish *Kalevala*, which were much greater in extent than the *Iliad*, if not equalling it in quality.

It has been well remarked that " Ireland would have been the richer had not the fears or bigotry of the priests discouraged the reading of pagan poems and romances, and thrown thousands of MSS. into the flames." St. Patrick is declared the destroyer of some hundreds of them. Though a number, yet preserved, are in Irish letter, the language is but Latin. The ancient *Domnagh Airgid*, in the Dublin Museum, is in Irish character, having portions of the Gospels in uncial Latin. That copy was *said* to have belonged to St. Patrick.

The reported ages of MSS. may be considered doubtful. Zeuss, the German philologist, puts the oldest at the ninth century ; but many are clearly copies of earlier ones, now lost. The fifth century has been claimed for some, and a pre-Christian period for a number of lost originals.

The *Cathach* of the O'Donnels, containing some psalms, is in a very ancient character. The *Leabhar-na-H-Uidhre*, or *Book of the Dun Cow*, has 138 pages on vellum. The *Leabhar Gabhala*, or *Book of Invasions*, is historical. The *Book of Kells* was ascribed to Columba, having its gospels beautifully illustrated. The *Seanchus Môr* is a storehouse of information. Psalters are ascribed to Cormac of Cashel, and others; the Psalter of *Tara* is taken from the one of Cashel. The latter records the fact that "Trosdan, a magician, advised the Irish army to bathe in the milk of one hundred and fifty white crumple-horned cows, as a sure antidote against the envenomed arrows of the Britons."

Among the lost MSS. may be named the *Calendar of Cashel*, the *Cuilmenn*, or *Book of Skins*, &c. The *Leabhar Leccan* has much about the Tuaths. Historical or mythological tales are numerous. There are *Annals* of Ulster, of Munster, Leinster, Innisfallen, Donegall, Tigharnoch, Clonmacnois, the Four Masters, &c. The *Book of Armagh* is very celebrated for its Irish character, mixed with Greek and Latin. There are the *Books* of Meath, of St. Kevin of Glendalough, of Leacan, of Kells, of the Isle of Saints, of Fermoy, of Dianna, of Clonmacnoise, of Mulling, of Dioma, of Howth, of Durrow, of Ballymote about Tuaths and Milesians, of Leinster, of Lismore, of Clogher, of Dunnseanchus by Amergin, &c. There are the *Book of Rights* or Leabhar na-g-Ceart by St. Benignus, the *Yellow Book of Ferns*, and the *Book of the Angel*. The *Book of Armagh*, containing the *Confessions* of St. Patrick, has 442 pages. The *Four Masters*, with some authorities, dates from the seventeenth century.

Dr. Petrie dates the *Feath Fiudha* or *Guardsman's Cry*, from the seventh century, though put much later by Todd, and in the twelfth century by the Rev. W. Kilbride. Of

291 words, 16 are Latin, and 30 are obsolete. The antiquarian authority, J. T. Gilbert, has doubts of any fifth century Latin Vulgate in Ireland. The *Lives of St. Patrick* are mostly of mediæval age.

The *Martyrology of Donegal* was by O'Clery, one of the " Four Masters," and gives an account of the Irish Saints. The *Saltair Chaisil* was seen by Sir W. Ware, though since lost. There are two copies of the *Book of Hymns*, eleventh century. The *Martyrology of Maolmuire O'Gormain* dates from 1167 ; the *Metrical Calendar* is put at the ninth century. St. Patrick's *Hymn to the Trinity* is declared of the sixth century. Among Foray or cattle-stealing poems may be cited the *Tain-Bo-Cuailgne*, written by St. Kiaran on the skin of his pet dun cow. Irish Triads were perhaps in imitation of the Welsh ones.

O'Curry had declared the *Tripartite Life* of St. Patrick to be of the seventh century. Arthur Clive finds it " was certainly written after the eleventh century. Such are the allusions to the kings and chieftains ; while the MS. called the *Book of Armagh* must have been written after the Norman Conquest, for it alludes to the Saxons as in occupation of the Island, and gives expression to a prophecy foretelling their final expulsion."

Gilbert, the Irish Archivist, in *Calendar of Ancient Records in Dublin*, tells us that " the early documents are in mediæval Latin, antique French, and Old or Middle English, written in obscure and contracted styles, replete with obsolete terms and archaic, undated." He finds the charters and grants are written in abbreviated Latin. The Irish was ever a puzzle. There were men to be found in Rome, it was said, who could speak every language but Irish. Lilly called it the Angels' language. Our James I. hated it, and declared his conviction that the Devil himself could not speak it. It might, therefore, on that account, be regretted that the Irish are more and more adopting English for Erse.

As the Erse has long been regarded as the "poor relation," among the Celtic family, the following from the *Edinburgh Magazine* for 1800 may be reassuring to Irishmen—

"The Scottish dialect of the Irish, corrupted as it was with Monkish Latin, and abundance of Danish, arrived in this country with the Dalriadæ. The Irish is the real mother-tongue, and retains a very long list of vocables, either now forgotten, or never used in Scotland. On the other hand, the Irish vocabulary contains all the words, a few modern corruptions excepted, to be found in the Scottish Gaelic."

Although Welsh enthusiasts claim the greatest antiquity for their tongue, many philologists lean to the Irish language. Elton affirms that it "seems to be of all the Celtic languages the farthest removed from the Latin"; and that "the oldest Irish is found to be the original, not merely of the modern Erse, but also of the Manx." Ussher found it nearest to Hebrew. O'Flaherty traced it to Phœnicia. Sir William Temple regarded it as an original language. H. O'Brien sees Hebrew derived from this primordial tongue. From Hamilco we should learn that the Carthaginians of his day thought more of the Sacred Island "extensively inhabited by the Hiberni," than they did of the Island of Albiones (Britain).

As to the writing itself, Todd believed in its pagan age; but Dr. Richey says, "It can scarcely be pretended that writing was known prior to the introduction of Christianity." The Greek character is seen in its semi-uncial state. Runic letters are absent, as the Vikings were using Roman ones when they began to plague the Irish coasts. Patrick has the credit, with some, of introducing Roman letters. Boece relates of the old Irish, that " in all their secret business they did not write with common letters used among other people, but with cyphers and figures of beasts."

Toland wrote—" The use of letters has been very ancient in Ireland, which at first were cut on the bark of trees, prepared for that purpose; or on smooth tables of birch wood, which were called *Taibhe Fileadh*, poets' tables; as their characters were in general named *Feadha*, twigs and branch letters, from this shape. Their alphabet was called *Beth-luis-nion*, from the three first letters of the same, B, L, N, *Beth*, *Luis*, *Nion*,—Birch, Quicken, and Ash; for the particular name of every letter was, for memory sake, from some tree or other vegetable."

" The Irish Beth-luis-nion is a living monument of a barbarous age," says Ledwich. At first he informs us they were stenographic, then steganographic, being called *Feadha*, or *woods*. O'Molloy gives seventeen letters, O'Conor eighteen, Lhuyd eighteen, with thirteen diphthongs. Ledwich was convinced that "the speech of the Irish became a fluctuating jargon." The aspen, fir, elder, broom, heath, willow, yew, ivy, vine, whitethorn, hazel, furze, and oak, gave names to letters. There was another alphabet, *Uraiceact-na-Neigeas*, called after men. Beechen tablets were used before parchment there. G. Massey says, " The Druidic sprigs belong to this ideographic stage. The Druids were in possession of the symbolic branch for the types of the youthful sun-god, who was annually reborn as the offshoot from the tree." The profane writing of the Druids was known as the *Bobel-loth*, from b, f, l, beginning the alphabet. The ordinary letters ran *b, l, n, s, f, h, d, t, c, m, g, p, r, a, o, u, e, i.*

Ogham writing demands some explanation. O'Curry will not have it derived from Scandinavian Runes. Sometimes the Latin beside it forms a bilingual. The ogham is made by notches on the edges of stones or wood, above, below, or upon a line. The strokes may be one below the line for *b*, one above for *h*, one across the fleasg, or medial line, for *m*. One small stroke across may be *a*, two strokes, *e*, three *i*, four *o*, five *u*. Some are in the form of a dart, or arrow-head. M. Gebelin was struck with the resemblance between the Irish Ogham and Persian Cuneiform.

There were thirteen single consonants, two double ones, five vowels, and five diphthongs. The key was found by Dr. Graves, Bishop of Limerick. The ogham has been claimed for the Welsh by Rhys. Dr. G. Moore sees that "the grammatical distinction of the letters indicates that —the oghams came from a southern and an oriental land." He regards oghams as sepulchral in pagan times. Crowe thinks them older than Sanscrit. The *craobh* was a branching ogham. The Brehon Law recognized the use of ogham as evidence of landownership. The Scythians had cryptic ciphers.

The *Book of Invasions* refers to "that ogum which is on the stone." Dr. Isaac Taylor would derive it from Runic of the eighth century. More likely, the characters came from the wedge letters on the angles of Babylonian bricks. Rhys thinks ogham came from the Phœnician alphabet. He finds "the ogham alphabet is of a double origin, forming a sort of compromise between the east and the west." Rolt Brash regards it as often pre-Christian. It is known on one hundred and seventy monuments; there being one hundred and forty-seven in Kerry, Cork, and Waterford. Tylor declares it very ancient, and not Runic; so said General Pitt-Rivers.

The derivation is unsettled. One writer in the Royal Irish Society gets it from *oe*, *ogh*, or *ogha*, a circle. Ogma was the father of the Tuath king, and was called Grianann, or, belonging to the sun. G. Mouncey Atkinson has the word from *Ghuaim*,—the guaim, or wisdom of birds. One of old styled it a cowboy's inscription. The *Book of Bally-mote* had an ogham tract.

In the *Tain-bo-Cuailgne* we read—"Cucullain cut an oak before him there, and he wrote an ogham on its side."—" He then made an *Id* (rod), and wrote an ogham in its side, and twisted it round the head of the pillar stone. The *Id* was put into the hands of Fergus Mac Roi, and he read the *Id*." O'Curry heard that in the third century there existed, at Tara, a book of wooden tablets of great age. The museums of Dublin, Edinburgh, and London have specimens of ogham writing.

THE LIA FAIL, OR THE STONE OF DESTINY.

ELSEWHERE, mention has been made of the Irish *Lia Fail*, Stone of Fate, Fatal Stone, or Stone of Destiny, generally believed to have been the Irish Kings' Inauguration Stone, afterwards used for Pictish and Scottish kings at Scone, ultimately becoming the Coronation Stone in Westminster Abbey.

Like other subjects connected with Irish history, this point has been considerably discussed. As the present work is mainly intended to give ordinary readers a citation of opinions upon ancient Irish religious topics, it is unnecessary to do more here than present various authorities upon this mysterious stone.

There are two competitors for the honour of authenticity, and both to be now seen ; one, a dozen feet long, standing erect, half out of the ground, on the Hill of Tara, in Ireland ; the other, twenty-six inches long, in the coronation chair at Westminster Abbey.

A legend in the *Scalacronica*, dated 1355, declared it was Simon Brec (a name of solar association) "who brought with him a stone on which the Kings of *Spain* were wont to be crowned, and placed it in the most sovereign beautiful place in Ireland, called to this day the Royal Place ; and Fergus, son of Ferchar, brought the Royal Stone before received, and placed it where it is now, the Abbey of Scone." The Royal Place was Fordun's *Themor*, and Blind Harry's *Canmor* or *Teamor ;* i. e. *Tara.*

Baldred Bisset, early in the fourteenth century, had another version ; saying, " The daughter of Pharaoh, King of Egypt, with an armed band, and a large fleet, goes to Ireland, and there being joined by a body of Irish, she sails to Scotland, taking with her the royal seat, which he, the King of England, with other insignia of the Kingdom of Scotland, carried with him, by violence, to England." This Bisset sought to gain the Pope's good offices for its restoration to Scone by our Edward I.

The Irish story in the *Leabhar Gabhala*, or *Book of Conquests*, mentions the bringing *to* Ireland, *from* Falias in Scotland, of the *Lia Fail*, by the Tuath de Danaans.

Upon this, W. F. Skene has stated—" The two legends at all events are quite antagonistic to each other, and there is one historic fact certain as to each. First, the *Lia Fail*, or Irish Stone, did not leave Tara, but was still there in the eleventh century ; and secondly, the Scotch one was not in Argyle during the existence of the Irish colony of the Dalriada, nor was used in the inauguration of their kings."

Wintownis Chronikel, written in St. Serf's monastery, of Inch, Loch Leven, about 1420, has this account—

> " A gret Stane this Kynge than had
> That for this Kynge's Sete was made ;
> And haldyne was a great Jowale
> Wytht in the kynryk of Spayne hale.
> This King bad this Simon (Brec) ta
> That Stane, and in-tyl Yrland ga,
> And wyn that land and occupy
> And halde that Stane perpetually,
> And make it his Sege thare
> As thai of Spayne did it of are,

> Broucht this Stane wytht in Scotland
> Fyrst gwhen he came and wane that land,
> And fyrst we set in Ikkolmkil,
> And Scune pare-estyr it wes broucht tyl ;
> And there it was syne mony day,
> Qwhyll Edward gert have it away,
> Nor will I the werd rehars
> As I fynd of that Stane in wers ;
> *Ne fallat fatum, Scoti quocung locatum,*
> *Invenient Lapidem, regnare tenentur ibidem ;*
> But gyf werdys faly hand be,
> Qwhare euer that Stane yhe segyt se
> Thare sall the Scottis be regnand,
> And Lorddys hale oure all that Land."

The Latin inscription said to have been on the stone has
been thus rendered by another—

> " Except old seers do feign,
>   And wizards' wits be blind,
>   The Scots in place must reign,
>   Where they this stone shall find."

This has been fulfilled, say some, by James VI. of Scotland,
but of Irish descent, becoming James I. of England ; or, by
so many Irish and Scotch holding official posts in England
and the colonies.

But James Mason did not believe the story, when he
called the stone in Westminster " a spurious relic, and
utterly worthless " ; as " not the ancient coronation stone
of Scotland at all," but a base imitation palmed off on
Edward I. That the Scots in their retreat should abandon
the real stone, is to him " the most monstrous of suppo-
sitions." Hidden awhile, it may have been lost sight of in
the subsequent wars, or lost by the death of the custodian,
as many another treasure has been.

Geikie, the geologist, who found it perfectly resemble
the sandstones of the Scone district, says, " To my eye the
stone appears as if it had been originally prepared for
building purposes, but had never been used." Even
Shakespeare in Richard III. called it

> " A base, foul stone, made precious by the foil
>   Of England's chair."

It is curious, also, that while the stone Holy Rood, containing a portion of the true cross, was given up by Edward at earnest Scottish solicitation, no pressing was used for the return of the Coronation Stone, not even after the crushing battle of Bannockburn.

It was, perhaps, intended to return the stone to Scotland, and a writ for the removal was dated July 1, 1328, according to the decision of a council at Northampton. Dalrymple states that it was further determined on at a conference between David I. and Edward III. in 1363. The Londoners, however, who accepted the belief of the stone being a national palladium, strongly objected to its leaving Westminster.

Irish, Scotch, Culdees, and Anglo-Israelites have honoured the stone from the fancy that it was the stone pillow of St. Columba, after having been the stone pillow of Jacob at Bethel, afterwards transferred to Scone. The material, however, is unlike the geological formation of either Judah or Iona, any more than of Ireland itself. But it is like that of Scone. McCulloch's *Western Isles* has this notice—" The stone in question is a calcareous sandstone, and exactly resembles that which forms the doorway of Dunstaffnage Castle."

How came Columba to have this Stone of Destiny for his nightly pillow? It is said, however, that when Fergus carried it from Ireland, it was placed in Iona, before being transferred to the monastery of Dunstaffnage. If it had been Jacob's pillow, the reported visit of the angels at night to Columba is easily accounted for.

In Camden's time, the Jacob theory was received. But the Scottish Reformer and Historian, Buchanan, left this testimony three hundred odd years ago—" The connecting this stone with the name of the patriarch Jacob was most likely a monkish invention, and not improbably had origin in this Abbey, since the most ancient document in which it was thus described appears to have been a tablet that was formerly suspended above the chair, but which has long ago partaken of the same fate as all the other written memorials that were in this chapel."

As to the nature of that one in our Abbey, Neale, in his *Westminster Abbey*, describes it as " chiefly quartz, with light and red-coloured felspar, light and dark mica, with probably some green hornblende, intermixed ; some fragments of a reddish-grey clay slate or schist are likewise included in its composition ; and, on the upper side, there is also a dark, brownish, red-coloured, flint pebble." Dean Stanley thought the stone certainly from Scotland. Scone is of Old Red Sandstone formation. The Dean had a piece of it tested in Percy's laboratory, when it was found to be slightly calcareous. Examined under the microscope, grains of quartz and small scales of mica were detected. Prof. Ramsay, 1865, had the like opinion of its geology.

Keepe's *Monumenta Westmonasteriensia*, in 1681, tells us—" Here is likewise on the west side the Feretory (shrine) of St. Edward, hard by the screan that separates the High Altar from the Chappel, the chair or seat whereon our Kings are accustomed to be inaugurated and crowned. It appears extreamly antient both in its fashion and materials, being made of solid, hard, firm wood, with a back and sides of the same, under whose seat, supported by four lions curiously carved, instead of feet, lies that so much famed Stone, whereon the patriarch Jacob is said to have reposed. —The ruines of this chair itself shows that heretofore it hath been fairly painted, and gilt with gold." The cost of the labours of carpenters, painters, and gilders upon the same, nearly seven hundred years ago, was £1 19s. 7d.

The chair itself is 6 ft. 9 in. by 3 ft. 2 in. The seat is 2 ft. 3 in. from the ground. There appears a groove in the stone. The circular iron handles, for lifting it, are fixed to a staple. A crack may be observed. The stone is 26 in. long, 16¾ broad, 10½ high.

Returning to its Scotch history, Skene discovers not a single example of a Pictish sovereign being crowned thereon ; and, supposing an instance were known, he wonders why the Scots, as racial foes of Picts, should have used it for the purpose. Robertson, the historian, traced Columba's relics to Dundalk, not Scone.

A work published about 1686 describes the stone as 22 in. long, 13 broad, and 11 deep; and says, "whereof history relates that it is the stone whereon Jacob is said to have lain his head in the Plain of Luga ; and that it was brought to Brigantia (Corunna) in the Kingdom of Spain, in which place Gathol, King of Scots, sat on it as his throne. Thence it was brought into Ireland by Simon Brec, first King of Scots, about 700 years before Christ's time, and from thence into Scotland about 300 years before Christ, and in A.D. 850 was placed in the Abbey Scone." Will. Rishanger mentions Milo, King of the Spanish Scots, giving it to his son Simon Brek.

Dr. O'Connor cites an Irish MS. which records the removal of *Lia Fail* from Tara to the Connaught Kings at Cruachan, and so it lost its sounding property till Con's day, second century ; that it was sent by Murtagh Mac Earca to his brother Fergus Mac Earca of Dalriada in Argyle. O'Flaherty, confounding its asserted removal from Iona to Scone in the ninth century, affirmed it was sent then by Aodh Finliath to his father-in-law, Kenneth Mac Alpin. Another version is, that Simon Brek (speckled sun) brought it up with his anchor off the west coast of Ireland.

Pennant narrates—"The stone which had first served Jacob for his pillow, was afterwards transported into Spain, where it was used as a seat of justice by Gathalus, contemporary with Moses." Boece declares this Gathalus was the son of Cecrops of Athens, and that he married Scota, daughter of Pharaoh. Haydn's *Dictionary of Dates* relates that "the *Lia Fail*, on which the Kings of Munster were crowned, was laid in the Cathedral of Cashel."

The Royal Irish Academy had the full Tara story from Dr. Petrie's pen. Referring to what he considered the Lia Fail, the author mentioned its position by the Mound of Hostages, though removed to the Forradh Rath in 1798, over some graves after the Tara fight. "But the mound," said he, "is still popularly called Bod Thearghais; that is, Penis Fergusii, an appellation derived from the form of this stone." Other MSS. "identify the Lia Fail with the stone on the Mound of the Hostages." Elsewhere he said—"Between the Irish and Scottish accounts of the history of this stone there is a total want of agreement, which shows that the Scottish writers, when they recorded their tradition, were not acquainted with, or disregarded, the accounts of it preserved by the Irish. The Irish accounts uniformly state that the Lia Fail was brought into Ireland from the north of Germany by the Tuatha de Danaan colony."

The conclusion of Dr. Petrie is as follows—"It is an interesting fact, that a large obeliscal pillar stone, in a prostrate position, occupied, till a recent period, the very situation, on the Hill of Tara, pointed out as the place of the Lia Fail by the Irish writers of the tenth, eleventh, and twelfth centuries ; and that this was a monument of pagan antiquity, an *idol stone*, as the Irish writers call it, seems evident from its form and character."

It is, in fact, the remnant of an ancient object of worship, the honouring of the symbol of production, or source of life.

One may smile at a clergyman, the Rev. Mr. Glover, saying of the stone of Jacob, that it was reverenced long by the Jews, and "being lost in the destruction of their sanctuary, 588 B.C., has appeared in Ireland as the precious *Liag Phail*, brought thither by Hebrew men in a ship of war, *cir.* 584." Mr. Hine, in *Leading the Nations to Glory*, regards that stone as "a witness to God's covenants in the future."

One may, also, smile at Dean Stanley's enthusiasm over the rival stone at Westminster, as a "link which unites the throne of England with the traditions of Tara and Iona."

Skene determines that the Lia Fail "never was anywhere but at Tara," while the other stone "never was anywhere but at Scone." Mr. G. Hudson rightly exclaims—"It is a matter of surprise that the Council of the Royal Irish Academy, if they believe this (at Tara) to be the Lia Fail, have made no effort to save such a relic." But Skene's conclusion upon this vexed question of, authenticity is as follows—

"There was no connection between the stone at Scone and the Lia Fail at Tara, and the legends of their wanderings, like those of the tribes with whom they were associated, are *nothing but myth and fable*."

It is uncomfortable to have one's pleasing romances disturbed ; and the *Stone of Destiny* has had to encounter the searching light of modern inquiry, to the destruction of many pretty fancies. It is good to be *happy ;* it is better to be *true*.

INDEX.

Ab Ithel. 63
About, quoted 184
Abury 8, 26, 178, 184
Adamnan 30, 280, 281, 282, 298
Adderstones as charms 106
Aeir, or long curse 81
Aengus, solar god 124, 137, 138
Aesar, a god 123, 129, 135
Ain, the seasons' course 130
Ainé, *Mater Deorum* 123, 230
Alphabet, the Irish 311
Amergin 18, 28, 39
America, Neo-Druidism in 3
Ammianus on Druidism 48, 64
Anderson (C.) 300
Anderson (Dr. J.) 215
Anglesey, Druidism in ... 8, 9, 20, 45, 70
Animal-worship ... ... 83, 224—231
Annwn, Sea of 7, 65, 294
Apollo and the Python 154, 165, 181, 184
Archdruid 1, 3, 7, 11, 14, 45, 46
Arkite theory of Druidism 62
Armagh 37, 52
Armstrong, Rev. 163
Arthur, King 7, 26, 287, 294
Astronomy and mythology 147—149, 180, 216
Atkinson (G. W.) 103
Aubrey, John 214
Augustine, St. 72, 127

Baal ... 149, 150, 195, 203, 204, 205, 206, 207, 270
Baalites, Irish sect of 151, 202
Baecker (L. de) 49, 79, 186
Balor 50, 82, 113, 143, 144
Banshee, the 91, 94, 95
Bards ... ... 12, 20, 33, 37—44
Baring Gould (Rev.) 79, 248
Barnard (Dr.) 113
Beads, Druidic 9
Beaudeau 47
Beaufort (Miss) 272
Bede, the Venerable 40, 171, 206, 266, 279, 283, 284, 305
Belenus, God of Gauls ... 125, 126, 159
Beletucadrus, Breton god 126
Belisana 126
Bells, holy ... ... 244—247, 273
Beltaine 194, 202, 205, 206, 207—209, 272
Benfey (Prof.) 215
Bergmann 157
Bevan (Prof.) 139
Birds in tradition ... 15, 59, 60, 123, 145, 225
Blackie (Prof.) lines on serpent 177
Blair (Dr.) 39, 132
Blavatsky (Mme.) ... 8, 33, 181, 200, 215
Blood drunk by Irish 82

Boethius 44
Bona Dea, Irish origin of 123
Borlase 39
Boscawen 117
Bourke (Canon) 34
Brahmins, Druids said to be 8
Brand 204
Brash (R.) 173, 255, 273, 312
Breastplate, Druidic 9, 17
Brehon Law 23, 43, 44, 229 312
Brehons 41, 43, 44
Bress 141, 145
Bridget, St. and goddess 13, 29, 81, 135, 1 1, 200, 235, 241, 243
Brittany 12, 45, 46, 184, 198, 209, 211, 984
Brooke, Miss 113, 278
Brougham, Lord 65
Bryant, Mrs. ... 35, 43, 87, 104, 105, 157, 158, 202
Buchanan 39, 317
Buddhism in Ireland 33, 67, 69, 152-4, 222, 250, 253, 255, 272, 273
Bullan stones 80, 81
Burial customs 291, 298, 299
Butler 77
Butterfly, the 66, 129

Cabiric religion ... 35, 57, 118, 135, 214
Cader Idris 5
Caesar ... 31, 40, 65, 67, 146, 226
Cairns 45
Camden 150, 169
Canute 118
Carpenter (Dr.) 280
Carrowmore, former people of 113
Cashel 18, 154, 165, 173, 174, 218, 226, 252, 266, 308
Ceara 125, 126
Chandruc de Crazannes 126
Christian missionaries, &c. 4, 20, 25, 29, 30, 69, 155, 158, 255, 280, 281, 301, 305
(*See* also Patrick and Columba, SS.)
Chyndonax 46, 128
Clark (Dr. D.) ... 133, 160, 208, 216, 254
Clement, St. 32, 172
Clement of Alex. 72, 180, 223
Clive (A.) 5, 20, 103, 112, 158, 206, 222, 309
Clogher 14, 37, 162
Clonmacnoise 250, 251, 252
Coleridge 288, 289
Colgan 30, 171
Columba, St. 30, 107, 172, 219, 225, 240, 246, 280, 281, 282, 284, 285, 304, 308, 316
Comparative mythology 49, 54, 91-3, 123, 125, 127-9, 130, 135, 140, 142, 144, 178—184, 190, 191, 196, 198, 252
Conchobar, a sun-god 134

Conder (Major) 155
Coquebert-Montbret 67
Cormac ... 51, 54, 58, 60, 154, 164, 266
Cory (I.) 130
Cosmology, Druidic 7, 18, 19
Cows, sacred ... 62, 113, 143, 227
Crete, free from snakes 169, 171
Croker 176, 241, 276
Crom, Irish god ... 121-2, 160, 161, 164
Cromduff Sunday 121, 163
Cromlechs 121, 212, 213, 257
Crosses 91, 104, 168, 173, 188, 229, 247—257
Crowe (O'Beirne) ... 12, 19, 42, 66, 90, 119,
    123, 129, 137, 163, 197, 297, 298, 312
Cuchulainn ... 36, 52, 83, 94, 119, 144, 296,
    297, 313
Culdees ... 20, 26, 206, 216, 279—286, 316
Curran (J. P.) 89
Cymry 6
Cyril, St. 32

Dagda Mor, the 103, 104, 114, 140-2, 296
Dallans, or Standing Stones 81, 216, 217,
    219, 258
Dana, the *Tuath* goddess ... 111, 141
Davies and *Arkite* theory 62
Days, Irish names of 148
Dechtere, mother of *Cuchulainn*. 94, 134, 144
Deemsters 45
Denis 171
D'Eremao (Dr.) 179
Dezobry 47
Diancecht 27, 108, 145
Diarmuid 51, 54, 60, 62, 134, 194
Diodorus 8, 40, 195, 271
Dion Chrysostom 32
Divination 11, 51, 53, 54, 61, 82, 110, 228,
    236, 240
Divorce 51
Dog-totem in Ireland 83
Donat, Bp. 169
Dormer 128
Dracolatreia; *see* Serpent-worship.
Druid, etymology of 235
Druidesses ... 15, 16, 33, 47, 48, 62, 94, 107
"Druidic" = magic 34, 45, 50
Druidism 2, 7, 10, 14, 20, 26, 35, 36, 42, 43,
    46, 49, 68, 69, 107, 214, 215, 216, 225,
    235, 241, 248, 256, 280
Druids, Irish 3, 7, 8, 9, 11, 13, 14, 16, 17,
    18, 20—27, 29, 31—34, 36, 45, 47, 48, 50,
    51, 61, 68, 69, 70, 83, 91, 105, 107, 183,
    223, 228, 230, 260, 282, 284, 285, 300
Druids' names 5, 13, 14, 15, 16, 18, 21, 27,
    28, 29, 30, 38, 39, 42, 43, 44, 46, 52, 55,
    56, 57, 58, 59, 60, 61, 106, 108, 109, 110,
    111, 113, 294
Dryden 89
Duff (R. J.) 103
Duffy (Sir C. J.) 304
Dundalk 22, 174

Earberg on ghosts 97
Easter ... 194, 203, 204, 281, 282, 283
Egg, Druidic 9, 32
Egypt and Druids 21, 34
Eisteddfods, Neo-Druidism at 4
Eliot, George 64
Elton 146
Ennius 158

Epics, credibility of Celtic 16
Eric, damages 109
Erse language, the 306, 309, 310
Eusebius 37, 125
Evil Eye, the 82

Fairies ... ... 90—94, 96, 137
Fenians, the 13, 174, 175, 195, 262, 263, 274,
    275, 276, 278, 296, 306, 307
Ferguson (Sir J.) 40, 153
Ferguson (Lady) 112
Ferguson (S.) 263
Fergusson (J.) 268, 269, 270
Fetch, the 99
Fetishism 79
Fili ; *see* Bards 18, 48
Fingalians 40
Finn 50, 53, 55, 60, 99, 105, 108, 174, 175,
    176, 230, 237, 277, 278, 301
Fintan 58, 66, 104, 106
Firbolgs 18, 102, 203, 300
Fire-worship ... ... 198—210
Flammarion 209
Fomorians, the ... 141—143, 145, 227, 300
Forlong ... 45, 177, 235, 236, 267
Fosbrooke 69, 196, 255
Four Masters, the 29, 30, 101, 138, 161, 199,
    283, 308, 309
Fraternities, Druidic 48
Frazer (J. G.) 61, 96, 225
Freemasons ... 24, 71, 74, 107, 248, 250, 267
Frogs in Ireland 169
Froude 24, 39, 78, 169

Geikie 315
Geoghegan (A. G.) 105
Ghosts ... ... 64, 96—100. 299
Giants 92, 218, 221
Gilbert (J. T.) 309
Giraldus Cambrensis 80, 170, 200, 221, 227,
    242, 283, 284, 285
Gladstone (W. E.) 97, 102, 228, 288
Glas, origin of 177
Glass ornaments 9, 17, 174
Glendalough 22, 81, 176, 195, 234, 252, 273
Glover (Rev. F. R. A.) ... 259, 260, 320
God, Druidic symbol for 7, 155, 222
Goddesses 129
Gods, names of, 103, 114, 122, 123, 124, 126,
    127, 128, 131, 132, 134, 135, 136, 139, 140,
    141, 144, 145, 152, 155, 160, 174, 183, 184
Gold ornaments 17
Gomme 5, 220, 231, 233, 243
Gorsedd, survival of the 36
Gould (R. F.) 71, 285
Gradwell 30, 265
Graves (Dr.) 249, 312
Greal, the Holy 7
Greek known to Druids ... 46, 48, 70
Grian and cognate sun-deities 125, 192, 194,
    312

Hackett 15, 62, 227, 230
Hades ; *see* Life
Hagiology, date of Irish 139
Hall (Mrs. S. C.) 266
Hanloy 153
Harmer (Rev. T.) 266
Harp, the 40
Harrington, Mrs. 89

Harttung (Prof.) 304
Healing powers of Druids ... 51, 57
Hebrides, customs, etc., in 82, 155, 197, 207,
209, 220
Heeren on Greek Bards 39
Hennessey, bard in 1804 39
Hennessey 140
Herder 77,
Hereditary professions 43
Hermand 68
Hermaphrodite deity, the 130
Herodian 162
Heroes changed into saints 136
Heus, or *Esus*, the Gallic god 123, 253, 256
Higgins 40, 266, 283, 286
Hislop (Rev. A.) 247, 255
History, Irish 11, 13, 305
Holbach (Baron d') 118
Hollinshed 261
Home (the Rev. John) 274
Hone 202
Horns 87, 143
Horse, the, in tradition 56, 58, 85, 86, 126
Howth 262, 263

Idolatry ... ... 116, 134, 157—168
Idols ... ... 134, 159—168, 174
Immortality, Druidic belief in 64
Inis na illuic 102
Injustice in judges 17, 43
Ireland, its races, antiquities, etc. 3, 20, 116,
120, 173

Irish MSS.; *see* Irish Literature.

Jebb (Prof.) 76
Jocelin 134, 170, 218
Johnson (Dr.) 97
Jones (Sir W.) 135, 156
Jormungandr, the 183
Joyce (J. W.) 50, 95, 112, 299
Jubainville (d'Arbois de) ... 48, 74, 114, 141,
142, 145, 223, 297

Keane (M.) 138, 173, 250, 252, 253, 264, 270
Kearney (N.) 86
Keating ... 43, 123, 169, 172, 177, 203, 205
Keens, laments for dead 87, 88
Keepe 317
Kenealy (Dr.) 35, 130, 153, 216
Kennedy (P.) 56, 96, 225
Kevin, St. 22, 156, 172
Kilkenny, Statute of 38, 39
Kirk 89

Laing (S.) 207
Lamariouze 68
Lang (A.) 78, 84, 96
Lanigan (Dr.) 4, 271
Le Blanc 126
Lecky (W.) 77, 293
Ledwich 35, 49, 156, 233, 258, 273, 304, 311
Leflocq 6, 31, 124, 157
Leland 306
Lenoir 130
Leslie (Col. F.) 215, 222
Lewis (K.) 189
Lia Fail, the ... ... 57, 223, 313—320
Life, the future ... ... 286—303
Literature, Irish ... 24, 120, 122, 303—313
Literature, Welsh 6, 12

Local names, Irish ... 90, 95, 102, 149, 152,
193, 194, 205, 211, 212, 213, 225, 227,
230, 234, 262, 263, 273
Logan stones 212
Lönnrot 41
Löttner 57
Lubbock 118, 145
Lucan 33, 146, 159, 195, 256
Lug, the *Tuath* god 143, 144

McAlpine 45
McCarthy (D. F.) poem 93
McCurtin 41
McFirbis 102
McGee (T. D.) 122
Maclean (L.) 36
Macpherson; see *Ossian.*
Mag Slecht, the 121, 122, 146, 160, 162, 163
Magh Tuireadh, battle of 14, 57, 102, 113,
267
Magic 13, 24, 25, 30, 52, 61, 83, 85, 218,
245, 259, 263, 280, 281
Manuscripts, Irish 10, 12, 67, 305, 306, 307
Manx Druidism ... 44, 45, 135, 136, 208
Martin (Henri) ... 45, 97, 99, 124, 167
Martin (M.) 20, 220
Mason (J.) 315
Massey (G.) 34, 111, 311
May-day mummeries 86, 202
Mellor, font at 234
Melville (H.) mythology explained by ... 148
Metempsychosis, Re-incarnation 58, 63
Meyrick (Sir S. R.) 125, 157
Milesians, the 18, 52, 102, 188, 230, 257,
300, 308
Milligan, Miss 80, 193, 241
Mistletoe, the ... ... 235—236
Mona; *see* Anglesey.
Montfaucon 159
Moore (S.) 232, 295
Morgan (Owen); *see* Morien.
Morien 4, 6, 7, 8, 36, 192, 214, 225, 294
Morrigan, the ... 90, 91, 123, 140, 141
Moryson 169
Müller (Max) 76, 131
Music 40, 41
Myfyr, Archdruid ... 3, 8, 36, 146, 215, 253
Mysticism ... ... 71—73, 131-2
Myth, growth of 78

Nash (D. W.) 9, 57
Nature-worship 117, 119
Neale 317
Nemidians, the 14
Nennius' tale of human sacrifice ... 146
Neo-druidism ... ... 3, 4, 62—64
New Grange 137, 174, 214, 222, 250, 257

Oak, the 234-5, 241, 248
O'Brennan (Dr.) 271
O'Brien (H.) 26, 125, 185, 251, 253, 266,
267, 272, 282, 310
O'Connor (Dr.) 16, 318
O'Curry (Prof.) 5, 11, 13, 14, 18, 33, 35, 36,
106, 146, 158, 221, 265, 306, 309, 311, 313
O'Donovan (Dr.) 81, 206, 246
O'Flaherty 58, 176, 310, 318
O'Flanagan (T.) 13, 102
Oghams 18, 103, 153, 237, 249, 255, 311—313
O'Grady (Hayes) 79

O'Grady (S.) 140
O'Kearney (N.) 65, 96, 98, 134, 144, 151,
    158, 202, 299
Oliver (Capt.) 248, 268, 269
O'Looney (Bryan) 295, 296
O'Neill 172
Ophiolatreia ; *see* Serpent Worship.
Ophites, the 179, 180
O'Reilly and Irish writers 39
Origen 32, 290
Ossian 42, 98, 132, 196, 202, 212, 274—279,
    290, 291, 296, 301

Pantheism 69, 119, 129
Parthalon 13, 140, 141, 298
Patrick, St. 12, 13, 16, 17, 28, 29, 30, 44, 53,
    55, 72, 106, 121, 122, 128, 137, 146, 151,
    158, 161, 170, 171, 187, 193, 203, 204,
    205, 218, 229, 232, 240, 245, 246, 259,
    266, 270, 278, 280, 285, 291, 301, 304,
    307, 310
Persians had no idols 147, 167
Petrie (W. M. F.) 180
Petrie (Dr. G.) ... 158, 258, 262, 265, 267,
    308, 319
Phallicism 8, 86, 123, 150, 164, 167, 177 184,
    185, 211, 216, 219, 239, 262, 267, 269,
    270, 271
Phené (Dr.) 186, 200
Phoenicians 37, 119, 125, 148, 149, 154, 156,
    193, 228, 267
Phookas 90, 94
Picart 214
Pictet 35, 118, 135, 156
Pigmy races 92
Pigs, magical and sacred ... 227—231, 255
Pitt-Rivers (Gen.) 244, 312
Pliny 16, 31, 117, 236
Plowden 45, 77, 208
Plutarch 13, 146
Pontypridd, Druids of 3, 8
Pownall (T.) 166, 167, 268
Pyrolatreia ; *see* Fire-worship.
Pythagoras 31, 48, 68

Quatrefages 41

Reeves (Dr.) 282, 283, 284
Re-incarnation 48, 58, 67
Religion ... 35, 76, 77, 116, 118, 120, 151
Renan 48
Reynaud (J.) 167
Rhind 221
Rhys (Prof.) 6, 20, 21, 53, 58, 63, 66, 68, 72,
    78, 83, 104, 111, 117, 122, 128, 130, 133,
    198, 242, 280, 294, 312
Rich on *Keening* in 1610 87
Richey (Dr.) ... 16, 19, 36, 66, 281, 310
Rivett-Carnac 216
Robertson-Smith 242-3
Romans on Celtic religion ... 120, 158
Ross (D.) 65, 98, 129, 193, 277
Round Towers ... ... 26, 263—274
Rowan wood 86, 111, 237
Ruskin 182, 233

Sabbath, the 37
Sacheverell 45
Sacrifice, human 47, 121, 145, 146, 147,
    241, 285

Saints, Irish 22, 107, 138, 139, 156, 172, 188,
    212, 218, 224, 225, 226, 263, 264, 266,
    270, 273, 285, 308, 309
Samhain, All Saints' Day 87, 153, 204, 205,
    206
Saronidae, or judges 8, 45
Sayce (Prof.) 37
Schmidt (Dr.) 37
Scotland, customs in 207, 226, 231, 233,
    239—240, 254
Sects, ancient Irish 7, 151
Senachies, or heralds 38
Serpent-stones 47, 48
Serpent-worship ... ... 151, 168—189
Serpents not in Ireland ... ... 169—171
Serpents on idols, etc. 18, 166, 173, 174, 178,
    183, 250, 254, 255, 256, 257, 273
Senchus Mor and Druidism 18
Shamrock, the ... ... 232—234
Shearman (Rev. J. F.) 16
Sheriffs, Brehons' successors 21
Sidh 95
Simpson (Prof.) 222
Skene 279, 305, 314, 318, 320
Sligo, Druidic remains in 113
Smiddy (Rev. R.) 103, 112, 130
Smith (A.) 67, 153
Solinus 82, 169
Sonnerat 210
Spencer (H.) 97
Spenser (E.) 82, 136, 137, 232, 305
Spiritualism of Druids 23, 56
Staff, Druidic 9, 18, 32, 54, 281
Stewart (Rev. A.) 207
Stokes (Miss M.) 246, 265, 267
Stokes (Prof.) 96
Stone-circles ... 26, 207, 211, 212, 244
Stone-worship ... ... 211—224
Stonehenge 2, 8, 26, 221, 223
Strabo 9, 70, 146
Straws as charms 116
Sun-worship 20, 21, 103, 104, 124, 125, 126,
    134, 189—198, 225, 266, 267
Superstitions, Irish 79—101, 163, 164, 196,
    217, 218, 226, 231, 241, 251
Sword-worship 56, 115, 136
Sydney (Sir P.) on bards 39

Taliesin 4, 19, 20, 133, 294
Tara 17, 28, 57, 219, 223, 257—262, 308,
    313, 314, 318, 319
Tate 222
Templars and mysticism 73
Tethra 114, 298, 300
Thanet, no snakes there 169, 171
Thierry (A.) 69, 70, 78
Thumb, chewing of the 50, 108
Tighernmas 134, 144
Tir-na-n-og 140, 291, 293, 299, 301
Todd (Dr.) ... 29, 80, 129, 282, 305, 308, 310
Toghairm 56
Toland (J.) ... 21, 22, 33, 34, 43, 161, 206
    306, 311
Tonsure, the 281, 282
Torques, Druidic 9, 17, 18
Totemism in Ireland 83
Train 44, 45, 208
Transformations 53, 59, 62, 65, 67, 73, 83,
    108—110, 230
(*See* also Re-incarnation.)

Triads, Irish and Welsh   63, 64, 72, 73, 131,
                                    143, 229
Tribal feeling   138
Trinity symbols 7, 155
Troyon   65
Tuan Mac Coireall 59, 65, 73
Tuatha de Danaan, the   ...   14, 24, 58, 101,
    102, 103, 106, 108, 111, 112, 115, 127, 128,
    137, 142, 219, 223, 230, 233, 237, 250, 251,
    260, 261, 263, 266, 271, 300, 308, 314, 319
Twelve, number   149
Tylor (Dr.) 159, 190, 312

Vallencey   ... 53, 36, 52, 104, 152, 158, 162,
                                    194, 222
Virgin, the Black   123
Vortigern's human sacrifice   146

Waddell (Dr.) 66, 133, 202, 277
Wakeman   249
Wales, Druidism, race, etc., in   2, 3, 4, 10,
                                    160, 240
Walhouse   220
Walker 37, 39, 41, 195
War-gods and goddesses   115, 127, 130, 140

Ware (Sir J.)   169
Weapons worshipped   115
Well-worship   ...   ...   237, 238—244
Wesley (J.) 88
Whately (Arbp.)   64
White (Capt.)   254
Wicklow gold-mines   17
Wilde 102, 115
Wilkes, Mrs.   139, 154, 169, 203, 205, 256,
                                    261, 272
Williams (J.); *see* Ab Ithel.
Windele 34, 188, 272
Windisch 278, 279
Winds, colours of 8, 18
Wise 21, 22
Witchcraft   84
Wolf-totem in Ireland   83
Woman, Druidic creation of   111
Women's Isles 15, 284, 285
Wood-Martin 113, 244, 281
Wordsworth on Pre-existence   64
Worth, an author   33
Wright   266

Zodiac, Irish signs of the 147, 224

AUTHORITIES CITED.

ADAMNAN : Libri III. de S. Columba.
Anderson (Dr. J.): Scotland in the Pagan Times.
Anecdota Oxon.
Armstrong (Dr.) : Gaelic Dictionary.
Aubrey (J.): Remaines of Gentilisme and Judaisme.

Baecker (L. de): De la Religion du Nord de la France avant le Christianisme.
Beaudeau : Mémoire à consulter pour les anciens Druides Gaulois.
Beda Venerabilis : Opera.
Bernard St. : Life of Malachy, Archbishop of Armagh.
Betham (Sir W.) : Gael and Cymbri.
Blavatsky (H. P.): Isis Unveiled, and Secret Doctrine.
Brash (R. R.): Sculptured Crosses of Ireland.
Brockham : Lexicon.
Brooke (Miss) : Reliques of Irish Poetry.
Bryant (J.): New System of Antient Mythology.
Bryant (Mrs.): Celtic Ireland.
Butler : Historical Memoirs of the English, Irish, and Scottish Catholics.

Caesar : Commentaries.
Camden (W.): Britannia.
Columba, Life of, 1827.
Conder (J.): The Modern Traveller.
    „   „   : View of all Religions.

Connelan (O.) : Translation of the Proceedings of the Great Bardic Institu-
    tion.
Cory (I. P.) : Ancient Fragments.
Courson (A. de) : Histoire des Peuples Brétons dans la Gaule et dans les
    Iles Britanniques.
Croker (T. C.) : Fairy Legends of Ireland, &c. &c.
Crowe (O'Beirne) : Religious Beliefs of the Pagan Irish.

Dalyell (Sir J. G.) : Darker Superstitions of Scotland.
Darwin (C. R.) : Descent of Man.
Davies (E.) : Celtic Researches on Origin, &c. of Ancient Britons.
De antiquitate Turrum Belanorum Pagana Kerriensi. 1605.
Denis : Le Monde Enchanté, Cosmographie et Histoire Naturelle Fantastiques
    du Moyen Age.
D'Eremao (Rev. Dr.) : Serpent of Eden.
Dormer : Origin of Primitive Superstitions.
Dudley : Symbolism.

Ferguson (Sir J.) : Lays of the Western Gael.
Ferguson (Lady) : Story of the Irish before the Conquest.
Fergusson (J.) : Tree and Serpent Worship.
Forlong (J. G. R.) : Rivers of Life.
Fosbrooke (Rev. T. D.) : British Monachism.
Frazer (J. G.) : The Golden Bough.

Giraldus Cambrensis : Opera.
Gladstone (W. E.) : Juventus Mundi.
Glennie (J. S. Stuart) : Arthurian Localities.
Gomme (G. L.) : Folk-Lore of Early Village Life.
Gould (R. F.) : History of Freemasonry.
Gradwell : Succat.
Grey (Sir G.) : Polynesian Mythology.
Guenebauld of Dijon : Le Reveil de Chyndonax, Prince des Vacies Druydes
    Celtiques Diionois.

Hall (S. C.) : Ireland. its Scenery, Character, &c. &c.
Hanmer : History of Ireland.
Hardiman : Irish Minstrelsy.
Harmer (Rev. T.) : Observations on various passages of Scripture.
Harp of Erin, the, (periodical). 1818.
Henderson : Folk-Lore of the Northern Counties of England, and of the
    Border.
Higgins : Celtic Druids.
Hislop (Rev. A.) : Two Babylons.
Hoare (Sir R. C.) : Tour through Ireland.
Hollinshed's Chronicle.
Hucher (Eug.) : L'Art Gaulois.

Inverness Gaelic Society, Transactions of the.
Ireland's Mirror. 1804.

James (Rev. Dr.) : The Patriarchal Religion of Britain.
Jocelin : Life and Acts of St. Patrick.
Joyce (J. W.) : Origin and History of Irish Names of Places.
Jubainville (D'Arbois de) : Cours de la littérature celtique.

Keane (M.) : Towers and Temples of Ancient Ireland.
Keating (G.) : History of Ireland.
Keepe : Monumenta Westmonasteriensia.
Kenealy : The Book of God.
Kennedy (P.) : Legendary Fictions of the Irish Celts.

Laing (S.) : Modern Science and Modern Thought.
Lanigan (Rev. J.) : Ecclesiastical History of Ireland.
La Villemarqué (Th. H. de) : Contes populaires des anciens Bretons.
Le Blanc (L.) : Etude sur le Symbolisme Druidique.
Ledwich : Antiquities of Ireland.
Leflocq : Etudes de la Mythologie Celtique.
Leslie (Lt.-Col. F.) : The Early Races of Scotland.
Lubbock (Sir J.) : Prehistoric Times.

McCulloch (J.) : The Highlands and W. Islands of Scotland.
Martin (H.) : Etudes d'archéologie celtique.
Martin (M.) : The W. Islands of Scotland.
Melville (H.) : Veritas.
Meyrick : Druidical Religion during the Residence of the Romans.
Milligan (S. & A.) : Glimpses of Erin.
Moran (Dr.) : Irish Saints.
Morgan (O.) or *Morien :* Light of Britannia.

Nash (Dr. W.) : Taliesin.
Neale (J. P.) : History and Antiquities of Westminster Abbey.

O'Brennan (Dr.) : Ancient Ireland.
O'Brien (H.) : Round Towers.
    ,,   ,,   : Phœnician Ireland.
O'Conor (Dr.) : Rerum Hibernicarum Scriptores Veteres.
O'Curry (Eng.) : Lectures on MS. materials of ancient Irish History.
    ,,   ,,   : Manners and Customs of the Ancient Irish.
O'Donovan (J.) : The Four Masters.
O'Flanagan (T.) : Translation of *Deirdri.*
O'Grady (S.) : History of Ireland.
O'Halloran (S.) : History and Antiquities of Ireland.
O'Hartigan : The Book of Ballymote.
O'Kearney (N.) : The Battle of Gabhra.
Oliver : Historical Landmarks and other Evidences of Freemasonry.
O'Neal : Irish Crosses
Ossian, Macpherson's.
Ossian Society, Transactions of the.
Otway (Rev. C.) : Sketches of Ireland, &c. &c.

Patrick, St., Tripartite Life of
Petrie (G.) : Ecclesiastical Architecture of Ireland.
Petrie (W. M. F.) : Ten Years' Digging in Egypt.
Phéné (Dr.) : Serpent Worship.
Picart (B.) : Ceremonies and Religious Customs of the Various Nations of the
    World.
Pictet (A.) : Les Origines Indo-Européennes.
Plowden (F.) : Historical Review of the State of Ireland.
Pownall (Govr.) : On the Study of Antiquities.

Revue Celtique, 1870 *et seq.*
Reynaud (J.) : Philosophie Religieuse, Terre et Ciel.
Rhys (Prof.) : Celtic Britain.
    ,,   ,, : Hibbert Lecture, &c. &c.
Richardson (Rev. J.) : Folly of Pilgrimages.
Richey (Dr.) : Lectures on the History of Ireland.
Robertson-Smith : Works.

Shaw (Dr.) : Gaelic Dictionary.
Shearman (J. F.) : Loca Patriciana.
Sirius (French).
Skene (W. F.) : Celtic Scotland.
Smiddy (Rev. R.) : Essays on the Druids.
Smith (W. A.) : Lewisiana.
Smith (W.) : Dictionary of the Bible.
Spenser (E.) : View of the State of Ireland.
Squier (E. G.) and Dr. E. H. Davis : Ancient Monuments of the Mississippi
    Valley.
Stevens (E. T.) : Flint Chips.
Stokes (Miss) : Early Christian Architecture in Ireland.
Stonyhurst Magazine.

Thierry (A.) : Histoire des Gaulois.
Tirechan : Life of St. Patrick.
Todd (J. H.) : St. Patrick, His Life and Mission.
    ,,   ,, : War of the Gaedhil with the Gaill.
Todd (Rev. W. G.) : The Church of St. Patrick.
Toland : History of the Druids.
Train : History of the Isle of Man.
Tylor (E. B.) : Researches into the Early History of Mankind.
Vallencey (Lt.-Col.) : Essay on the Antiquity of the Irish Language.
    ,,   ,, : Vindication of the Ancient History of Ireland.

Waddel (Rev. Dr.) : Ossian and the Clyde.
Wakeman (W. E.) : Archæologia Hibernica.
Walker : Irish Bards.
Westropp (H. M.) and C. S. Wake : Ancient Symbol Worship.
Wilkes (Mrs. A.) : Ireland, the Ur of the Chaldees.
Wood-Martin : Antiquities of Sligo.
Wright (T.) : Essays on Archæological Subjects.